Endorsements of *When Anger Hurts, 1st edition*

"A good book ... practical and down to earth ... it will prove quite helpful to a great many readers."

—Albert Ellis, Ph.D., founder of Rational Emotional
Therapy, and author, *A New Guide to Rational Living*

"A fine job! ... I very much like its practical, applicable techniques, the friendly constructive tone."

—Carol Tarvis, author, *Anger—The Misunderstood Emotion*

WHEN ANGER HURTS

SECOND EDITION

QUIETING THE STORM WITHIN

Matthew McKay, Ph.D.

Peter D. Rogers, Ph.D.

Judith McKay, RN

New Harbinger Publications, Inc.

Publisher's Note

This publication is designed to provide accurate and authoritative information in regard to the subject matter covered. It is sold with the understanding that the publisher is not engaged in rendering psychological, financial, legal, or other professional services. If expert assistance or counseling is needed, the services of a competent professional should be sought.

For Our Children

Dana, Noah, Jordan, and Rebekah

Élan and Becky

Contents

Preface to the Second Edition

By now, *When Anger Hurts* has sold 250,000 copies. It's used all over the world in clinics, as well as anger management groups and classes. Hundreds of therapists regularly recommend it to clients, and thousands of readers have found and bought it, hoping to change their lives.

In the fourteen years since the book originally appeared we've gotten a great deal of feedback, and we are honored that our book has proven useful to so many. But since it was introduced many things in our field have changed. Research, particularly the work of Jerry Deffenbacher, has pointed the way to more effective treatment protocols. So we have put them in this book—adding new chapters on 24-Hour Anger Management, Anger Inoculation, Problem Solving, Assessing the Cost of Your Anger, and Road Rage.

There have also been major changes made to the chapters on Anger and Children, Controlling Stress Step by Step, and Coping Through Healthy Self-Talk. And there have been deletions—notably the chapter on thought stopping that recent research has shown to be a questionable technique.

We believe this extensively revised second edition will give you an opportunity to learn the crucial skills you must have to change your life. Everything you need is here to alter even lifelong patterns of anger and reactivity. To the therapists and clinicians who've used the first edition, we wish to express our thanks. And we offer the promise that this second edition will be even more effective, more helpful. To those who are just discovering *When Anger Hurts*, we invite you to make a commitment to change, by making the commitment to work your way through each step of this program. It is true that doing the exercises will take time and energy. But your reward, in the coin of stronger, healthier, more loving relationships, will be more than worth it.

> —Matthew McKay, Ph.D.
> Nance's Hot Springs
> Calistoga, California

1

How to Use This Book

Anger has enormous costs. The impulse that felt so right at the moment, so justified, becomes in the quiet hours another source of guilt and regret. What seemed so worthy of blame passes. What remains are the scars, the hurt, and the alienation.

If you are often angry, every one of your relationships may be affected. Marriage can become a minefield. Distance grows. Walls thicken. Children may become hardened, resistant, while carrying deep feelings of worthlessness. Coworkers may withdraw or sabotage you, bosses become critical. A bitterness may grow with certain friends.

And anger affects your health. A twenty-five-year followup study of law students who had taken a test measuring hostility revealed a startling fact. Twenty percent of those who had scored in the top quarter on the hostility scale had died, compared to a death rate of only five percent for students who had scored in the lowest quarter on the same test (*New York Times* 1989). Frequent anger is damaging to your body and increases the death rate from nearly every cause.

When Anger Hurts

This book is for people who are concerned about their anger, who've grown tired of the emotional and physical toll that anger takes. It's for those who want less anger in their relationships, who seek better ways of expressing needs and solving problems.

This is a self-help book—which means that you are in for a lot of work. You can't achieve anger control without learning and practicing crucial coping skills. A passive reading of the text will prove disappointing. Nothing will change in your life.

A real change in your experience and expression of anger can be achieved only by doing the exercises, trying the techniques, and practicing your new skills on a daily basis. Whether you are learning stress reduction or a system to alter your anger-triggering thoughts, the book can help only if you master each step and then apply what you've learned to real events in your life.

The work will pay off. The skills you'll learn in this book can help you achieve these important benefits:

1. The ability to control destructive anger venting. And the chance to protect and rebuild relationships that have been damaged by venting in the past.

2. A reduction in the frequency and intensity of your physiological anger response. There is a wealth of scientific data that anger damages your health (see chapter 3). The less anger you experience, the longer you live.

3. A change in the beliefs, assumptions, and attitudes that trigger chronic anger. As you learn to restructure anger-triggering thoughts, you'll find that fewer and fewer things upset you.

4. Identification of the stresses and needs that lie *below* your anger. When you're clear about the real problem, you can move past anger to decision making.

5. The ability to cope effectively with your stress. Instead of exploding when stress exceeds your tolerance threshold, you can employ specific relaxation tools.

6. Greater effectiveness in meeting your needs. Anger generates resistance and resentment in others. You may get short-term cooperation. But in the long run your needs will be ignored and you will be avoided. Problem solving and communication tools can help you get what you want *without* anger.

When Anger Helps

Despite its costs, anger can be adaptive. It's a warning signal that something is wrong. Just as physical pain can be a warning ("this stove is hot—move your hand right now"), anger can warn you of imminent trauma. Anger can provide the energy to resist emotional or physical threats. The following exceptional situations are examples of when anger helps:

1. Perhaps the most obvious situation in which anger can be helpful is that of *physical threat* or actual attack. Anger can mobilize you to defend yourself or escape.

A few years ago Iris, a middle-aged woman living in New York, heard footsteps following her as she was returning home alone from the theater. She was frightened, of course, but then she became angry at the thought of being victimized. She slowed down. Then, when the footsteps came near, she whirled around and shouted at the top of her voice, "Get away from me you son of a bitch—or I'll kill you!" The would-be attacker fled.

2. Anger can be adaptive when your *boundaries are violated*. This type of infringement can take a variety of forms. At work, Sally's boss often asked her to bring him coffee, although food service is not part of her job description. Jim's boss expects him to put in hours of unpaid overtime each day. A personal boundary can be violated by relatives or friends who drop in without calling, by a neighbor who consistently borrows tools, or by a lover who demands a kind of sexuality you find repulsive.

Anger can help you mobilize your resources to set appropriate limits. You don't need to get hostile or aggressive with your boss. But you can learn to be very assertive. In your personal life, anger can help you set limits and give you the strength to resist threatening demands.

3. Many people struggle with the task of *separation and individuation*. Some children live most of their lives in the shadow of intrusive or abusive parents. And even when the child thinks she's escaped by marrying and having her own family, the intrusiveness continues.

Penny is a case in point. When she and her husband and newborn baby moved to the other coast, they thought they had bought a measure of independence. Not so. Weekly telephone calls full of interrogation and criticism were followed by overlong visits where Penny's mother completely "took over." Finally, Penny (supported by her husband) took the risk and confronted her mother. She didn't yell and scream. But her controlled anger allowed her to communicate the intensity of her need to raise her child *her* way. Penny's mother felt hurt and angry. But eventually she learned to appreciate her daughter as an individual.

Adolescence is a trying and troubled time for all concerned. Richard was a fairly "good" boy. When he got to high school he started using the nickname "Gandi" (short for Gandalf), and his parents noticed a change. He began to have and voice opinions. He was openly critical of the president and made disparaging remarks about capitalism. When his Republican parents objected to these new political values, his first response was sullen withdrawal. After a while his anger energized him to take bolder action. He told his parents off: "I have a right to my beliefs. Lay off or you'll have a war right in your own house." His parents were shocked, but decided to give him "more space."

Chris and Sandy met and fell in love. After a whirlwind courtship they moved in together. It was wine and roses for a couple of weeks, but soon Chris began to feel trapped.

Sandy kept demanding more and more attention until Chris felt drained. In the end, Sandy was following him around like a lost puppy. This was the last straw. Fully experiencing his anger enabled Chris to set firm limits. Eventually, the couple had to separate entirely. However nourishing it had been at first, the relationship was stifling both of their lives and not allowing them to grow.

4. One of the most difficult problems to deal with is *sexual or physical abuse* as a child. Sexual molestation, whether by a parent, grandparent, sibling, or next door neighbor, is a devastating experience. Equally devastating is physical or continued verbal and emotional abuse. Children who experience these kinds of maltreatment are traumatized and carry huge reservoirs of grief and anger into adulthood.

   For survivors of child abuse, recovery means allowing more and more of the child's buried feelings to surface: First the pain, the humiliation, the sense of wrongness. Next comes the anger and a realization that one's innocence was violated. Finally the deep feeling of grief. If ever the words "legitimate," "valid," or "appropriate" could be used in connection with anger, this is the best example.

   For victims of child abuse, catharsis in a safe therapeutic environment is an essential requirement for "moving on." Getting in touch with the victimized child's anger is a major step in the recovery process.

5. Anger helps overcome the *fear of asserting your needs*. Many people believe they don't have a right to ask for what they want. They believe they don't deserve to be happy. Without the mobilizing effects of anger, they would simply never have the courage to communicate their needs.

   Cindy is a case in point. She was always being put down, even as a child. Her family's message was: "You're not important." "Your sister needs braces on her teeth, she's going to be in the school play. Your teeth are okay. So what if they're a little bit crooked?" "We're sending your brother to college, he's the bright one. You'll get a job till you get married."

   There came a time when Cindy finally stood up for herself. Her anger strengthened and supported her as she confronted her parents. In a loud voice she told them that she was finished being second-best, finished with the "Cinderella shit." Some things started to change. For one, her mother apologized. And her father offered to pay for books and tuition at the local community college.

Using This Book

Although anger can serve vital functions to protect and defend the integrity of the self, it is too frequently an instrument that destroys and abuses. Chronic anger does not make you strong and safe. It weakens you. It encourages attack. The truth is that anger begets anger. The more you shout, the more you invite shouting. The more you rage, the more you invite rage.

There are two kinds of anger: anger at yourself and anger directed toward others. Anger at yourself triggers depression and damages your self-esteem. Self-directed anger is not within the scope of this book. If this is a significant issue for you, it is suggested that you read *Self-Esteem* (McKay and Fanning 2000) for a thorough cognitive behavioral treatment of the problem.

This book is focused on anger directed toward others. Whether you tend to vent your feelings (*anger-out*) or silently seethe (*anger-in*), you will find help here.

Chapters 2 through 5 contain basic information about what anger is and isn't and what it costs you physiologically and interpersonally. Chapter 6 shows how anger is *always a choice*. You can control anger by controlling your anger-triggering thoughts. Chapter 7 explores the issue of responsibility. For the angry person, someone else is always responsible for the pain. Anger control means taking responsibility for *everything* that stresses, hurts, or frustrates you. Chapters 8 through 17 are skill-building chapters. It's vital to apply the information in these chapters—not just read them. Do the exercises, try the techniques, find out what works best for you. Chapter 18 deals with road rage which has become an important problem in anger management nationwide. Chapters 19 and 20 focus on the special problems of anger with children and spouse abuse. Chapter 20 has been designed to function on its own, as a component of a spouse abuse treatment program. To this end, key strategies presented at length in earlier chapters are summarized in a section on anger control. For professionals, an appendix contains a protocol for leading Response Choice Rehearsal groups.

Your Anger Journal

Keeping an anger journal is a recommended part of using this book. You will be instructed at various points to observe and record specific aspects of your anger. For example, we will ask you to monitor the patterns of chronic tension in your body, your physiological anger response, and your anger-triggering thoughts. You'll track the most frequent targets of your anger. You'll notice and record the images and remembered scenes that most incite you.

The journal is important because it enables you to apply the book to your specific situation. Rather than passively reading about stress, you will explore the patterns of tension in your own body. Instead of absorbing abstractions and concepts, you will learn about your own trigger thoughts and anger imagery.

Coping with anger is an active process. And the time to start the process of change is now. Buy yourself a spiral notebook. Put it on your desk or bedside table (wherever you're more likely to use it). Today and every day until you've worked your way through all the chapters in this book, make the following notations.

1. The number of times you got angry in the last twenty-four hours.

2. How aroused you felt when you were at your angriest during the past twenty-four hours. Use a scale of 1 to 10, where 1 is minimal arousal and 10 is the most anger arousal you've ever felt.

3. How aggressively you acted when you were at your angriest during the last twenty-four hours. Again use a 1 to 10 scale, where 1 is minimal aggression and 10 is the most aggression you have ever displayed.

A typical entry might look like this:

Dec. 4   4 times.   Arousal 6.   Aggression 2.

Dec. 5   3 times.   Arousal 7.   Aggression 5.

Monitoring your anger in this way may teach you quite a lot about yourself. It will also provide you with a measure of your progress. Over the weeks you will be able to observe yourself change both the frequency and intensity of your anger. Seeing progress documented in this way will reinforce your efforts enormously.

2

The Myths of Anger

Anger, Shakespeare's "full hot horse," has been both praised and maligned, but mainly misunderstood. Whether it is "the sinew of the soul" (Thomas Fuller, *Of Anger*) or that which "resteth in the bosom of fools" (*Ecclesiastes*), anger has been the subject of speculation and discussion from the beginning of time.

Have you ever gotten angry and had a friend reassure you that "it's good to get it out?" Have you been to a therapist who advised you to stop holding your anger in? Have you sometimes had the feeling that anger is inevitable, that you better find a way to let off steam before you burst? These are all common experiences. But these common sense beliefs about anger, accepted even by mental health professionals, have turned out to be, in a word, wrong. This chapter examines the four basic myths of anger and describes some of the research that is now uncovering the truth.

Myth 1: Anger is a biochemically determined event.

Myth 2: Anger and aggression are instinctual to humans.

Myth 3: Frustration leads to aggression.

Myth 4: It's healthy to ventilate.

Each of these myths supports the unfortunate conclusion that anger and aggression are a *necessary* part of being human. By suggesting that anger and aggression are determined by instinct and biology, that they are basic to human adaptation, these myths make anger seem inescapable. The end result is an era in the history of psychology during which the expression of anger has been encouraged and even praised. People are assumed to be naturally angry. And they are told that expressing their anger, letting it out, is the royal road to mental health.

The truth is that anger is rarely unavoidable and seldom necessary. But that's getting ahead of the story. Right now it will be helpful to examine, one by one, the myths of anger.

Myth 1: Anger Is a Biochemically Determined Event

It is a common belief, mainly held by the biomedical community, that anger is largely a biochemical process. Specifically, anger is thought to be the result of hormonal changes or activity in the limbic system (e.g., the hypothalamus and amygdala).

Anger and Hormones

Some researchers have linked the hormone prolactin (which stimulates the production of mother's milk) to high levels of anger. Kellner et al. (1984) found that women with hyperprolactinemic amenorrhea (a condition characterized by increased levels of prolactin in the blood and absence of menstrual periods) had higher hostility scores than women with normal prolactin levels. When hyperprolactinemic women were given a prolactin-lowering drug, a significant and progressive decrease in hostility followed. In a related study, postpartum women who had high prolactin levels were significantly more hostile than a control group and equally as hostile as hyperprolactinemic women.

Testosterone has also been linked to hostility. Scaramella and Brown (1978) found that testosterone correlated with aggressive behavior. Konner (1962) found that male prison inmates with the highest levels of testosterone had the earliest age of first arrest. However, testosterone levels have also been found to be subject to environmental influences. When a monkey was introduced into a cage where rival males had established dominance, Konner noted that the newcomer exhibited a rapid drop of plasma testosterone. On the other hand, when a male subject was placed in a cage of females in heat, testosterone levels rose sharply.

Norepinephrine has long been implicated in the anger picture. Friedman et al. (1960) reported that aggressive, hostile individuals were found to excrete more norepinephrine than the passive and anxious subjects to whom they were compared. However, this research suffers from the "chicken-egg" problem. It is unclear whether the secretion of norepinephrine is a product of anger, or whether the subjects were angrier because they had higher levels of norepinephrine in their system.

There is no question that hormones are associated with emotion. But although physiological arousal may be a necessary component of any emotional response, it usually cannot, by itself, make you angry. Your cognitive awareness and interpretation of an emotion-provoking event or situation is a second, equally important component.

The work of Stanley Schachter best demonstrated the importance of the cognitive point of view. Building on the research of Maranon (1924), Schachter proposed a "two-factor" theory of emotion. According to this theory, the labeling (or attribution) of an emotion is based on a physiological change *plus* a cognitive interpretation of that change.

In a classic series of experiments exploring this point of view (Schachter and Singer 1962), subjects received what they thought to be vitamin injections. Actually, the injections were adrenaline. One group of subjects was told that the "vitamin" would produce certain side effects, such as heart palpitations and tremor (which are real side effects of adrenaline). Other groups were led to expect no side effects or ones not usually associated with adrenaline.

While waiting for a "vision test," each subject sat in a room with another person who was actually a confederate of the experimenters. In some cases, the "stooge" appeared euphoric and silly, throwing paper airplanes, laughing, and playing with a hula hoop. In other cases, the stooge acted annoyed and angry, finally tearing up a questionnaire he was supposed to fill out.

The purpose of the study was to see whether subjects under these different experimental conditions would assign different emotional labels to the physiological sensations produced by the adrenaline. The major finding was that subjects who did not expect the arousal produced by adrenaline, and thus had no way of explaining the physiological changes they were experiencing, tended to use the emotion displayed by the confederate as a label of their own feelings. They too expressed euphoria or anger, depending on the model provided them by the stooge. In contrast, subjects who were told to expect side effects were less likely to share the confederate's feelings.

Many other experiments (Schachter 1971) have lent support to the notion that cognitions tend to override the effects of sheer arousal. Anger authority Ray Rosenman (1985) concluded that "It is primarily the perception of an event that determines the emotional response and hence the psychophysiological consequences. . . . Anger is a cognitive response that is associated with personal appraisal and interpretation."

Carol Tavris, author of the seminal book, *Anger—The Misunderstood Emotion*, agrees that hormonally induced arousal is not enough to *cause* emotion. "It needs a psychological component before heat is transformed into hostility, uncertainty into fear, general distress into depression or rage. Adrenaline does not become the anger hormone until it is attached to a provocation, perception of injustice, or some interpretation of events" (Tavris 1982).

Anger and the Limbic System

The area of the brain that neurologists believe governs violent behavior is the limbic system. This system is located in the oldest part of the brain and includes among other components the amygdala and the hypothalamus. The amygdala, in particular, has been fingered as a major culprit in aggressive behavior.

Elliot (1976) has suggested that brain diseases affecting the limbic system may result in something called the "dyscontrol syndrome." He believes that this syndrome is "an important cause of wife and child battery, senseless assaults, motiveless homicides, self-injury, dangerously aggressive driving, domestic infelicity, divorce," and so on. Vivid case histories of the dyscontrol syndrome have been cited that involve brutality of all kinds, sexual assault, and reckless-ness. The syndrome also appears to be implicated in the tragic case of Charles Whitman, the "Texas Tower" murderer of seventeen people. After his death, an autopsy revealed a tumor the size of a walnut located in his amygdala.

Although the limbic system, and particularly the amygdala, is identified with aggression, Rosenman (1985) points out that the relationship is not a straightforward one. "The amygdala's existence does not necessarily mean that the brain is programmed instinctively for aggression. Thus, its stimulation in animals does not elicit aggres-sive behaviors *unless they were previously learned.* Moreover, its stimu-lation in human subjects variously causes anxiety, depression, anger, fright, and horror. . . ."

Other researchers agree. Deschner points out that the amygdala evaluates incoming stimuli for their life-threatening or life-enhancing potential.

> These primitive "good-bad" evaluations seem to control access to the anger programs in the hypothalamus. Fortunately, incoming stimuli must first be received and interpreted by the appropriate areas in the cerebral hemispheres specialized to handle sights, sounds, and so on. *Therefore the amygdala passes judgment on stimuli that have first been filtered through the conscious parts of the mind,* where all inputs are registered; compared with past memories, beliefs and expectations; and interpreted. This simple anatomical fact serves to screen the midbrain from the world and is the built-in basis for cognitive regulation of anger reactions (Deschner 1984).

Myth 2: Anger and Aggression Are Instinctual to Humans

The idea that humans are endowed with a basic instinct for aggression received quasi-scientific support in the work of Raymond Dart. His analysis of the findings in the South African caves, particularly Makapansgat, led him to describe early hominid ancestors in vivid terms.

> Man's predecessors differed from living apes in being confirmed killers: carnivorous creatures that seized living quarries by violence, battered them to death, tore apart their broken bodies, dismembered them limb from limb, slaking their ravenous thirst with the hot blood of [their] victims (Quoted in Leakey 1981, p. 221).

When Dart continued his work with a detailed examination of the fossil remains of the australopithecines in the caves, he found that these also bore the unmistakable marks of violence. In a 1953 essay, he summarized his view of human origins by proclaiming that "the blood-bespattered, slaughter-gutted archives of human history from the earliest Sumerian records to the most recent atrocities of the Second World War accord with early universal cannibalism ... this predacious habit, this mark of Cain separates man dietetically from his anthropoidal relatives and allies him rather with the deadliest of Carnivora" (ibid.).

Dart's conclusions were expanded upon by his disciple, Robert Ardrey, in such books as *African Genesis* and *The Territorial Imperative*. Ardrey's vivid portrayal of a prehistory rife with predatory, carnivorous, and cannibalistic scenarios was instrumental in furthering the idea that humans cannot escape their aggressive instincts and that they are, in fact, "... predator[s] whose instinct is to kill with a weapon."

The result of modern scientific inquiry tends to refute the claims on which Dart and Ardrey based their descriptions of our bloody past. The principal investigator in this area is Bob Brain, working from the Transvaal Museum in Pretoria. Brain discovered that fossils buried close to the bottom of a deep cave may have as much as 100 feet of sediment resting over them. This weight has the effect of flattening and distorting the hominid fossils. If a hard pointed object lies close to the skull, the pressure can push the point into the bone, causing a localized compound fracture which can resemble the effects of a deadly blow to the head.

Brain capitalized on the results of a "natural experiment" when he discovered a large number of goat bone fragments in a Hottentot village. Goat was the primary source of meat in that region, and the leftovers were thrown to the dogs. When he collected and sorted the remains, he found that only the toughest and most resistant part of the skeleton survived. This bone collection was remarkably similar to that found at the Makapansgat site. It now appears that the fossils Dart interpreted as weapons of a prehistoric culture are more likely the leftovers of many carnivore meals.

Perhaps the most popular proponent of the evolutionary basis for human aggression was Konrad Lorenz. Best known for his book *On Aggression*, he relates human aggressiveness to a universal territorial instinct in biology. Throughout the animal world, territories are established and maintained by ritualized displays of aggression. According to Lorenz, our ancestors acquired weapons and turned these rituals into bloody combats, which were heightened by a primal lust for killing.

The Lorenzian school suggests that aggression is a basic part of the territorial animal's survival mechanism and is fueled by a continuous pressure for expression. According to Lorenz, aggression may be released by an appropriate cue, such as the appearance of a threat from another animal. But if no such threat appears, the internal pressure will eventually reach a "critical point," and the aggressive behavior will burst out spontaneously. This theory could be used to explain anything from marital spats to nuclear war, as biological pressures push human beings past some built-in anger threshold.

Anthropologist Richard Leakey (1981) disagrees with the Lorenzian hypothesis. He suggests, to begin with, that animals are territorial for a reason, usually to protect resources or a reproductive area. The lunging behavior by sticklebacks and the morning cacophany of the gibbons both are displays announcing ownership of territory. Intruders are met with these ritualized confrontations in which the more biologically fit of the two inevitably wins without inflicting physical damage.

These forms of "aggression" are, in fact, an exercise in competitive display, as opposed to physical violence. The biological advantage of this behavior is obvious. A species which settles its disputes through violence will reduce its overall fitness and be less likely to survive in an environment that is difficult enough already. This fact is deeply embedded in the nature of survival, and evolutionary success depends on it. An animal that is unable to restrain its murderous lust puts itself and its species in a disadvantageous evolutionary position.

Our ancestors probably lived in small bands of closely related members. Nearby bands were also similarly related. Any act of murder would probably have involved someone who was kin to the murderer, and since evolutionary success requires the production of as many descendants as possible, an innate unrestrained aggressiveness would have doomed the human species.

The principal factor in successful evolution is cooperation rather than conflict. Even in primates, most fighting is a ritualized process that preserves the species. Thus the evolution of *Homo sapiens* would appear to stem from our ability to live in effective groups, unlike other protohominids who failed in this endeavor.

Leakey concludes that territoriality and aggression are not universal instincts. Territorial behavior is triggered, as required, by scarcity in food supplies or mating spaces. It is inevitable that some of the weakest individuals will fail to secure food or a mate. This is the harsh lesson of natural selection or "survival of the fittest."

In 1986, a remarkable group of twenty distinguished behavioral scientists gathered in Seville, Spain. This group included psychologists, neurophysiologists, and ethologists from twelve different nations. The conference concluded that there is no scientific evidence to support the belief that humans are innately aggressive and warlike. The "Seville Statement" that resulted from their deliberations has since been endorsed by the American Psychological Association and the American Anthropological Association, among others. The following excerpts from that document (*Psychology Today* 1988) served to summarize their position:

1. *It is scientifically incorrect to say that we have inherited a tendency to make war from our animal ancestors. Warfare is a peculiarly human phenomenon and does not occur in other animals. War is biologically possible, but it is not inevitable.*

2. *It is scientifically incorrect to say that war or any other violent behavior is genetically programmed into our human nature. Except for rare pathologies the genes do not produce individuals necessarily predisposed to violence.*

3. *It is scientifically incorrect to say that in the course of human evolution there has been a selection for aggressive behavior. In all well-studied species, status within the group is achieved by the ability to cooperate.*

4. *It is scientifically incorrect to say that humans have a "violent brain." While we do have the neural apparatus to act violently, there is nothing in our neurophysiology that compels us to do so.*

The group concluded that "biology does not condemn humanity to war, and that humanity can be freed from the bondage of biological pessimism. Violence is neither in our evolutionary legacy nor in our genes."

Myth 3: Frustration Leads to Aggression

According to Freud, individuals are born with an innate aggressive instinct. He further argues that when this instinctual urge is blocked or "frustrated" it will lead to a hostile attack. When the real object of the anger is perceived as being too risky to attack, the anger is displaced. Thus a child displaces aggression toward its parents by fighting with a sibling or talking back to a teacher.

In 1939, Dollard et al. formulated the *frustration-aggression hypothesis*. They believed that "aggression is always a consequence of frustration. More specifically the proposition is that the occurrence of aggressive behavior always presupposes the existence of frustration and, contrariwise, that the existence of frustration always leads to some form of aggression."

Although there is a great deal of evidence for the usefulness of the frustration-aggression hypothesis, it requires careful qualification. While frustration may lead to aggression, reports from many different cultures throughout the world indicate that this transfer is by no means inevitable. For example, the Kwoma of New Guinea may respond to frustration by submission, dependence, or avoidance, as well as anger (Whitting 1941). The Balinese are also unlikely to respond angrily to frustration (Bateson 1941). A more common response is for the Balinese man to withdraw from all contact and go without food or water for days. The Semai (a Senoi tribe) are renowned for their nonviolence (Dentan 1968). Semai children are taught to deal with frustration by using their dreams to work out alternatives.

Alternative responses to frustration may be found in our own culture as well. Losing money to a coffee machine may provoke some people to cursing and kicking behavior. Others will simply write down the name and address of the vending company and mail a request to get their money back.

The second part of the hypothesis, that frustration invariably precedes aggression, has also been called into question. One need only think about hired mercenaries who kill in cold blood or children who imitate violence on TV to see the problems with this formulation.

Frustration is definitely related to anger arousal, but a cognitive factor is involved. Frustration can occur only when you have an expectation that is not fulfilled. Disappointment requires cognitions that include memory and imagination. In addition, a frustrated person will not act in an aggressive way unless the setting is perceived as appropriate for the expression of hostility. Whether on the battlefield or in a domestic argument, aggression only occurs if it is considered appropriate or acceptable for the situation at hand.

It must be noted that Neal Miller did modify the famous hypothesis in 1941. Miller's reformulation stated that frustration instigates many forms of behavior, and that only one of these is aggression. This clearly more realistic assessment lacks the dramatic flair of the original and hence has received much less attention.

Many people use the "frustration leads to aggression" myth to explain and excuse their anger. Since frustration is seen as invariably provoking anger and aggression, these individuals view anger as automatic and uncontrollable. When frustrated, they assume that anger is the only response possible. This myth leads to the belief that you have no choice. When things go wrong, anger is seen as the natural response, the only response to frustrated drives. In truth, anger is only one possible response to frustration. This book will offer you a whole new range of choices and ways to cope when your needs are not met and you are experiencing frustration.

Myth 4: It's Healthy to Ventilate

Much of the current misunderstanding about anger can be traced back to the work of Sigmund Freud and his disciples. Freud used a number of metaphors to describe his view of psychological processes. He regarded these as useful aids to understanding, and cautioned his readers that these models should not be regarded as established scientific facts. He looked forward to the eventual discovery of the basic psychological mechanism that would validate his assumptions. Unfortunately, many of Freud's disciples took his metaphors to be reality, and these transitional notions took on a life of their own.

One of these concepts is the so-called "hydraulic model." Freud conceptualized the libido as the source of energy that fuels internal conflicts between id, ego, and superego. If the energy is blocked or dammed up, it will either find alternative routes of expression or eventually spill over the hypothetical "reservoir" and flood the system. Similarly, Freud described *repression* as the unconscious "damming" process that keeps dangerous material from coming into awareness, thereby producing a host of neurotic symptoms.

Although psychoanalysis was designed to alleviate neurotic symptoms by bringing to light this repressed material, Freud did not believe that suppression of aggressive instincts was undesirable. In fact, he believed that their suppression and sublimation were necessary for the survival of society as a whole. He would have been appalled to find his theories used as a justification for the modern injunction to "let it all hang out."

The *catharsis hypothesis* is perhaps the best known theory for the reduction of aggression. This idea also stems from Freud (in collaboration with J. Breuer). For Freud, this hypothesis explained why there are relatively few instances of violent acting out of aggressive instincts. Catharsis was a way of emptying emotional reservoirs (as in the hydraulic model) that could be accomplished in a variety of ways. The range of cathartic activities included fantasies, tears, angry words, and the destruction of objects.

The past twenty years have seen the rise of many new psychological schools and theories. The notion that it is unhealthy to bottle up feelings is common to many of these, ranging from the encounter group movement to Janov's "primal scream." Advocates of this point of view have been termed "ventilationists" by Leonard Berkowitz. Many therapists of this school would agree with Adelaide Bry:

> I've seen how suppressed anger festers in the mind and body of the individual, creating both emotional and physical ailments; how it insinuates itself between husband and wife, and between friend and friend, dissolving all the good warm feelings that first brought them together; how it poisons relationships at work, at school, at play, in love, in all of life itself (Bry 1976).

Further on, she enumerates the virtues of expressing anger. These include making you feel better about yourself, making your relationships more meaningful and *real*, relieving both physical and emotional stress, and finally, whetting your sexual appetite.

This point of view cannot be dismissed as a far-out fringe position in psychological circles. Well-known psychoanalyst Theodore Isaac Rubin proposes a similar point of view in *The Angry Book* (1969). The "message" of the book includes a number of related points: (1) by expressing anger you are working in the service of healthier and happier communication, (2) expressing anger gives you a "good, clean feel" and increases self-esteem, and (3) the purpose of "warm, healthy anger" is to clear the air and make corrections and reparations if necessary.

Even outside the psychological community, the general belief is that expressing feelings or "blowing off steam" is beneficial. But after summarizing the major research on anger, Carol Tavris (1989) notes that people who are most prone to vent their rages get angrier, not less angry. And the recipients of this rage get angry, too. The typical stages of a "ventilating" marital argument involve a precipitating event, an angry outburst, shouted arguments, screaming or crying, a crescendo (perhaps including physical violence), and exhaustion, followed by withdrawal or apology. This cycle is replayed *ad nauseum*, and no decrease in anger is apparent.

Jack Hokanson (1970) has done extensive research in the area of catharsis theory for the past twenty years. His original finding was that aggression was cathartic (in that it lowered blood pressure), but only when directed against peers. Expressing anger to a superior was actually anxiety producing, adding a new dimension to the anger rather than reducing it. In a related series of experiments, Hokanson discovered that while aggression was cathartic for anger in men, friendliness was cathartic for women. Even when directed toward a peer, aggression was as upsetting for women as aggression toward authority was for men.

These findings led Hokanson to speculate that catharsis is not a natural consequence of anger, but a learned reaction. In a follow-up series of experiments, he paired students matched for gender and age in a situation where they could administer either shocks or rewards. Male subjects responded to shocks by giving back shocks and experienced cathartic relief. Women, on the other hand, responded to shocks by giving a friendly response, thereby also experiencing cathartic relief. Cathartic relief was measured by physiological monitors hooked up to the subjects.

The experiment continued. In stage two, men were rewarded every time they gave a friendly response to a shock. Women were rewarded every time they were aggressive in response to a shock. Rapid learning occurred and the traditional form of catharsis for each sex was reversed. Women showed a reduction in blood pressure when they responded aggressively, and men now showed a cathartic response to friendliness rather than belligerence.

Seymour Feshbach (1956) had a group of nonaggressive children play with violent toys and "run amok" during free playtime. These boys, rather than behaving in a less aggressive way (as catharsis theory would predict), in fact became more hostile and destructive than previously observed. The same principles of anger and aggression were observed in adults by Murray Straus (1974). He found that couples who yell at each other feel more angry afterward, not less.

Yelling or even talking out an emotion doesn't reduce it. What actually happens is that you are rehearsing for more of the same. Ebbesen, Duncan, and Konecni (1975) conducted exit interviews with men who had been laid off from an aerospace project, comparing them to others who had voluntarily quit at the same time. The finding was that "ventilation" of anger during the interview did not act as catharsis in any way. In fact, men who had taken an angry stance became even more hostile toward the company.

Tavris (1982) found in study after study that ventilation could serve to "freeze" a hostile attitude or opinion. This was true even among children who were encouraged to express their anger toward a child who had frustrated them in an experimental situation (Mallick and McCandles 1966). These children later expressed less liking toward that child than the children who were not permitted to express their anger. Similarly, college students remained angrier with someone who had irritated them when they were allowed a catharsis of their feelings (Kahn 1966).

Experimental studies consistently point out that the popular remedy for anger, ventilation, is really worse than useless. In fact, the reverse seems to be true: expressing anger tends to make you even angrier and solidifies an angry attitude.

There are, of course, exceptional cases. The incest victim who confronts her tormentor may experience real satisfaction. Cathartic experiences of this kind do not feel good simply because a psychic reservoir has been "emptied." Rather, the depth of the individual's emotional response is an outgrowth of facing and conquering a real situation involving objective instances of conflict, injustice, coercion, and so on.

The belief that anger and violence is unavoidable is psychologically attractive for many people. It allows individuals to excuse and justify acts of aggression by suggesting that they have little choice in the matter. Belief in the four myths discussed above makes anger and violence seem natural and even healthy.

In fact, the opposite is the case. Anger is basically a matter of choice. It is determined by your thoughts and beliefs far more than your biochemistry or genetic heritage. Venting anger rarely leads to any real relief or any lasting catharsis. It leads instead to more anger, tension, and arousal.

3

The Physiological
Costs of Anger

Stella is standing in line at the bank. It is 1:20, and she's due back at the office at 1:30. She could make it in time if she is lucky and the line moves along at a brisk pace. But it doesn't look good. Two of the five tellers close their windows. "How dare they take a break when there are people still waiting?" she thinks. One customer is buying travelers' checks. "Why don't they have a special window for that kind of service?" Stella asks the person behind her in line. The customer slowly signs each check while cheerfully discussing her upcoming vacation. "Who cares about Florida in April? Just sign the damned checks and get going, for Christ's sake," Stella mutters under her breath. By now, Stella is impatiently opening and closing the snap on her purse. "This could take all day!" she sighs in exasperation.

The noise of the other people's conversations is annoying, and the two men standing behind her in line are too close. A young man counts out the money the teller gave him and carefully tucks it into his wallet before he leaves the window. "Good grief! Don't take all day! Just move it!" she thinks.

By the time it's her turn at the window, at 1:29, Stella is in a rage. Her heart is pounding, she is breathing heavily, her mouth is dry, and her hands are shaking. She's mad at the stupid, slow patrons and the inconsiderate bank tellers. She's mad at her boss for making her feel guilty if she's even one minute late, and she resents her job for allowing only a one-hour lunch break. She's also angry at the restaurant for its slow, inefficient service and the undigested food she can still taste. Her lunch, which she bolted down half an hour ago, sits like a rock in her stomach.

For Stella, feeling so angry is not uncommon. In fact, it would be fair to say that Stella is angry most of the time. There's nothing wrong with occasional, moderate anger. It creates no lasting harm. But chronic, sustained anger can be a serious problem, because it puts your body on red alert—always ready to fight. By keeping the body in a constant state of emergency, chronic anger can contribute to hypertension, heart disease, and increased mortality from all causes. This chapter will begin by exploring what we know about how anger impacts your health. In chapters 4 and 5 we'll look at the emotional and interpersonal costs of chronic anger.

The physiological experience of anger proceeds automatically once it is triggered, but getting angry is by no means automatic. Stella's anger is triggered by things that she tells herself while standing in line: "Tellers shouldn't take breaks while people are waiting . . . They should have a special window . . . Who cares about Florida? . . . This could take all day . . . Damn rigid boss . . . Bad service . . . Hideous food . . . ," and so on. It is Stella's thoughts that actually start the emotional ball rolling, signaling her body to prepare for battle. Later chapters will have more to say about the role of thoughts. Right now it's important to understand what happens to you physically when you get angry.

Early research into the physiology of emotion indicated that all strong emotions grew out of the same physical reaction. This reaction was dubbed the *stress response.*

The Stress Response

Walter Cannon (1929) first documented the physiological reactions of different organs to stress of all kinds. In experiments with animals, he observed a similarity in their physical responses to pain, anxiety, heat, starvation, and so on. When he performed autopsies on these poor creatures, he saw the same characteristic organ abnormalities in all the animals, no matter what kind of stress they had been exposed to. Their adrenal glands were enlarged, they had stomach ulcers, their thymus glands were small, and their livers were pale.

Hans Selye (1936), considered the father of stress theory, called this whole pattern of organ abnormalities the "stress syndrome." He believed that the stress syndrome was an alarm reaction—a general call to arms of the body's defensive forces. He recognized that the body's efforts to deal with both the stress and the hormones released in response to stress affected all of its tissues and cells. Selye was convinced that stress accounted for the wide assortment of "diseases of adaptation" found in humans and other animals, diseases such as peptic ulcers, high blood pressure, heart attacks, and nervous disorders.

Of course the stress response isn't all bad. It acts as the body's alarm system, and enables the threatened person to run faster, climb higher, shout louder, see more clearly, hit harder, endure more pain, and do what must be done to survive an attack. The same hormonal response helps (or hinders) athletes, dancers, actors, and speakers. And it is that response that gives a horrified mother the strength to lift a car off of her child trapped beneath it. Clearly in an emergency the stress response is highly adaptive. But Selye also demonstrated that if the body's alarm system is turned on chronically, serious organic damage will inevitably occur.

In Selye's day, it wasn't possible to measure the levels of hormones in the body directly. Today, new technologies make it possible to measure hormones and endocrine levels at the very moment a subject is reacting. These more exact measurements have made it clear that each strong emotion has a characteristic physiological reaction and that emotions are *not* just variants of a single stress response. Although the sympathetic nervous system is involved in all strong emotions producing epinephrine and norepinephrine, it is the mixture of types, amounts, and balance of hormones that cause important differences in the body's reaction. For example, fear and distress cause an increase in heart rate and blood pressure, constriction of blood vessels in the skin, and the shunting (diverting) of blood to the skeletal muscles. The frightened, distressed person looks ashen, cold, clammy, and tremulous. On the other hand, situations that are challenging and exciting result in the constriction of blood vessels in the skeletal muscles, and less change in heart and respiration rates.

The Physiology of Anger

Many studies show that the stress of anger produces a unique and specific hormonal response, one that is particularly dangerous. Anger results in elevated levels of testosterone (for men), epinephrine, norepinephrine, and cortisol. Chronically high levels of testosterone and cortisol contribute to the development of atherosclerosis, the most common cause of coronary artery disease. Cortisol also depresses the immune system and reduces the body's ability to fight infection. Epinephrine and norepinephrine stimulate the sympathetic nervous system to shunt blood from the skin, liver, and digestive tract to the heart, lungs, and skeletal muscles. Blood pressure is elevated, and glucose increases in the blood system to provide energy for confrontation or escape. When blood is shunted away from the liver, it becomes less efficient at clearing cholesterol from the blood, thus contributing to fatty deposits in the arteries. Elevated blood pressure also damages the arteries and the heart. Hypertension forces the heart to work harder and creates a large and less efficient heart muscle. Turbulence caused by the high pressure of the blood flow also damages the arteries. Tiny tears develop on the artery walls. Fatty deposits cover the tears, but eventually these can grow to fill the artery and stop the flow of blood.

Anger and Hypertension

Doctors always suspected that there was an association between anger and high blood pressure. It turned out they were right. To understand how anger raises blood pressure, it's important to first understand how the vascular system works. Blood pressure is simply the pressure exerted by the flow of blood on the walls of the blood vessels. It is really two different pressures and is expressed in two numbers such as 120/80 or 140/90. The higher number represents the *systolic pressure* of your blood as it surges through your arteries during each heartbeat. You feel that wave of pressure when you touch the pulse in your wrist. The lower number is a measurement of the *diastolic pressure* in the artery between heartbeats. A blood pressure of 120/80 means that the pressure in the arteries is 120 at the time of the heart's contraction and 80 at the times between heartbeats.

"High" blood pressure can be understood by thinking about garden hoses. Let's say that you have two garden hoses, one a half-inch in diameter and the other a quarter-inch in diameter. If you attach the half-inch hose to the faucet and turn the valve all the way, you will get a steady stream of water. However, if you attach the quarter-inch hose to the same faucet, and turn the valve all the way as before, you will get a much stronger stream. When the diameter of the hose is smaller, that is, "constricted," the water pressure increases. Anger is associated with high levels of norepinephrine, which tends to constrict blood vessels. This can raise your blood pressure as surely as if you had switched to a smaller diameter hose.

The association between anger and high blood pressure has been demonstrated by many studies on many different patient populations. Schwartz, Weinberger, and Singer (1981) compared changes in blood pressure as their subjects experienced fear, happiness, anxiety, and anger. They found that anger caused the greatest response in the heart and blood vessels and the greatest increase in blood pressure.

Anger-In and High Blood Pressure

The idea that unexpressed anger (anger-in) could lead to high blood pressure has been circulating for more than half a century. In 1939, Franz Alexander suspected that his hypertensive patients were having trouble with feelings of anger and an inability to express them. This failure to express angry feelings, he argued, could lead to chronic activation of the sympathetic nervous system and to high blood pressure. Research as early as 1942, by Hamilton, confirmed that unexpressed anger was inextricably linked to hypertension.

Alexander's hypothesis that unexpressed anger (anger-in) was linked to elevated blood pressure was confirmed again and again in studies of hypertensive young adults and middle-aged populations (Harburg et al. 1964, 1973; Kahn et al. 1972; Esler et al. 1977; Miller and Grimm 1979).

In 1982, Diamond reviewed four decades of research involving the role of anger and hostility in essential (chronic) hypertension and coronary heart disease. He described the hypertensive individual as someone "ridden with hostility and constantly guarding against impulse expression." In the same year, Gentry studied the effects of habitual anger coping styles on more than a thousand subjects. With this larger sample, he showed categorically that chronic suppressed anger increased the risk for hypertension.

Research by Dimsdale and associates (1986) confirmed once again that higher blood pressure is significantly related to suppressed anger. In fact, those with normal blood pressure were twice as likely as those with high blood pressure to be free of suppressed anger. All in all, there are dozens of studies linking anger-in with hypertension.

It's clear from the research literature that the inability (or unwillingness) to express anger contributes to the development of hypertension for many susceptible people. But that's only half the story. As it turns out, people who tend to exhibit more hostility and act more aggressively toward others (anger-out) also have higher blood pressure rates than normal.

Anger-Out and High Blood Pressure

While the weight of the evidence points to anger-in as a major culprit in hypertension, other studies have found that people with high blood pressure tend to show more hostility and behave more aggressively than people with normal blood pressure (Schacter 1957; Kaplan et al. 1961; Baer et al. 1969; Mann 1977). In 1979, Harburg, Blakelock, and Roeper did an interesting study in which they asked people how they would deal with an angry and arbitrary boss. Some subjects reported that they would just walk away from the situation (anger-in). Others said that they would protest, confront the boss, and might even report him to the union (anger-out). Still another group stated that they would try to talk it over later, after the boss had cooled off. The researchers called this coping style "reflection." They found that the subjects who chose to express their anger to the boss had the highest blood pressure. Subjects who used reflection had the lowest blood pressure, prompting Harburg and his colleagues to suggest that reflection was a coping style that could be taught to hypertensives.

Anger and Heart Disease

Research evidence amassed over the past fifty years has strongly established the link between anger and heart disease. To understand how this link works, let's begin by looking at what creates a heart attack.

What Is a Heart Attack?

The heart muscle, like every other part of the body, needs oxygen and nutrients to keep its cells alive. These essentials are supplied by the coronary arteries. Between each heartbeat, the coronary arteries feed the heart cells with oxygen-rich blood.

Anything that interferes with coronary artery function is potentially life threatening. When cholesterol is deposited in the lining of the essential coronary arteries, the resulting plaques can irritate the artery and cause spasm (experienced as angina pain). But something more serious also can happen. The rough lining of the coronary arteries may cause the formation of a clot that completely occludes (blocks) the artery. This condition is called a heart attack, or myocardial infarction. In a heart attack, all muscle tissue downstream from the clot dies. Whether or not a person survives a heart attack depends on how much of the muscle tissue has died, and if the remaining undamaged part of the heart can still continue to function.

The Discovery of Type A

In the 1950s, Friedman and Rosenman, two San Francisco cardiologists, were trying to determine what put individuals at risk for coronary heart disease. Who was most likely to have blocked arteries, heart attacks, and angina pain? They found that people who had heart attacks had several factors in common, such as high blood cholesterol levels, hypertension, and some bad habits like smoking or sedentary lifestyles. But when they examined their patients' personality patterns, Friedman and Rosenman hit the jackpot. They found a cluster of personality traits that appeared to be linked to heart disease.

In their famous book, *Type A Behavior and Your Heart* (1974), Friedman and Rosenman made the revolutionary suggestion that the high-risk cardiac symptoms and habits were not due to diet, activity level, or stress, but were actually a personality style. They identified the Type A person as having the personality traits of time urgency, competitiveness, high ambition, hyperaggressiveness, and free-floating hostility. They observed that this form of hyper-aggressiveness was the desire not just to win, but to dominate. It was as if the hostility was always present and took any opportunity to attach itself to a person or a situation. The Type A person was full of anger—anger looking for an excuse to get out.

Laboratory Evidence

Friedman and Rosenman did many experiments on lab animals to try to recreate the physical changes that take place during anger (Friedman and Ulmer 1984). In an experiment on rats whose hypotha-lamuses were electrically stimulated in such a way as to create rage, they found something very reminiscent of Hans Selye's early work. Autopsies showed that the rats had very pale liver tissue. Since anger diverts blood away from the digestive system, the pale livers of these raging rats showed the effect of constant sympathetic nervous system stimulation. Friedman and Rosenman recognized these liver changes as one of the major contributors to heart disease. Because the liver is the organ that removes cholesterol from the blood, a restricted supply of blood to the liver tends to elevate cholesterol levels.

Confirming Studies

Many studies have documented the association between Type A behavior and heart disease. Between 1960 and 1969, Friedman and Rosenman (1974) conducted the Western Collaborative Group Study on 3,500 healthy men. First, they found that 113 of the original group already had heart disease and that 80 percent of these men could be classified as Type A. Over the course of eight and a half years, Type A men were twice as likely to have heart attacks as Type B's. In the Framingham Heart Study (Haynes, Feinleib, and Kannel 1980), 5,500 men and women were tested. An analysis of data collected between 1950 and 1980 again revealed a significant link between Type A patterns and heart disease. A study supervised by Redford Williams at Duke University Medical Center (Blumenthal et al. 1978) showed that Type A patients undergoing diagnostic coronary angiography (X-rays of the heart's blood supply) had more severe atherosclerosis that Type B's. And more than 90 percent of individuals with severe coronary artery disease were shown to have Type A personalities.

Heart disease starts early for those who are chronically angry. Grunbaum and his research group (1997) studied the association between anger or hostility and coronary heart disease in children and adolescents. Their review of epidemiological studies uncovered a strong connection between anger and pathologic changes in the arteries of school-age children.

In a recent study, Williams et al. (2000) followed a group of 12,986 black and white men and women for a period of fifty-three months. All subjects were initially disease free. They found that anger, as measured by Spielberger's Trait Anger Scale (1988), independent of biological risk factors, put these *normotensive* subjects (having blood pressure typical of the group to which they belong) at significant risk for coronary heart disease and death.

The Real Culprit: Hostility

In recent years, Rosenman, working at the Stanford Research Institute, concluded that of all the personality traits found in Type A, the key predictor of coronary disease is the potential for hostility. He and others reanalyzed data from the Western Collaborative Group Study (Rosenman 1985) and found that the anger-hostility dimension proved to be "the dominant characteristic among the coronary prone Type A behaviors."

Corroborating evidence came from a study of 1,877 men at the Western Electric Company in Chicago (Shekelle et al. 1983). Men who scored high on a hostility scale were one and a half times more likely to have a heart attack than men who had lower hostility scores. Barefoot, Dahlstrom, and Williams (1983) did a follow-up study of 255 male physicians who had completed the Hostility Scale twenty-five years earlier, while they were in medical school. Men who scored at the median or below in hostility had one sixth the incidence of coronary heart disease of men who had scored higher on the scale. Williams et al. (1980) tested 424 patients who were referred for coronary angiography. Forty-eight percent of patients with low hostility scores were found to have coronary atherosclerosis. But 70 percent of patients with higher scores had significant atherosclerosis.

The Finnish Twin Cohort study (Koskenvuo et al. 1988) provides corroborating evidence from a different culture. Using a simple three-item hostility measure and a sample of 3,750 men, they found that high self-ratings of hostility were associated with increased all-cause mortality over a three-year follow-up program.

Kawachi and associates (1996) conducted a seven-year follow-up study of 1,305 men. They concluded that high levels of expressed anger are a risk factor for cardiac disease among older men. Siegman and associates (1987) found that the degree of expressed hostility was related to the severity of coronary artery disease in patients sixty years or younger.

The evidence is clear. Chronic hostility and anger can damage your heart and arteries.

Anger and Digestion

Anger has a dramatic impact on your stomach. Wolff and Wolf (1967) noticed that anger produces physiological effects quite different from those produced by depression or fear. Angry subjects manifested red stomach linings with increased rhythmic contractions and increased secretion of hydrochloric acid. People who were depressed or frightened had pale stomach linings, and decreased contractions and acid secretion. Anger's role in increasing acid secretion is very significant. Because hyperacidity is associated with the development of gastritis and ulcers, chronic anger may increase your risk for these diseases.

Anger may also be implicated in the development of ulcerative colitis. Researchers Lewis and Lewis (1972) have argued that "predisposed persons" may show symptoms of colitis when they maintain and hold in chronic resentment and anger. The mucus membrane of the colon reacts sharply to suppressed anger. It becomes engorged with blood and peristaltic activity is increased.

Beyond the Anger Response

It seems that it doesn't matter whether anger is expressed or suppressed. It's just plain bad for you. Chronic anger that is expressed is bad for you because it feeds on itself. It prolongs and supercharges all the associated hormonal changes. Chronic suppressed anger is damaging because it mobilizes the sympathetic nervous system responses without providing any release of the tension. The effect is the same as flooring the accelerator of your car at the same time as slamming on the brakes.

Although anger is an unhealthy habit, it's one you can change with awareness and effort. Remember Stella at the beginning of the chapter? If her distress waiting in line at the bank is part of a chronic anger response, eventually she may be at risk for a serious illness. But Stella is not the helpless victim of an anger-triggering hormonal storm. She has a choice. The potential for anger resides far more in how she interprets and thinks about events than in the events themselves. Later chapters will show how your perceptions, assessments, and interpretations of the world are learned responses. Anger can be controlled by changing the habitual ways that you perceive, assess, and interpret what goes on around you. A traffic jam, a long line at the bank, incompetent, stupid, or even malicious people need not trigger the deadly physical reaction of the anger response.

You can learn to live without anger. And learning to do so will be good for your health.

4

The Interpersonal
Costs of Anger

Sometimes expressing anger can feel enormously relieving. And though it can act as a powerful tool for influence or control, expressing anger comes with a price tag. This chapter details the toll anger takes on your relationships, what it costs you in the currency of support and satisfaction.

The price you pay for anger may seem obvious. A cooling friendship, coworkers who keep their distance. A marriage where you have each become vigilant, always on the alert for another bitter round. Other costs may be more subtle. A friend's decision not to give you the vital feedback you really need. A colleague who recommends your work, but without enthusiasm. A lover who keeps quiet rather than attempt some risky problem solving. It comes down to this: each angry episode you have cuts into the fabric of goodwill, care, and appreciation that's vital to your relationships. Angry people are experienced as dangerous, and they are handled like a loaded gun—with caution or downright avoidance.

Anger stuns. It frightens. It makes people feel bad about themselves. And, of course, it warns them to stop doing whatever is offending you. But people gradually become inured and resistant. As soon as they see you, they put on their emotional armor in preparation for the next upset. The more anger you express, the less effective your anger becomes, the less you are listened to, and the more cut off you may begin to feel from genuine closeness.

Anger has its place. There are times when it is healthy, even necessary, but those times are rare. In general, the more frequent and intense your anger, the more likely you are to sustain irremediable damage in your relationships.

Tafrate, Kassinove, and Dundin (2002)* studied anger episodes in adults. A total of 228 adults over the age of twenty-five were recruited and tested with the Trait Anger Scale. One-hundred and twenty-nine subjects met the criteria for either high trait anger (HTA) or low trait anger (LTA). In analyzing their sample they found that although the two cohorts were similar in most demographic variables, the HTA subjects were less likely to be married and more likely to be unemployed.

When asked to describe an anger episode and its consequences, additional differences were noted. In general, anger episodes appeared to have little or no impact on the relationships of LTA adults. With HTA adults, however, the results were different. These subjects experienced significantly more anger-related damage to relationships, and spent less time with the source of their anger following the episode.

Raising Defenses

With its genius for the obvious, psychological research has confirmed what most people already knew: anger leads to hostility as well as to physiological and verbal aggression (Rule and Nesdale 1976). The angrier you feel, the more likely you are to act it out in the form of an attack. And here's the kicker. Aggression begets hostility, anger, and more aggression. The more you behave aggressively, the angrier you become, and the more you want to keep up the assault. As Carol Tavris (1984) concluded after an exhaustive review of the anger literature, "a primary result of aggressive behavior seems to be to stimulate both parties to continued aggression."

That's what makes the aggressive expression of anger so damaging—it doesn't stop. Once you permit verbal or physical aggression to enter your relationships, you develop a tendency to return again and again to the hostile, aggressive response. Each episode breeds new fuel to generate attacks. A relationship that started with hope and trust slowly devolves into each partner's list of sins and transgressions.

Anger-fueled hostility and aggression cuts and scars the tissue of relationships. Scar tissue isn't healthy tissue. It's thick and hard and inelastic. It serves to cover and protect, but it blocks out feeling. Jerry Deffenbacher and his colleagues (1996) have done the most extensive research on how chronic anger affects personal and work relationships. Among other results, Deffenbacher (1992) found that

---

* Many thanks to Chip Tafrate for making available a prepublication copy of this journal article.

angry individuals suffer significant disruptions in work or school performance, and that high anger people drink more alcohol and get drunk more often. Houston and Kelley (1989) also reported a strong relationship between anger scores and overall levels of conflict in both the family of origin and current marriages.

Anger and Rigidity

As frequency of anger increases, there is a corresponding decrease in tolerance and flexibility (Biaggio 1980). That's because angry relationships spawn an atmosphere of vigilance and fear. Your energy gets channeled into erecting barriers, rather than into communication and problem solving. The barriers defend you against hurt, but they also create a maze of psychological mines and trenches that make it impossible for angry people to reach each other—even with genuine feelings of love and support.

Typical defenses against anger include numbness, judging, irritability, attack, withdrawal, revenge, and extreme restriction of response. Once set in place, these barriers cause you to become rigid and trigger-happy. It's hard to switch from defense to appreciation, from vigilance to any kind of trust. You'll tend to stay in the bunker, rather than risk real openness. And your tolerance for mistakes and criticism can fall so low that even the slightest flaw or hint of disapproval can make you blow up.

Anger and Resistance

Because anger is so often used to coerce change in others, people erect defenses not only to shield themselves from hurt, but also to keep from feeling controlled. They resist the angry person's demands by means of avoidance, discounting, counterblaming, derailing, passive-aggressive sabotage, and a host of other defensive maneuvers.

People fight to maintain their boundaries and limits. Losing the capacity to say no, to have choice, to make independent decisions is a kind of psychological death. You feel as if you're being engulfed or suffocated, as if the framework of the self were being crushed. No matter how frightening coercive anger becomes, it can never be as scary as the loss of self. So people resist anger that is used to pressure change.

When you use anger to influence the behavior of others, it often works extremely well. At least at the first, or even the second time. But soon enough those others learn to push you and your anger away. It's simply too scary for them to surrender control of their own behavior.

Losing the Sense of Well-Being

Chronically expressed anger tends to chip away at the quality of people's lives. Chronically angry people tend to feel more helpless than others and they find less satisfaction in every part of their lives.

Helplessness

Angry people often express a sense of helplessness. Nothing ever seems to go as they would like. Friends are selfish and insensitive, employers are tightwads and tyrants, a lover is unappreciative or withholding. Underlying these complaints is a genuine despair of ever feeling good, of ever feeling nurtured in relationships.

Anger leads to helplessness in four simple steps.

1. You tell yourself, "I'm in pain, something is wrong or lacking."

2. You tell yourself, "Others should fix or provide it."

3. You express your anger with aggression.

4. Your anger is met by resistance and withdrawal.

After step 4, the angry person feels frustrated: something is wrong, something is lacking. And the whole cycle starts again. This process continues, cycle after cycle, until a deep sense of hopelessness and cynicism begins to form. Each relationship seems to reach the inevitable stage where disappointments overtake the earlier enjoyment, and chronic upsets make it too aversive to go on.

In truth, helplessness is self-induced, and despair is unnecessary. A sense of entitlement really starts the cycle: "I should never feel pain, but if I do, you must fix it." The angry person puts the responsibility on others to meet his basic needs and gives up his own power in the process. The problem is compounded when he or she uses anger as a preferred strategy to make others change. As the others increasingly resist, the angry person feels his or her life sliding out of control. Nothing seems to work. No one really cares. No one seems good enough.

Diminished Satisfaction

Anger takes the pleasure out of life. As relationships become more defensive and distant, they offer fewer and fewer opportunities for warmth and nurturing. Very simply, the more one demands, the less one gets. This was documented in a survey of more than 1,000 patients referred for coronary angiography. Hostile people were shown to have the same number of social contacts as those who are not hostile. But hostile people experience their social contacts as lower in quality and less satisfying (Tavris 1984).

Clearly, feelings of entitlement and anger diminish your ability to really feel good with others. The myriad discomforts and little losses you experience all seem to be "their fault." And efforts to solve these problems with anger often serve only to make matters worse.

Self-Defeating Behaviors

Anger can have a negative effect on the decision-making process, and may lead to self-defeating behaviors. For example, Kassinove, Roth, Owens, and Fuller (reported in Tafrate, Kassinove, and Dundin 2002) studied subjects engaged in a simulated Wartime Prisoner's Dilemma game. High trait anger players made more attack responses that resulted in losses. It was concluded that high trait anger and anger control difficulties could be factors in poor decision making. Deffenbacher et al. (2000) offered correlational evidence that high trait anger is related to risky driving behavior that results in increased close calls and minor accidents.

Problems on the Job

Dr. Myer Friedman, one of the two men who identified the type A personality, has determined that hostile, hard-driving people fail far more than they succeed in the workplace. "Type A behavior, far from bringing about success in the factory, office, laboratory or marketplace, is actually responsible for repeated disasters—careers and lives wrecked, whole businesses and large enterprises threatened with ruin." All too common are the type A's who have "simply burned themselves out in pointless struggle, impatience, and anger" (Friedman and Ulmer 1984, pp. 62-63).

Anger doesn't work any better at the office than it does with friends or family. The results are exactly the same: defensiveness, counterattack, and withdrawal. Although sometimes anger can be used to motivate subordinates, it has the long-term effect of driving people away—to other departments or other jobs. Or they begin to drag their feet in subtle ways—nothing the angry supervisor can really point to, but just enough to make the unit a little less productive or the boss's stress level a little higher. People talk. They know who blames, who becomes upset at any imperfection. So angry individuals get less business, fewer referrals, less help from the typing pool, more noncompliance with requests. The list goes on. And so will your difficulties at work if you are frequently angry.

Isolation

For many people, the price of anger is isolation. Friendships are distant, love relationships severed. Tavris (1984) observes that hostile type A's "freely ventilate their wrath at anyone who displeases them and . . . thereby block off an important route to close friendships."

Greenglass (1996) studied a sample of 252 male and 65 female managers in Canada. Those with high scores on anger reported receiving less support from family members. They also reported less trust in their close relationships.

Hazaleus and Deffenbacher (1986) found that 45 percent of angry males in their sample had suffered a terminated or damaged relationship during the previous year. And a study by psychologist Debra Weaver and Darlene Shaw at the medical school of South Carolina found that hostile type A women had significantly worse marriages than type B's (reported in Wood 1986).

Barbour et al. (1998) studied anger and marital violence. They found that men who were violent in their marriage scored higher on trait anger. Not surprisingly, they also found that these men scored higher on anger expressed outwardly, and lower on anger control.

Loneliness

Anger has been associated with loneliness by a number of researchers. One study that reviewed much of the previous research on loneliness found that anger cuts people off from social support in two ways. First, cynical attitudes toward others can result in the failure to recognize that real support is available. Second, unrealistic and overly demanding expectations can make available support seem lacking in important respects or worthless. In either case, the angry person cannot feel or access the support that may exist. No matter how sincerely interested others may be in him or her, the judging, angry person simply doesn't see or appreciate it (Hansson, Jones, and Carpenter 1984).

Jones, Freeman, and Gasewick (1981) found that hostility, alienation, and negativistic attitudes were linked to such factors as low self-esteem and loneliness. An angry, unaccepting view of humanity, and a picture of the world as an unjust place, are associated with greater isolation.

It's clear that angry people keep others at arm's length. And in so doing they experience less support, less enjoyment, and a greater feeling of loneliness than their less hostile counterparts.

Isolation and Illness

Anger-induced isolation affects you physically as well as psychologically. Although the hormonal changes associated with chronic anger have been directly linked to cardiovascular and gastric disease, these are by no means the only physiological effects of anger.

Anger affects your body indirectly because people who lose or have weak social ties are far more susceptible to disease of all types. In their fine book, *The Healing Brain*, Ornstein and Sobel (1987) point out that the incidence of infections, cancer, tuberculosis, arthritis, and problems during pregnancy are all higher for people who have fewer social supports. Other researchers have added diabetes, hypertension, and asthma to the list (Hansson, Jones and Carpenter 1984). People who are divorced, separated, or have few close friends have a death rate two to five times that of married peers (Berkman and Syme 1979).

The relationship between isolation and a broad range of illness may explain why hostile people have higher death rates from all causes (Barefoot, Dahlstrom, and Williams, 1983). As social supports weaken due to chronic anger, so do the body's defenses against a host of infections and diseases.

5

Assessing the Cost
of Your Anger

Anger costs. And before you embark on any anger management program, it's important that you take the time to find out what that cost actually is. You may be paying for your anger in the coin of damaged relationships, damaged health, damage to your career, or actual financial losses from jobs or work relationships that went awry.

To understand the toll your anger may be taking, we want you to carefully go through the worksheet and assessment exercise that follow. The Anger Expression Worksheet will help you identify which of the ten key domains are affected by your anger—and *how* you express anger in each of them. The Anger Impact Inventory will help you rate the *degree* of negative impact that your anger has on your life.

Anger Expression Worksheet

In the spaces provided below, write brief descriptions of how anger has affected you in each area. Then identify the main anger behaviors you used in each domain (1) physical threats, (2) emotional threats, (3) blaming/accusing, (4) criticism/put-downs, (5) name calling/negative labeling, (6) expletives/profanity, (7) belittling/sarcasm/mocking, (8) dismissing/negating, (9) angry withdrawal, and (10) withholding.

1. How my anger has affected my work relationships (include jobs lost or jeopardized):

_____

_____

_____

_____

2. How my anger has affected the relationships with my family of origin (including parents, siblings, and extended family):

_____

_____

_____

_____

3. How my anger has affected my marriage or intimate/romantic relationships:

_____

_____

_____

_____

4. How my anger has affected my children:

_____

_____

_____

_____

5. How my anger has affected my friendships (including lost friends and strained relationships):

_____

_____

_____

_____

6. How my anger has harmed people who aren't family or friends (including the names of all the people my anger has hurt—on a separate sheet if necessary):

_____

_____

_____

_____

7. How my anger has affected my health and physical well-being (including stress-related illnesses/problems and physical discomfort from anger reactions):

_____

_____

_____

_____

8. How my anger has endangered me (including reckless driving, physical fights, hurting myself by hitting things, legal problems, etc.):

_____

_____

_____

_____

9. How my anger has affected me financially (including bad decisions made in anger as well as material objects broken or damaged):

_____

_____

_____

_____

10. How my anger has affected me spiritually (including bad behavior that goes against my personal code of ethics or my sense of right and wrong, my conscience):

_____

_____

_____

_____

Adapted from *The Anger Control Workbook* by Matthew McKay and Peter Rogers, New Harbinger Publications, 2000.

The worksheet you've just completed has given you an opportunity to examine two things. You first looked at specific negative outcomes from anger in ten areas of your life. Some of these domains may be untouched by your anger. But in others, you may have paid dearly for explosive moments you'd give anything to undo. The second thing you explored on this worksheet was your modes for anger expression. This can tell you about your anger style, and whether your methods of anger expression vary from situation to situation.

Here are some questions to think about as you review what you've written on the worksheet:

1. Where is anger affecting you most? What relationships, what aspects of your life have been most damaged?

2. Are there particular outcomes that occur over and over across domains? For example, being rejected or avoided by others.

3. Are there things you can no longer do or places you are no longer welcome because of your anger?

4. How permanent is the damage? Are any of these outcomes reparable?

5. How many of these anger outcomes are still affecting you emotionally today?

6. What are your predominant forms of anger expression?

7. What anger behaviors have cost you the most (i.e., been the most damaging)?

8. Do you tend to use different anger behaviors with different people and situations, or is your anger expression consistent across domains?

9. What anger behavior would you most like to change?

10. Which of the ten domains would you like to focus on initially for changing your anger behavior?

Anger Impact Inventory

0 = No Effect

1 = Minor Effect

2 = Moderate Effect

3 = Very Significant Effect

4 = Major Effect

Instructions: Using the five-point scale above, rate the degree of impact your anger has on the following:

Rating

1. Relationships with authorities (teachers, bosses, police, government, and so on)   _____

2. Relationships with peers and colleagues at work   _____

3. Relationships with subordinates at work   _____

4. Relationships with customers, clients, business associates and so on   _____

5. Relationships with children   _____

6. Relationships with children's teachers, other parents   _____

7. Relationships with spouse or lover   _____

8. Relationships with previous spouse or lover   _____

9. Relationships with in-laws   _____

10. Relationships with parents   _____

11. Relationships with other family members   _____

12. Relationships with current friends   _____

13. Relationships with former friends   _____

14. Relationships with neighbors   _____

15. The role of anger in lost relationships   _____

16. Relationships with recreational groups or organizations   _____

17. Relationships to religious groups or organizations   _____

18. Relationships with political and other groups   _____

19. Impact of anger episodes on your health   _____

20. Effect of anger symptoms (rapid heart rate, tension, shoulder and neck pain, headache, irritability, feeling of pressure, restlessness, insomnia, brooding, and so on)   _____

21. Time lost to angry feelings   _____

22. Anger intrusion into relaxing or pleasurable activities (sex, sports, hobbies, day in the country, vacations, and so on)   _____

23. Effect of anger on drinking or drug use   _____

24. Effect of anger on creativity or productivity   _____

25. Effect of anger on experience while driving   _____

26. Accidents, errors, and mistakes   _____

As you examine the inventory, see whether any patterns emerge. Is your anger having an impact on intimate relationships more than on distant ones? Is your anger more damaging in relationship to authorities, parents, or peers? Notice the items with a score of 2 or higher. These are your trouble spots. They may require special attention as you begin to practice the anger management skills you will learn later in this book.

Now add up your total score. If your score is between 10 and 14, it indicates a *moderate* problem with anger. This is a good time to learn new behavior patterns—before more damage is done. If your score is between 15 and 19, the impact of anger on your life is *very significant*. It needs to be addressed immediately, particularly if any items are rated 3 or 4. If your score is 20 or above, your anger is having a *major impact* on your life. Furthermore, if any items were rated 3 or above, you should consider your anger problem to be of great urgency.

The time to do something about your anger is *now*. Your future will be determined by what you decide in this moment. What has happened in the past is beyond reach, beyond changing. What is about to happen is still yours to control. We urge you to identify immediately the areas of your life where anger has been most hurtful. Then commit yourself to using this book for change. Wishes and good intentions won't be enough. It'll take a bold decision. Not tomorrow. Not the next day. Now.

6

Anger as a Choice: The Two-Step Model of Anger

It's late afternoon. The TV is on. The kitchen is hot and full of oven smells. James and his mother, Sarah, begin the opening round of a familiar conflict.

Sarah: Is your homework done yet?

James: It's only six o'clock. I have all night to do it.

Sarah: Everybody has a job to do. This is my job right here, making dinner. You think I like standing in this hot kitchen? Your job is your schoolwork, and I don't see you doing it.

James: Look, I'm chilling out from school. Leave me alone.

Sarah: I want you to turn off the television and do your schoolwork. I'm sick of telling you. Just do your job like everybody else.

James: You think your job is to be the field marshal around here. Leave me alone. Go hassle Dad when he comes in.

Sarah: (*starting to shout*) I'm sick of your mouth. Turn off the television, I said. You're lazy, you let your work go to the last minute, and then it's slipshod crap.

James: (*shouting*) Stuff it, just stuff it. And you know where. You can't stand it when I relax; you never let me relax for a second. I guess you want everybody to be as crazy and screwed up as you are.

At this point a key is heard turning in the front door. James's father, Leonard, walks the short way to the kitchen. He leans against the counter and begins speaking in a quiet, compressed voice.

Leonard: What's going on in here? What's the matter with you? I'm walking up thinking, "finally I can relax," and I hear you screaming like banshees in here. (*He grows louder.*) James, did I hear you calling your mother crazy? Is that a way to talk? Do you want to shout? Why don't you shout at me? (*He moves towards James.*) Why don't you shout at me, huh? Why don't you try it? See how it feels. (*He pushes James backward.*) Nothing? You don't want to shout? (*He turns to Sarah.*) What's the matter with the two of you? What's wrong in this house? (*He shouts.*) Why don't you learn to talk to each other? Bickering, bickering. This place is like a damn asylum!

None of the participants wanted this fight. In retrospect, James described it as "spontaneous combustion—like we're a pile of dry leaves waiting for a spark." But Sarah, James, and Leonard are caught in a pattern that is anything but spontaneous. Each of them brings to the conflict a unique and largely unacknowledged group of stresses. Stress is the fuel of anger, because it creates high levels of physiological arousal that must be discharged. But stress does not, by itself, create anger. Each combatant also must bring a set of "trigger thoughts" that act as psychological flint to ignite the anger and aggression.

You can see how this works by viewing a *cognitive replay* of Sarah, James, and Leonard's fight. A cognitive replay documents the internal processes of each participant, as reconstructed during a family therapy session.

Sarah's most immediate stresses are heat and fatigue. Additional stress comes from her unspoken fear that James is using drugs, a fear that she uses to explain his decreasing interest in schoolwork. Sarah also lives with a chronic level of frustration and sadness that she and James are not as close these days and he reveals little about himself. She is hurt, too, that her husband has been distant and sexually unresponsive for the past several months. The decision to get angry occurs as Sarah listens to the sound of television in the living room. She uses two kinds of trigger thoughts to start her anger: *shoulds* and *blamers.*

Shoulds:

"Everyone must do his job."

"No one should watch television in the afternoon, it's lazy."

Blamers:

"He lets his work go to the last minute."

"His work is slipshod crap."

Sarah says variations of these four statements to herself throughout the fight with James. Each statement is like pushing down the handle of an emotional whirling top; she feels more and more righteous and angry.

James's stresses include muscle tension from a school day in which he felt unprepared for several classes and pain from a chronic knee injury aggravated during soccer practice.

James is also experiencing moderate levels of guilt over recent inattentiveness to his schoolwork. At the moment that the fight begins, he is experiencing high anxiety over a decision to call an attractive girl for a date. His strong drive to relax this tension is frustrated by his mother when she asks about his homework.

James triggers his anger with three blamers:

Blamers:

"You're trying to control me."

"You're deliberately preventing me from relaxing so I'll feel as bad as you do."

"You're crazy and screwed up."

Leonard's stresses include chronic tension in his neck and shoulders and rising anxiety over a recent symptom of skipped heartbeats. He is physically aroused from a rushed day filled with anxiety over new high production quotas instituted three months earlier. Leonard has a strong fear of rejection; the raised voices he hears as he walks in sound like threats that he will be hurt or abandoned.

Leonard triggers his anger with three blamers and two shoulds:

Blamers:

"They deny me a chance to relax."

"This house is crazy with bickering, a damn asylum."

"James is turning into a sullen, withdrawn ingrate."

Shoulds:

"James should never attack his mother."

"They should learn to talk to each other."

Sarah, James, and Leonard were each in pain. They each made an independent decision to cope with that physical and emotional stress by using anger-triggering thoughts to ignite a hostile outpouring. For a few moments the anger felt very good, the stress was masked or discharged. There was a release. In a while, the stress would be back—this time in the form of guilt or hurt or frustration. But in those few moments of discharge and relief, the strategy of anger was reinforced. When in pain, they would return again to the attack.

The Function of Anger

The sole function of anger is to stop stress. It does this by discharging or blocking awareness of painful levels of emotional or physical arousal. There are four kinds of stress that anger serves to dissipate.

1. **Painful affect.** Anger can block off painful emotions so that they are literally pushed out of your awareness. It can also discharge high levels of arousal experienced during periods of anxiety, hurt, guilt, and so on.

2. **Painful sensation.** Stress is often experienced as a physical sensation. The most common form is muscle tension, but stressful arousal may also stem from physical pain or sympathetic nervous system activity.

3. **Frustrated drive.** Anger can discharge stress that develops when you are frustrated in the search for something you need or want. It functions to vent high arousal levels that inevitably grow when your desires are blocked.

4. **Threat.** Any perceived threat, either to your physical or psychological well-being, creates immediate arousal. The arousal mobilizes you and generates a very strong push for some stress-reduction activity.

Each of the four types of stress sets off a psychological alarm mechanism that tells you something is not right. As the arousal builds, so too does your need to cope with it, to stop the pain. As you'll soon discover, anger is just one of many coping strategies available to you to discharge stressful arousal.

How Anger Stops Stress

To understand how anger stops stress, it will be helpful to return to the four types of stressful arousal.

Painful Affect

Anxiety and fear. Consider the mother who, seeing her child run into the street, shakes him and shouts about his carelessness. Anger blocks and discharges her surge of fear so that the enormous terror of losing a child is hardly experienced before the rush of angry words. In the fight that opened this chapter, Leonard is afraid of failing at work and worries that there is something wrong with his heart. The arousal generated by these concerns is discharged for a while by his outburst.

Loss and depression. The stress is quieter, more aching here. But sadness creates a tension that is every bit as painful as fear and a need to escape the pain every bit as great. Consider the man whose girlfriend has announced her desire to date other people. The loss of intimacy and of sharing consumes him for days. At work he upbraids his secretary for excessive typos, and there is a brief tension release until he resumes his sad review of lovely moments in his relationship.

Hurt. The pain of hurt can be so acute that anger is employed as a blocking mechanism almost immediately. A woman is criticized by her husband for being careless with money. She feels humiliated and dismissed. But within a few seconds her arousal is so high and so painful that she explodes in order to block any further awareness of it. You may remember that Sarah had been hurt by her husband's distance and sexual withdrawal. Some of that pain was discharged in her battles with her son.

Guilt and shame. Anger erases guilt. It is not you who has done wrong, but the other person. A woman comes home at six o'clock to find her son already in bed, lights out, surrounded by all his stuffed animals. When she asks what he's doing, he tells her that he's lonely. A wave of guilt surges up. As the arousal reaches intolerable levels, she reminds herself that his father never visits, and that's the real source of the problem. Now she is righteous and angry, discharging her guilt in a stream of silent condemnations. In the opening fight, James's guilt over inattentiveness to his schoolwork was neatly buried under anger at his mother.

Feelings of failure, badness, and unworthiness. Consider the young man who shows some of his poetry to an English teacher. The teacher shows him how the lines don't communicate. For the next fifteen minutes the young man wanders the halls, clutching his meaningless blather, feeling a deep worthlessness. The pain accelerates until he seizes on the teacher's accent and mannerisms to condemn him as an "affected twit." Many people have at their core a sense of wrongness or badness that can be activated with the smallest criticism or remark. Anger is a popular strategy to block awareness of these feelings and discharge any consciously felt pain that they might trigger.

Painful Sensation

Rushing. Leonard comes home after rushing to meet production quotas all day. He discharges stress by going on the attack.

Physical pain. You have undoubtedly noticed that when you hurt, you become tense. And with little effort, you can find something to get angry at. Imagine the scene where a man is dozing on the beach.

His sons are kicking and chasing a beachball. One of them trips and falls on him. The man sits bolt upright and cuffs his boy because he has learned to relieve pain with anger.

Overstimulation. Too much excitement, too intense a conversation, the success of a great presentation at the board meeting, or a lucky day in the casino can all take their toll. The arousal from the good times may reach stressful levels. When you come home from a day of drama and intensity, anger may be your way of cooling down, of discharging the energy.

Muscle tension. In the process of coping with the day, most people gather tension in zones of vulnerability. The forehead, jaw, shoulders, and abdomen are the most common of these zones. Anger can sometimes relieve muscle tension by discharging energy until, in the aftermath, you finally relax.

Tiredness and overwork. Fatigue creates stress. Lactic acid builds up in your muscles until your discomfort forces you into some arousal-reduction strategy.

Frustrated Drive

Arousal from blocked needs or desires. This is the human condition, the struggle to have what there isn't enough of. Waiting and wanting. Consider the woman whose vacation is again and again delayed because coworkers fall unexpectedly ill and she is needed to fill in during their absence. Finally she is aroused to such a pitch that she attacks her boss as "uncaring and incompetent." She feels good. There is a moment of discharge. Then she is given her two week's notice. In the opening fight, James's need for recreation was frustrated when his mother demanded that he stop watching television. Anger was his chosen strategy to cope.

Things are not as they should be. Here the frustration is to one's sense of order, "oughtness," perfection. Your picture of a world in which people act in good and correct ways is often violated. A checker puts your groceries in a single, flimsy bag. Your silent condemnation of his "wrongness" and "stupidness" creates painful arousal. Your daughter arrives home with a man friend dressed in purple leather. There is something wrong with this picture. As your tension rises, you wonder where she found this cross between a hippie and a motorcycle punk.

The sense of being forced. Not only aren't you getting your way, but you are being made to do something that's opposed to your needs or values. A man's lover insists on discussing "the problem of commitment" in their relationship. He knows from experience that she will feel hurt and withdraw if the issue is not explored. As the discussion continues, his tension rises until he blurts out something quite uncomplimentary about her recent haircut.

Threat

Feeling attacked. Here arousal is immediate. Anger is used to push away the threat so you can return to a relaxed state. Your boss announces that you are among a group of people who will be laid off. Your reaction is shock and a sudden surge in stress level. "Wait a minute, this isn't fair." You start to raise your voice. The anger helps you block awareness of the fear and tightness in your stomach.

Feeling engulfed. The experience is one of being controlled, of not having the right to set limits or say no. A teenager who felt overwhelmed by his father's rules and strictures could not bring himself to insist on greater freedom. He dealt with these threats to his autonomy by secretly burning important papers belonging to his father. A woman whose husband insisted that she forego all male friendships experienced this threat as tension in her diaphragm. "I felt I had to go along with it, but sometimes I'd want to scream. I knew if I screamed, I would feel better, so I imagined screaming the most horrible things at him."

Feeling abandoned. For a child, this is a threat to survival. Many adults experience abandonment as threatening in the very same way—as if their very existence were in danger, as if abandonment were death. Anger helps block awareness of the fear of loss and aloneness while mobilizing you to end the threat: to leave them before they leave you, to shake some sense into them, to make them hear your pain.

Alternative Stress-Reduction Strategies

There are many ways to discharge high levels of stress besides anger. Some of them are healthy, some are destructive. Any one of these can be used *instead of anger* when you are stressed. The following list is by no means inclusive, but will give you some ideas.

Crying. This is the first strategy you learn to cope with pain. Crying helps you discharge tension and discomfort, it relaxes tight muscles, it helps you communicate your needs.

Exercising. Walking, dancing, tennis, swimming—literally any aerobic reduces stress. (See chapter 10.)

Intense work activity. Chores like washing the dishes and vacuuming, cooking, painting, fixing, and building, all function to reduce stress by channeling your energy into a focused task.

Humor. Looking at the light side, the absurdity of a situation. Poking fun at things. Reframing the stress as something much less serious, even silly.

Writing. Poetry and journal writing are effective vehicles for expressing and discharging feelings.

Relaxation exercises. Among the most effective are meditation, progressive muscle relaxation, deep breathing, autogenics, and self-hypnosis. (See chapter 10.)

Verbalizing pain. The act of saying out loud that you hurt reduces painful stress. Even if you're shouting in your car or on an empty beach, just saying it is calming and sometimes even healing.

Recreation. Reading, TV, games, and hobbies act as psychological sponges that sop up stress.

Sex. Sex works well in two ways. First, it blocks awareness of painful feelings. Second, an orgasm has an enormous capacity to reduce tension from any source.

Problem-solving activities. Directing your energy toward fixing what's wrong reduces stress because you're dealing with the root problem. You anticipate some relief, you feel less helpless. (See chapter 11.)

Problem-solving communication. Letting the other person know your needs, feelings, and limits reduces stress born of frustration. (See chapter 16.)

Pillow and bed beating. This is a great way to have a private blow-out. Sometimes using a tennis racket can make the pummeling louder and more satisfying.

Music. Whatever your taste or preference in decibels, music can be profoundly calming. A little time alone with a favorite recording is a nearly surefire strategy for reducing stress from any source.

Resting. A period of no activity can be very helpful. Even brief rest periods, like counting or taking a deep sigh before making a response, can bring a moment of relative calm.

There are also many arousal-reduction strategies that are effective, but self-destructive. Included here are alcohol and drugs, recklessness and danger seeking, and compulsive sex. All of these can block, numb, or reduce pain, but their effectiveness is outweighed by obvious negative consequences.

The number of alternative stress-reduction strategies should make it clear that anger is only one of many possible responses to painful levels of arousal. In fact, anger is among the least effective of the listed strategies. It costs too much because it takes such a huge toll on you physiologically and because it damages relationships. The truth is that anger is rarely necessary. There are better ways to cope with stress than to go on the attack. Anger is usually effective only in the short term as a stress-reduction strategy. In the long run, it harms your health and isolates you. This book will help you develop more effective strategies to cope with the stress that underlies your anger.

Why You Choose Anger to Reduce Stress

There are three factors influencing the choice of any stress-reduction strategy, whether it's crying, relaxing, problem solving, or anger. The first is *physiological predisposition.*

You are born with a set of constitutional tendencies that make some responses easier or more rewarding than others. Some people are neurologically wired in such a way that anger tends to work better for arousal reduction than certain other strategies they have tried. However, a predisposition is just that. It's a tendency, a response that may be a little easier than other responses. Although anger may be constitutionally somewhat easier or more effective for you in temporary stress reduction, you *can* learn other strategies.

The second major influence on the choice of a stress-reduction strategy is *instrumental conditioning.* This is the process by which, as a child, certain behaviors were reinforced while others were discouraged. If you had a tantrum and were given what you wanted, the effect was to reinforce tantrum behavior. If you demanded your sister's block set and she refused and you then hit her and she acquiesced, you were reinforced for hitting. If your mother gave in when you shouted, you learned that shouting was rewarded. At the same time, as a child, you could have been rewarded for any of the other stress-reduction strategies. Intense work activity or problem-solving communication or verbalizing your pain could have been reinforced. Everyone responds in ways that he or she has learned to be effective. Anger is nothing more than a learned response to certain kinds of stress. In your family, anger worked well enough for it to become part of your adult strategic arsenal.

The last major factor in determining your choice of stress-reduction strategies is *social learning.* Social learning involves the skills and behaviors that you acquired through *modeling.* This is the process by which you imitate how parents and significant peers act.

You try to do it like they do. You strive to look and sound and behave like your role model. If you grew up in a family where people coped with their pain by getting angry, no doubt you modeled some of your behavior on what you observed. If your parents were loud and threatening or blaming when they felt bad, then you are likely to use the same strategies when you feel bad. The old cliche "like father like son" is unfortunately true in terms of anger responses. Children very quickly learn how their parents cope and begin making it part of their own behavior patterns.

You use anger to control stress because of a unique combination of physiological predisposition, reinforcement, and social learning. But you do have a choice. This book offers new tools and skills for coping with painful levels of arousal. It is a matter of trying them to see which ones work best for you.

How You Create Anger

Anger is a two-step process. It usually starts with stress and the subjective experience of arousal that stress of any kind generates. Stress motivates you to begin coping. You want to lower or block these uncomfortable feelings. The *first step* in anger production concludes when your awareness of stress leads to a coping decision. Although coping could include tears, relaxation, exercise, music, verbalizing, or problem solving, too frequently you may find yourself choosing to block and discharge pain through anger.

As you've seen, stress is not a sufficient cause for anger. You need the psychological flint of anger-triggering thoughts to convert stress into hostile affect. *Step two* in anger production is the process by which you focus on either *blamers* or *shoulds*.

Blamers. Here the generic thought is, "you deliberately did _____ to me." The key idea is that you have been intentionally harmed by the wrong behavior of another.

Shoulds. The generic thought here is, "you should not have _____ but instead you should have _____ ." The implication is that the person knows or should know how to act correctly and has, out of stupidity or selfishness, broken the rules of reasonable conduct.

Both kinds of trigger thoughts have, as a core belief, a perception of the other person as bad, wrong, and deserving of punishment. When Leonard says to himself, "They deny me the chance to relax," the implication is that Sarah and James are deliberately harming him. They are bad and should be punished. When Sarah says to herself, "Everyone must do his job," she sees James as breaking a basic rule of life. He is doing wrong and should be punished. When James blames his mother for trying to control him, he sees her as the "field marshal" deliberately inflicting harm. His response is to want to hurt her back.

Stress (painful arousal) plus trigger thoughts equal anger. You cannot have anger without both components being present. Trigger thoughts without arousal produce a judgment without emotion. Arousal without trigger thoughts leaves you in a chronic state of pain until you choose an alternative stress-reduction strategy.

The Anger Cycles

The anger cycle can start in two ways.

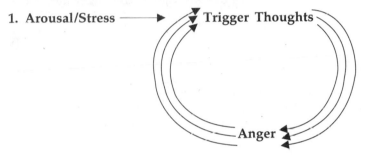

This is the conventional cycle described throughout this chapter. Notice that stress begets trigger thoughts, which beget anger, more trigger thoughts, more anger, and so on. Your thoughts and angry feelings become a feedback loop which can be self-perpetuating. The feedback loop is what keeps your anger simmering for hours or even days without letup.

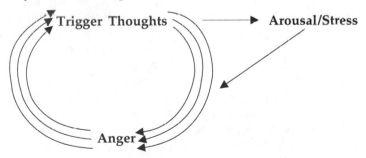

In cycle two, the trigger thoughts create a stress reaction (however brief), which then fuels anger. Some trigger thoughts are sufficiently provocative to create arousal where none previously existed. Arthur wonders if his wife will work long hours at her law office again tonight. The image of himself sitting through news shows and sitcoms waiting for her key in the door triggers a deep sense of abandonment. But he thinks that the pain is her fault. Almost instantly he converts the stressful feeling into anger. Now the anger stirs more trigger thoughts: "She doesn't care really about our marriage—there's that weekend where she decided to go away by herself, and her habit of reading in bed, and the fights about who was supposed to shop." Arthur is now caught in the feedback loop. Trigger thoughts breed more anger, which sets off more trigger thoughts, followed by more anger, and so on.

In cycle two, there is always an intervening moment of pain (loss, rejection, despair, fear, frustration, hurt, abandonment) between the trigger thought and the anger. But the perception that the pain is someone else's fault quickly ignites the anger and establishes the feedback loop.

Implications

As you come to understand the two-step process in anger production, it may affect some of your basic assumptions about the emotion. Consider the following implications of this model.

There Is Nothing Inherently Right or Legitimate About Anger

The only thing true and indisputable when you feel angry is that you are in pain and trying to do something about it. The trigger thoughts that you use to generate your anger may be false, or at best very debatable, and your anger may therefore have no legitimate basis. When Leonard tells himself that his son is a "sullen, withdrawn ingrate," these are global generalities that grossly exaggerate aspects of his son's behavior. This triggering thought is just plain wrong, and Leonard's feeling that James deserves punishment is equally wrong. His anger is not legitimate, it is not "right." When James decides that his mother is keeping him from relaxing because she wants him to feel as bad as she does, he is falsely assuming that his mother wishes him to feel pain. His decision to punish and attack her is based on an erroneous premise. Again, his anger has no legitimate basis.

The computer world uses the catch phrase "garbage in, garbage out." The same is true of your emotions. If you use triggering statements that are false or distorted versions of reality, the emotional storm that erupts is a response not to a real issue, but to an imagined violation. In the next chapter, you'll see that much of your anger may fall into this category.

Remember, your real motivation in getting angry is to reduce or discharge the arousal that comes from stress. The triggering statements you use may be quite arbitrary; they may even be total self-deceptions that you would deplore in a calmer moment. But at the time, you're not particularly concerned if your perceptions are true. What you want is to release or to block the pain.

Ventilationists claim that anger should be expressed because feelings have inherent legitimacy. As you've seen, a moment of anger can be fueled by many different, simultaneous experiences of stress. Although the pain is important, and perhaps even the expression of pain is important, the anger is usually destructive. It is not the anger that needs to come out, but the pain (stress) that underlies the anger. It is not the anger that is legitimate and right, but the human suffering that must be acknowledged and explored.

The Dam of Anger

The ventilationists would have you believe that there is a great dam inside you, holding back a reservoir of anger and angry impulses. In this "hydraulic theory" of anger, unexpressed angry feelings build and build. Finally the accumulated weight bursts through, shattering your mask of calmness. The ventilationists are wrong. It is not anger that builds, but stress. Stress of all types and from all sources: emotional pain, physical pain, frustration, and threat. As long as stress persists without remedy, you will continue to feel tension and arousal. The stress grows. Anger, as you have seen, is merely one of many possible strategies you can use to cope. Failing to express your anger *does not build up more anger*. It does not, in itself, increase your stress. Choosing not to express anger merely means that the arousal will continue at painful levels until you find a way to reduce it.

If Sarah had decided not to express anger, she might have reduced the stress in other ways. She might have suggested eating out that night to escape the hot kitchen. She might have chosen to discuss her fears about drug use with James or to share with him her feeling of being excluded from his life. Or she might have done some problem solving around television and homework. Holding in her anger would not create more anger. In fact, her anger is keeping her from really doing something about the causes of her stress. It masks the pain without really changing anything.

The same is true for Leonard. He is tense and scared about failing at work and having a heart attack. Choosing not to express his anger won't have the effect of damming up his rage for some later, more destructive explosion. It would merely mean having to live with the stress for a while until he finds another way to cope: a medical exam, seeking feedback from his boss, relaxation exercises for his shoulder spasms, and so on. Leonard's anger masks the real problem and obscures the path to real solutions.

Forget Displacement

Displacement theory holds that there is an appropriate target for your anger. In healthy anger, you express your feelings to the appropriate person or in the appropriate setting. Displacement is seen as a less healthy alternative. Here you take anger that belongs with one target and direct it to another less threatening target. You can't shout at your boss, so you go home and scream at your wife. You can't say it to your girlfriend, so you take it out on your mother.

In the two-step model of anger, displacement is an irrelevant issue. Anger is a response to stress, and its function is to discharge or block awareness of that stress. It may feel somewhat more cathartic to express anger to the person you associate with your pain, but as you have seen with Sarah, James, and Leonard, the anger is rarely about the real issues anyway. All anger usually does is temporarily reduce tension. Whether you ventilate to the appropriate person or displace your feelings onto a less threatening object, the underlying stress is rarely addressed in a constructive way. Angry people become too defensive to engage in real problem solving. So don't ask yourself, "Did I get angry at the right person?" Ask yourself, "Did I express the pain in a way that may lead to a solution?"

You Choose to Be Angry

It may seem like a revolutionary thought, but you do *choose* to feel angry. Up to now, the choice has been largely unconscious. It's a habit, based on years of conditioning. Anger is a strategy you use to cope with many kinds of stress because to some degree and at some times it works for you. Now what was hidden can be observed. What was unconscious can be consciously experienced. When you feel stress, you can choose not to take the second step. You can begin consciously turning away from anger-triggering thoughts.

Developing the awareness that you choose trigger thoughts to cope with stress is easier said than done. Right now, this is an abstract idea. Interesting, perhaps. Maybe a little threatening. You can make this real for you by studying your own process and developing an intimate awareness of how your anger works. To accomplish this essential task you will need to do more work in your anger journal.

New Entries for Your Anger Journal

The anger journal is an important part of the work you'll do to change your anger (see chapter 1). For the next two days at least, make an entry in your journal on each occasion that you feel angry.

Sometimes you won't be able to take notes right away, but please go back and try to reconstruct the processes leading to your anger.

There are four questions you need to ask in your journal in order to more fully understand each occasion of anger.

1. **What stresses preexisted your anger?** Prior to the moment of anger, were you aware of any painful feelings such as hurt, anxiety, sadness, or guilt? Did you experience any sense of threat, frustration, or uncomfortable physical sensations?

2. **What trigger thoughts did you use?** Think back to exactly what was on your mind at the moment you became aware of the anger. What were the thoughts that ignited your feelings? Try to recall any shoulds. Remember, the generic should statement is: "You should not have _____ , but instead you should have _____ ." The should statement carries the implication that the other person is bad and must be made to admit his or her wrongdoing. Also, try to recall any blamers: "You deliberately did _____ to me." Note your assumption that the other person is culpable, that he or she has harmed you with intent. Can you identify the point where the trigger thoughts turn your stress into anger?

3. **Were you angry or were you feeling some other kind of stress before the trigger statements?** In some cases, this may seem very hard to answer. Anger has a strange halo effect, seeming to bathe the entire memory in a feeling of outrage and wrongness. The trigger thoughts lead you to the perception that you are a victim, that you have been "done to" by someone. It's hard to go back to the moment you decided that someone was "responsible" for your pain. However, it is that very moment where the anger began. Your stress was transformed then into hostile affect.

4. **Was some of your preexisting stress blocked or discharged by the anger?** Note in your journal whether you felt better, even for a few brief moments after you became angry. The stress certainly may have come back, but did the anger give you even a few seconds of relief? Such relief, no matter how short in duration, is highly reinforcing.

Do your journal work before reading the next chapter. It will help give you a foundation of awareness to build on as you learn more about the many specific cognitive triggers for anger and begin developing skills to resist them.

Anger Journal

For each anger incident you experience complete the following:

Date/time: _____

Brief description of the event:

Degree of peak arousal (minimum = 1, maximum = 10): _____

Degree of peak aggressive behavior (minimum = 1, maximum = 10):

_____

Pre-existing stressors (e.g., feeling hurt, anxious, or muscle tension):

Trigger thoughts (e.g., "shoulds" or blaming statements):

Result of anger episode (e.g., "felt relief" or "felt excited"):

Sample Anger Journal

For each anger incident you experience complete the following:

Date/time: *3/18 lunchtime*

Brief description of the event: *I'm waiting on line at the Deli.
Everybody wants some kind of special sandwich, all I want is a pas-
trami on rye. This is taking all day. Now the sandwich guy is flirting
with a cute customer. When I finally get to the counter, the sandwich
guy takes a telephone call and keeps yakking. I yell, "Hey come on,
let's go."*

Degree of peak arousal (minimum = 1, maximum = 10):   5

Degree of peak aggressive behavior (minimum = 1, maximum = 10):

  4

Pre-existing stressors (e.g., feeling hurt, anxious, or muscle tension):

*I'm having a bad day Boss chewed me out for coming to work a lousy
five minutes late.*

Trigger thoughts (e.g., "shoulds" or blaming statements):

*They should have more people working the counter. They don't give a
shit about their customers. It's going to be their fault if I'm late again
today.*

Result of anger episode (e.g., "felt relief" or "felt excited"):

No relief at all. And I felt guilty later for acting like a jerk.

7

Who's Responsible

When you're in pain, you very often ask yourself, "Who did this to me, who's responsible?" The impulse to assign blame lies at the root of chronic anger. As soon as you decide that someone is responsible for your anxiety or hurt or physical tension, you feel justified in discharging your stress with anger. The perception that someone has caused your pain turns you into a victim. You see yourself as threatened, under siege by another's wrongdoing.

There is a pleasure in blaming. When someone else is responsible, you can turn your focus away from your pain and concentrate on listing the sins and the injustices that you have suffered. The stress is blocked or discharged and for a while you feel better.

But there's a problem with the habit of finding others responsible for your pain. It isn't true. You are solely responsible for the quality of your life. Whether you are in pain or not, whether your needs are met or not, whether your relationships feel good or not, is entirely determined by the choices you make. There are four reasons why you, and only you, are responsible for your experience.

1. **You are the only one who really knows and understands your own needs.** You are the expert on what feels good and what feels bad to you: your tastes and aversions, the subtle hurts, the hidden dreams, the slight but important difference between kinds of touching. Others can only guess about what rewards you and where you are vulnerable. They are hopelessly locked outside of your inner experience.

   Much of what seems obvious to you about your needs is hidden from even your intimates. Consider the man who feels great resentment because his wife rarely touches his penis during foreplay. He has told her several times during the past year that "it would be nice" if she touched his genitals more often. But his wife has no way of knowing how deep his desire is or precisely what sort of touching feels most stimulating to him. Nonetheless, he blames her for not really caring about his pleasure.

2. **It is appropriate for others to focus on meeting their own needs.** Their first responsibility must be to take care of themselves, to minimize pain, to provide for their own emotional nourishment, and to pursue those experiences that they find most satisfying. It is *not* the responsibility of others to take care of you. If others place your needs above their own, then they must neglect their own first responsibility of preserving their own lives and well-being.

If you feel that others should be willing to endure pain so that you won't have to, or give up what is emotionally or physically nourishing so that you can be nourished, then you are expecting a degree of altruism that is rarely encountered. Even the Christian ethic of loving others as yourself assumes that you first provide for your own needs (by loving yourself) before you give to others. Consider the woman who wanted her husband to give up watching sports on the weekend so that they could take drives in the country. She was enraged that he wouldn't "do something I would enjoy." The fact was that he despised driving because he spent long hours on the road during his workweek. Only when she came to accept that her husband's responsibility was to take care of his needs, and not hers, was she able to generate real solutions to her problem. By organizing weekend trips to Napa Valley (winetasting was one of his hobbies), she was finally able to entice him into a car.

3. **Peoples' needs inevitably conflict.** Everyone on the planet struggles to get basic needs met, and the struggle often leads to disagreement and competition. Every relationship must come to terms with this basic reality: the pursuit of one person's needs will frequently mean discomfort and frustration for the other. You may be tempted to ignore this reality by redefining your needs as "doing what's right" while dismissing the needs of others as a selfish indulgence. But this view belies the fact that your need to feel good and avoid pain is no more important than anyone else's.

The solution that usually works best for conflicting needs is compromise, giving something to get something. Helen, a thirty-four-year-old mother of two, was angered because her ex-husband brought the children home late from visits. While she waited for her kids, anxiety rose as she imagined them being abducted. The fear was unnerving, so Helen pushed it away with her anger. When she reframed the problem as a collision of needs, steps toward a solution began to present themselves. In a discussion with her ex-husband, she learned that he tended to return late because he wanted to spend more time with the children. He told her that he especially enjoyed taking them on day-long outings, and so he often had a hard time meeting her three o'clock deadline. Her need was predictability; his need was more time. He proposed a seven o'clock deadline, and after some bargaining they agreed to a six o'clock limit with a phone call if he were going to be late.

4. **Your overall life satisfaction depends on the effectiveness of your strategies for meeting needs and avoiding pain.** By making others responsible for your needs, you are obscuring this basic law of human interaction. If you're unhappy, it means that the strategies that you typically use to get emotional nourishment aren't working.

Consider the case of Al, whose girlfriend said he never listened. He reacted by expressing anger and withdrawing. Al's strategy wasn't effective because his girlfriend only became angry in turn and intensified her criticism. The problem doesn't lie with the criticism, but with the effectiveness of Al's strategy for dealing with it. Eventually he developed a better way of coping: he responded by expressing hurt rather than anger and then encouraged his girlfriend to express the specific needs underlying her global criticism. The same analysis can be made of his girlfriend's side in the exchange. She needed attention, but her strategy of blame and anger triggered Al's withdrawal. Only when she developed a more effective way of coping would there be any real chance for improvement in the relationship.

The Principle of Personal Responsibility

To understand how the principle of personal responsibility can change your anger, start with the assumption (whether you believe it or not) that (1) *you are responsible for your own pain,* and (2) *you are the one who must change your coping strategies to better meet your needs.* Applying this rule can revolutionize your attitude toward problematic situations as it allows you to shift from helpless anger to an awareness of the control that you have in each situation. Consider the following real cases.

Case 1. Irene describes Ms. Late and Loquacious.

"Nora arrives half an hour to an hour late for everything. You sit in the restaurant, the waiter brings you endless cups of coffee while you twiddle your thumbs. Finally she blows in with a hundred apologies and you make your biggest mistake of the day: you ask her how she is. Thus begins the litany, the anecdotes, the meanderings. The next time you open your mouth it's to ask the waiter for a dessert menu. It's interesting, I'll grant you, but Nora's talked for forty-five minutes nonstop without asking a single thing about me." Irene was so angry that she considered getting up and walking out on the luncheon. Let's use the two-step model of anger to examine her experience.

Stress: Irene is hurt and frustrated in her desire for attention and acknowledgment. "It's like I wasn't even there."

Trigger thoughts: "Nora's a self-centered motor-mouth ... doesn't give a damn if she's late ... doesn't care a bit about anybody but herself."

The trigger thoughts created a reality in which Irene felt victimized by the wrong and selfish behavior of her friend. When Irene learned the principle of personal responsibility, she began to accept that Nora was neither right nor wrong, but merely had very different needs. The activities that delayed Nora were simply a higher priority for her than being on time. And Nora's need to talk about her experience was considerably larger than her need to hear the experience of others. With the luncheon interaction reframed as a problem of conflicting needs, Irene was able to give up the expectation that Nora would take care of her and begin to develop new strategies to meet her own needs. Here's what she decided.

1. I'm really responsible here because I'm the one who chooses whether to see Nora or not. I have choices about how to structure the visit and how I act in the course of the conversation.

2. I can choose to have lunch with Nora only in a group so it doesn't matter if she's late. Or I can pick her up at her house. Or I can bring a good book so that I won't mind waiting. I know that she'll usually be late, so it's up to me to take care of myself.

3. Nora's conversational style isn't going to change, so I'll have to interrupt her to get my own stories in. I'll just barge in by saying "That reminds me of the time ..." I can break in rather than politely waiting for her to finish or ask me a question.

Notice that the rule of personal responsibility creates new options for problem solving. None of these solutions could possibly come to mind while focusing on trigger thoughts and the feeling of being victimized. When you're a victim, the responsibility always seems to be on the *other* person to change and make things better.

Case 2. Arthur describes the Jungian work junkie.

"Sylvia lives at the typewriter. They keep asking her to present papers and she keeps saying yes. Case studies, monographs, even something on Jung's garden. She's a slave to it, and we find ourselves nodding in the hall on our way to our respective studies. Pleasing every Tom, Dick, and Harry who has a sand tray is more important to her than our relationship. Some pitifully irrelevant paper matters more than a nice weekend together or going dancing."

Stress: Arthur feels hurt and lonely; he has a frustrated need for recreation.

Trigger thoughts: "Sylvia doesn't care about me ... she chooses to please others at the expense of our relationship ... she prepares trivial lectures and papers rather than making time for us to enjoy each other."

The trigger statements turn Arthur into a victim. He is helpless, while Sylvia's behavior is labeled wrong and outrageous. The trigger statements are an absolution that relieves Arthur of any responsibility for an empty marriage. After exploring the principle of personal responsibility, Arthur was able to reframe the problem as a conflict between his need for emotional closeness and his wife's need for social approval. He began to recognize that no one was to blame, but if he wanted to change the situation he would have to use new coping strategies. By taking responsibility for his own wants he was able to make the following decisions:

1. I'll buy that book on bed and breakfast inns and make reservations far in advance for weekend trips.

2. The only way to get Sylvia away from the typewriter is to create something more attractive, so I'll whip together a romantic candlelit dinner once a week.

3. Racquetball is the one sport we share. With a family membership in a racquetball club, I'm sure she'd be willing to schedule one night a week to play.

4. We haven't done much with the massage class we took. I'll schedule time with her each week for mutual massage.

5. Sylvia's needs are such that I don't think she'll cut down on the academic work (unless she gets too busy having fun). But I'll ask that she travel to conferences and training seminars no more than once every three months. If she doesn't like that, I'll try the fallback position of traveling with her to weekend conferences.

Case 3. Dumping Marty.

"I've known this guy since high school. We're close. Sean and I get together once or twice a week, play cards or backgammon, eat dinner, talk about his life, my life. But every damn time he gets interested in a woman the whole thing evaporates. It's like he's saying, 'Forget it guy, first things first.' I feel like he doesn't give a shit. Like it's okay hanging out with me until something better comes along. I saw him last week and he ran off to her right after dinner. And what gets me is I know when things don't work out it'll be like old times again."

Stress: Marty has feelings of loss and abandonment.

Trigger thoughts: "He doesn't give a shit . . . I'm a fill-in till something better comes along . . . I'm being used."

Marty made Sean responsible for his own feeling of loss. Like an animal in winter, he saw himself malnourished, living on scraps. He was helpless during the seasons of closeness and distance. The principle of personal responsibility made it possible for Marty to change his perspective and explore new ways to cope. It was important to face, without blame or judgment, that Sean had a very high need for sexual intimacy. Sean was merely taking care of himself, and Marty needed to do the same. After a good deal of thought, he made the following decisions.

1. I can't put all my eggs in one basket. I'm going to develop my friendships with John and Louise, schedule regular lunches, movies, and so on.

2. I'm responsible for getting my needs met, I'll have to create a situation where Sean will want to spend time with me. I know his new girlfriend is busy Saturday afternoon teaching piano. I'll suggest we get together at that time. Sean likes to play pool, and we can meet down at Town and Country for a few racks and some lunch.

3. I can also be frank with him and say I feel somewhat discarded with each new relationship. I can tell him that I would like to see him at least once a week and find out if he sees any way of doing that.

Case 4. Joan, the reluctant accountant.

"Since I spend my life balancing books, Bob and I agreed that he'd pay our bills and handle the checkbook. But he's unbelievably lazy about it. The bills lie around unpaid, we get late notices, we get collection notices! I can't believe it, he's willing to destroy our credit rating because he can't get off his ass and pay some bills. Bob doesn't even pay the mortgage, and I worry that some day I'll find a notice of intent to repossess buried in the pile. It's a nightmare, and he's such an irresponsible jerk about it."

Stress: Joan feels anxiety about the bills not getting paid.

Trigger thoughts: "He's lazy . . . irresponsible . . . he's destroying our credit rating and could lose us the house."

Joan's anger was built on her assumption that she was a victim of Bob's irresponsibility. By learning to take 100 percent responsibility for her need to reduce financial anxiety, she began to consider the following options.

1. Do the bills myself.

2. Give my husband reinforcement for doing them. For example, we could set deadlines for the bills and take a nice weekend trip if he gets them done.

3. I could pay someone I know to balance the accounts and write the checks. All we'd have to do is sign them.

4. I could negotiate. If Bob would do the bills by an agreed deadline, I could offer something in return.

Case 5. Julie's emptiness.

"There are times I just feel lonely. Even though he's there I just feel it. It's worse when I have deadlines, and it's worse with the hideous PMS. It's funny, Richard always seems to choose those times to withdraw. Every time I say I need more support he gets angry and accuses me of demanding too much. So I tell him that he deliberately withholds support at the very time I need it most. Then Richard gets more upset and shouts that I'm a demanding bitch. I tell him he's a self-centered, vulgar asshole. Then we really start shouting and sometimes we even slap each other. It's the same thing over and over: I tell him I'm lonely or ask him why he's so far away; he gets very mean, very brutal."

Stress: Julie has feelings of emptiness, rushing, abdominal cramping.

Trigger thoughts: "He deliberately withholds ... he's uncaring ... doesn't care ... selfish asshole ... vulgar and brutal."

Julie believed that her husband was responsible for her pain. Her main strategy for getting support was to remind him that he was withholding in the hope that he'd be moved to change. Despite consistent failure with this strategy, Julie continued to use blaming-style attacks because she saw Richard having all the power to give or withhold what she needed.

The principle of personal responsibility changed Julie's perspective. She began to accept that her pain was her responsibility. She was the only one who really understood her needs and it was her job to develop strategies to meet them. She learned that the failure of one strategy meant only that she would have to develop a more effective one. She decided on the following course of action.

1. Get medical help for the PMS.

2. My old way of asking for support is too vague. It always ends up sounding like a complaint. From now on I won't comment on how distant or unavailable Richard is. I'll merely suggest doing different things that I know will feel good to me.

3. If he's unwilling to do anything that moment, I'll suggest scheduling something where we'll have a lot of contact, such as dinner out. In the meantime, I'll get support from a friend so I feel less focused on his withdrawal.

4. I'll give myself three months to work on better strategies to help me feel closer. If I still experience strong bouts of loneliness, I'll insist on therapy.

5. If he resists therapy, I'll need to consider the possibility of separating.

Case 6. Ariel, the good daughter.

"He's got his beacon-red nose and this funny high step from losing feeling in his feet. And he's killing my mother with his demands, his screaming criticism if she makes a microscopic mistake. Drunk or sober, he's relentlessly cruel. I'm doing his laundry, taking him to the doctor, running from store to store helping him find the right wingtips. But I can't not do it. If I tell him to stuff it, the whole burden of his selfish ass will fall on my mother. He's the kind of father who belongs in a Dickens novel. Always putting me down, always angry, and he gets meaner on booze. She'll never leave him because she feels she has no way of supporting herself. So I have to take care of that old disgusting man. I can't leave her to cope with him alone."

Stress: Ariel feels hurt, threatened, and forced.

Trigger thoughts: "He's a mean drunk . . . cruel . . . disgusting . . . selfish. He's trapped my mother and he's trapping me."

Ariel *is* trapped, but not by her father. She is held captive by the perception that her father is responsible for her pain. She sees her mother and herself as victims of a punishing and demanding monster. In blaming her father for her pain, she has handed control of her life to a very toxic person. When Ariel was introduced to the principle of personal responsibility, she resisted the concept. "How am I responsible for the pain this man causes me? I love my mother, and my love for her obligates me to protect her as best I can."

What Ariel didn't grasp was that the principle of personal responsibility applied to her mother as well as herself. Her mother, too, was responsible for the decision to stay in this painful relationship. She had not been willing to pay the financial and emotional price to free herself from this angry man. By seeing her mother as a victim (denying the real choices that her mother had made), Ariel maintained her own identity as victim.

If Ariel took responsibility for her pain, she would arrange private visits with her mother while curtailing contact with her father. Her mother would have to make the best decisions she could in dealing with the angry man she had married.

Six Steps to Responsibility

In the cases just discussed, taking responsibility resulted in making important decisions that changed the situation. There are six ways to exercise responsible decision making when you are unhappy with someone's behavior.

1. **Develop more effective strategies for reinforcing others.** In Case 2, Arthur decided to schedule pleasurable weekend trips and join a racquetball club with his wife. He knew that these activities were reinforcing to her and might be an enticement away from academic pursuits. Likewise, in Case 4, Joan considered the strategy of making fun weekend trips contingent on Bob finishing the bills.

2. **Take care of the need yourself.** Again in Case 4, Joan considered taking over responsibility for the bills, rather than waiting helplessly for Bob to send them out. In Case 1, Irene decided to bring a book, pick up her friend, or meet her friend only in groups so that the problem of lateness wouldn't bother her.

3. **Develop new sources of support, nourishment, and appreciation.** Here the emphasis is on going elsewhere for what you need, rather than continuing to make demands on someone who is unable or unwilling to give you what you want. In Case 3, Marty goes on to develop alternative relationships, rather than keep "all of his eggs in one basket." In Case 5, Julie decides to seek the company of friends while waiting to set up an intimate evening with her husband.

4. **Set limits.** This is the art of saying no. Anger so often comes from feeling pressure to do specific things for others. Your trigger thoughts may include the notion that people have no right to ask certain things of you, or that they want too much. The problem is not the requests that people make of you—they're entitled to ask for anything they want—the problem is your unwillingness to set limits. It's your responsibility to say no to the things you prefer not to do. If you don't give yourself permission to say no, you'll

often wind up using anger as protection from the wants and needs of others.

Some people are very demanding. They've learned to be that way because it gets results. Taking responsibility means that you rarely waste time blaming people for their obnoxious or manipulative styles. You focus instead on how to get across the message that you have limits and are willing to do only so much. Limits are like good fences. They act as strict boundary lines to keep others from crossing into your territory. But while fences are plain to see, only you know your own limits. Only you can make them clear by saying them out loud. Remember in Case 6, Ariel's reluctance to set limits for her father results in being used and abused.

5. **Negotiate assertively.** This is the process of directly asking for what you want. Since your needs often conflict with the needs of others, simply making requests is often not enough. You may have to offer something in exchange or make compromises so that each party in the negotiation feels satisfied. In Case 5, Julie decides to request shared activities that would bring her closer to Richard. If he resists, her fallback suggestion is to schedule something fun for later.

6. **Let go.** There are two ways of letting go. The first is to accept that the situation is not going to change and you will have to live with it. Resisting it or railing against it will only add to your frustration and unhappiness. Again in Case 5, Julie may eventually have to accept that her husband is much less supportive than she would prefer him to be. This may be an unavoidable negative in a relationship that has many positives that make it worth keeping. If Julie can accept this unchanging aspect of Richard's personality, it may reduce her overall sense of pain and alienation.

The second kind of letting go involves recognition of those situations and relationships that are unrewarding or toxic for you. Letting go involves facing first that the situation will not change, and second that it is costing you more than the benefits are worth. Ariel in Case 6 needs literally to let go of the relationship with her father. To do that, she will also have to give up some of the caretaking aspects of her relationship with her mother. Letting go is usually the choice reserved for those times when other pathways to responsibility have not worked. Yet it is perhaps the most important of your options. It is your ultimate protection, your last response to a closing helplessness where nothing seems to change and you are in pain.

Like Ariel, many angry people are afraid to face this option. They survive unhappily in marriages and jobs. They rage to drive away the pain. Of course, they have reasons for staying: someone depends on them, someone would be hurt, they would be alone, it would be a big financial loss, they would be rejected and disapproved of, and so on. But all the reasons reduce to a common thread: the angry person is unwilling to pay the price of letting go. He or she does not want to feel the loss, the rejection, the disapproval, the money fears, the guilt, or the loneliness. And so they're left with the stuck feeling, the sense of being a victim. Taking care of yourself often exacts a high price. But if you are unwilling to pay it, you are nonetheless responsible for that choice.

Taking Responsibility: An Exercise

This is your chance to examine some of the situations in which you have responded with anger. Think back to a recent occasion, ideally one that you have written down in your anger journal and one that you recall well. Now, in your anger journal, write down your answers to the following questions. The first two help you identify the "cause" of your anger. The last six questions will help you take responsibility by changing the focus from others to yourself.

1. **What stress underlay my anger?** When thinking about this question, look at both your antecedent stresses (those that preceded and contributed to the anger situation) and your immediate stresses (those that grew directly out of the anger situation). Keep in mind the general categories of painful feelings, painful sensations, threats, and frustrated needs. (Refer back to chapter 6 for a more detailed list.)

2. **What were my trigger thoughts?** Here write down all the things you said to yourself that inflamed your anger.

3. **Are there more effective strategies than anger for reinforcing others to meet my needs?** Since anger is frequently met with defensiveness, avoidance, or yet more anger, are there ways that you can reward people for doing what you want rather than punishing or attacking them? What can you offer the other person to reinforce desired behavior in this situation?

4. **What can I do to meet my own needs (or reduce my stress)?** Is there independent action you can take without relying on someone else?

5. **Can I find other sources of support, nourishment, or appreciation besides the person with whom I feel angry?** Are there other

people or other situations that will give you some of what you need (or help you reduce your stress level)?

6. **What limits do I want to set but feel afraid to acknowledge or insist on?** Do you need to say no or reduce your involvement?

7. **How can I negotiate for what I want?** Can you make a direct, nonblaming request of the other person? Are you prepared to compromise, make counter suggestions, or offer something in return for the desired behavior? Write out your request and some possible compromises.

8. **How might I eventually let go?** If other strategies fail, you will have to let go of either your expectations in the situation or the person with whom you're struggling. In this case, which one will you choose? How will you implement your choice?

You probably found some of these questions difficult to answer. They go against the grain, because when you're angry you want to change the other person, not yourself. You have been turning to others to meet your needs and take away your pain. It's hard to reclaim this task as solely your own. Now, using the format below, try applying these eight questions to other anger-producing situations in your life.

Analyzing My Anger

1. *Stresses*

    A. *Antecedent stresses:*
       Painful emotions
       Painful sensations
       Frustrated needs
       Threats

    B. *Immediate stresses:*
       Painful emotions
       Painful sensations
       Frustrated needs
       Threats

2. *Trigger thoughts*
    Blamers
    Shoulds
    They did something to me

3. Are there more effective strategies than anger for reinforcing others to meet my needs?

4. What can I do to meet my own needs (or reduce stress)?

5. Can I find other sources of support, nourishment, and appreciation besides the person with whom I feel angry?

6. What limits do I want to set but feel afraid to acknowledge or insist on?

7. How can I negotiate for what I want?
   My request: _____

   _____

   Possible compromises: _____

   _____

8. How might I eventually let go in the situation (if other strategies fail)?

Why It's Preferable to Take Responsibility

The first reason for taking responsibility is that anger costs you too much. Physically, anger makes you prey to ulcers, high blood pressure, and cardiovascular diseases. As you read in chapter 3, anger releases powerful hormones in your body that prepare you to act aggressively. This is perfectly adaptive if you live in a primitive community where you must fight off threatening animals or other aggressive tribes. Those events are time-limited and the anger hormones quickly dissipate. But chronic, simmering anger is another matter. Your body is always revving up to fight, and this continuous arousal can eventually create illness.

Anger not only causes damage to your body, but also damages your relationships. Chapter 4 shows how angry people find themselves increasingly isolated. Friends and family get fed up with the tension and hostility. At first they become defensive, then grow less and less accommodating. Finally, they withdraw altogether. Most people are simply not willing to be pushed around by anger for an extended period of time. It's too painful. It makes them feel controlled and hypervigilant for the first signs of a flareup.

The second reason for taking responsibility is that anger is an ineffective long-term strategy for changing others. In the short run, anger often works. People are hurt or shocked and they may exhibit temporary changes to avoid your wrath. But eventually, if you continue to use anger to coerce, people become inured to your attacks. They will resist or avoid you.

Consider the case of Julia. Shortly after getting married, she discovered that her husband was a couch potato. He spent the weekend drinking beer and watching sports. Julia felt lonely and frustrated in the desire to share more activities with her husband. She triggered anger by thinking of her husband as lazy and uncaring. "I really let him have it to get him off that couch. There were projects to do around the house and I wanted to have picnics and go hiking together." Julia was using her anger as a coercive force to make her husband change. And for most of the first year it worked. He felt scared and rejected each time she went on the warpath and he'd make efforts to appease her. After a time, however, he began to resist. In therapy, he described his reaction: "I always felt I had to do what she wanted or she'd be angry. I got resentful, I guess, and I didn't enjoy being with her as much. I got to the point where she accused me of not caring and she was right, I didn't care. I'd stay away from the house, I'd leave my clothes on the floor to deliberately annoy her, I'd make comments about her clothes—that really got her." As long as Julia's husband enjoyed her and wanted to please her, the anger worked. But soon enough he became desensitized to the upsets and less concerned about her feelings. He began to enjoy small passive-aggressive revenges. Within a matter of months Julia's strategy had backfired and the new marriage was deteriorating.

Seth used anger to "make the children behave." He was a single parent during the summer months when his children traveled three-thousand miles to live with him. The initial camaraderie and good feeling changed for Seth as he realized that his daughters took no responsibility around the house. They spent the day on the phone or watching soap operas. The background noise of the TV was literally painful to him, and Seth experienced fatigue from the extra cooking, cleaning, and supervision of two children. He triggered his anger by telling himself that they *should* help more. Instead they were filling their heads with "video crap." When Seth used anger as a motivator to push the children into taking more responsibility, the initial response was frenetic cleaning and a surprise spaghetti dinner after work one night. Very gratifying. But in a week his daughters slacked off and Seth was angry again. He told the girls that they were testing him and they wouldn't get away with it. After a dozen angry go-rounds, the following response pattern emerged: sullenness and shouting back, followed by grudging help—the bare minimum. Following a summer of fighting, the girls left early for their mother's house. A week later, Seth got a letter from his ex-wife. No stranger herself to anger, she wrote:

> Nice going, Seth. You ruined their summer. You know as much about parenting as you did about marriage. The way you get kids to do chores is to praise them. Make allowances and TV watching something they get *after* the work is done.

Some people learn faster than others that anger doesn't succeed as a long-term change strategy. Sherry wanted her husband to fold the laundry. After a month of argument and nagging, he had folded the laundry exactly once. She decided to switch strategies and make something he wanted contingent on something she wanted. She told him she would do his laundry only if he would participate by folding it. Two days after running out of shirts he was on the job.

Implications of the Principle of Personal Responsibility

1. **You are responsible for the outcome of all interactions.** If you are dissatisfied with how people are treating you, only you can make the necessary modifications in your behavior for the outcome to change. You are the one who knows what you want. And it is in your interest, not the other person's, that things change.

2. **If one strategy doesn't work to meet your needs or solve a problem, there is absolutely no point in blaming.** It's your responsibility to keep trying new strategies until something does work.

3. **The appropriate question is not "Who's responsible for my pain?" but "What can I do about it?"**

4. **The amount of support, appreciation, and help you are getting is all you can get, given the current strategies you are using.** No one will willingly give you more than you now receive if you continue your current methods. Moreover, if you use coercive strategies such as anger on a long-term basis, you can expect the support and appreciation you receive to diminish over time.

5. **You can't expect other people to change or to be different.** They are using the best problem-solving strategies available to them at the moment. These strategies may be painful to you or they may frustrate your needs, but they represent the other person's best coping solution given his or her stresses, skills, and available resources. The other person will change only with the perception that new behavior is in his or her best interest. Don't fight this one. It's a law of nature. Accepting it will make you far more effective in taking care of your own needs.

6. **All relationships come down to two basic choices: adapt or let go.** If your needs remain unmet, if the painful aspects of the relationship are unremitting, letting go is your only healthy choice. The alternative is chronic anger or depression. You can let go of either your expectations or of the relationship itself. In a basically rewarding relationship, where you have tried and failed to meet

an important need, you may decide to let go of the expectation that things will change. On the other hand, if the pain and frustration in a relationship outweighs its rewards, letting go will involve a movement away from the other person.

7. **You are never a victim.** The only true victims are children, because they have so little control over the shape of their lives. An adult chooses to be a victim, because an adult has choice. Ariel, in Case 6, saw herself victimized by her father's alcoholism. As a child she was a victim. As an adult, however, she could *choose* the degree of involvement that she wanted with different members of her family.

Coping Mantras

A coping mantra is something you can say to yourself when you're beginning to feel angry that will calm you and help you look for more adaptive choices. Mantras are usually contained in single sentences that distill an important truth or awareness. Read the following mantras and choose one or more of them to memorize and use in situations where you are responding with anger. They will help you remember to take responsibility.

1. I am responsible for what happens between us.

2. No point in blaming, try a new strategy.

3. What can I do about this?

4. The amount of support, help, and emotional nourishment I am now getting is all I can get, given the strategies I am using.

5. People won't change unless I make it in their interest.

6. How can I reinforce him or her to change in this situation?

7. I may not like it, but he or she is using the best problem-solving strategy available right now.

8. Everyone is responsible for taking care of his or her own needs.

9. My choice is to adapt or let go.

10. Only children are victims, I always have a choice.

8

24-Hour Anger Management

If you are reading this book you know how uncontrolled anger is interfering with your life. It may be interfering with your role as a parent and partner, it may be affecting your success at work or sabotaging your friendships. Previous attempts to deal with this problem may not have been successful, and you ended up blaming yourself. This may have created feelings of unworthiness and shame—triggering more anger. This is a merry-go-round you have to get off.

The first step toward breaking free is to understand how anger works. Here are the basic facts about anger:

1. Anger is a *response that you learned* early in life to help you cope with pain. You may have learned this coping style from a family member who used rage to control others. You may have learned it as a way of surviving a hostile environment when you were a child. The sources of your pain may have changed over the years, but you're still using anger to block it.

2. Expressing anger *temporarily helps* you overcome feelings of helplessness and lack of control. But it disrupts relationships and makes you feel even more helpless and out-of-control—a vicious cycle.

3. *Anger is a habit,* one that you can learn to break. It will take time and practice. Many people who are trying to break a habit or overcome a dependency (alcoholism, gambling, food and drug addictions, etc.) talk about taking it "one day at a time." With anger management you need to do even more. You need to take it "one situation at a time."

Taking the First Step: A 24-Hour Commitment to Act Calmly

Although it may take some time to completely break the anger habit, there is something you can do today—right now—to take control.

Make a commitment to *act* in a calm manner for a 24-hour period, no matter what. Don't expect that you will *feel* calm; just that you will act that way—no matter what the provocation is, and no matter how justified you feel. When you make this commitment, that means that you will observe the following restrictions:

- No raised voice or shouting
- No angry driving, speeding, or tailgating
- No physical threats or actions
- No verbal attacks

Given how strong and habitual the anger habit is, making a commitment for a longer period of time (say, one week or a month) may be unrealistic. If you prepare for just one day—24 hours—without anger, you have a good chance of being successful. Here's how to make it work.

1. **Clarify your goals.** If you are going to be successful in managing your anger, you have to focus on *what is in it for you*. Clarify what specific goal *you* want to achieve.

   Do you want to have a closer relationship with your partner or your children?

   Do you want to be able to enjoy the people at work, collaborate more successfully, be considered for promotion or a management positions?

   Do you just want to physically feel better, calmer, in control, no matter what challenges or frustrations life sends you?

   Do you want to feel more pride and self-worth when you handle difficulties without anger, instead of the shame and regret you feel when you "lose it"?

   Write down a few goals that you want to accomplish by getting control over your anger. You can post them in places where you will be reminded about them during the day. Tape the goals on your refrigerator, your bathroom mirror, the dashboard in your car, on the corner of your computer screen. When you look at them, say them aloud.

2. **Tell people about your plan.** Tell the significant people in your life (at home and at work) that you are absolutely committed to refrain from acting angry for a 24-hour period starting

_____ , and ending _____ . You will not raise your voice, blame, slam things, or act aggressively in any way during that period.

Telling others about your commitment helps you keep your resolve and provides you with more motivation. They'll be watching, interested in your success, and can be a source of encouragement and support.

3. **Recruit an ally.** You need more than others' good wishes. You need two people (a trusted friend at work, and a family member at home) on your side to help watch for any early signs that you are starting to get angry. They may be able to pick up a change in your tone of voice, or some physical behavior that in the past was the prelude to an angry outburst.

Decide ahead of time on a nonverbal signal that the person can give you if you are looking or sounding angry. It could be a football "time-out" hand signal, or a hand slowly lowering that reminds you to relax, calm down, take it easy.

4. **Preview the day.** Once you have committed to an anger-free day, review in detail the typical problem times, people, or situations you will face.

Problem times:

There may be a particular time of day when you are more reactive, more vulnerable to feeling out of control. For instance, getting the kids up and out to school is a common source of frustration and a high risk time for an outburst. You may feel more irritable when you are hungry, if you are overtired, or when you drink alcohol.

Problem people:

There may be a person at work who is particularly annoying, or who seems to enjoy provoking you to become upset. There may be a family member who you "lose it" with frequently and predictably.

There may be people who set you off because of their personalities, habits, or communication style (whiny, dishonest, self-centered, abrasive, etc.). They may remind you of a problem person from your past. They may even remind you of yourself.

Problem situations:

There may be situations that always put you on edge. You may find that driving in rush hour traffic sets you off, so that by the time you arrive at your destination, you are already in a rage. Other anger triggers could be pressure from deadlines, noise (blaring TV, loud music, ringing phone, shrieking kids' voices, playing or fighting), traveling, being late for an appointment, and so on.

5. Make a coping plan. Right now, consider the problem events, people, and environments you are likely to encounter during your 24 hours. Once you have listed the possible anger triggers, see what you can do to *minimize, eliminate, or avoid as many as possible.* Write down the potential problem and your plan to deal with it. For example:

Problem: Early morning hassles with children

Plan: Wake the kids up earlier. Do as much as you can the night before so the morning goes smoothly (pre-pack lunches, set out clothes and breakfast food, get gas in the car, sign notes, hunt for the gym clothes and soccer equipment, locate your keys, etc).

Problem: Road rage, traffic jams, lateness, incompetent drivers

Plan: Leave earlier, listen to morning traffic and weather warnings before you leave so you can avoid problems. Bring along calming music, or a book on tape to distract you from the morning craziness on the road.

Problem: Irritating people, noise, and fatigue at work

Plan: Delay stressful encounters with coworkers whom you know will push your buttons. This is not the day for a performance evaluation with the employee you wish you never hired. This is not the day to solve long-standing and frustrating problems. Instead, do some stretches every hour to ease the tension and fatigue.

Problem: After-work fatigue, hunger, distraction, noise, etc.

Plan: Sit quietly in your car *before* entering into the activities, noise, and commotion of your family. Don't bring the problems of your work environment home with you. Recounting stories about the idiotic (stupid, self-serving, deceitful, short-sighted) things your coworkers did can pollute the atmosphere and ruin an evening.

Talk to your partner, roommate, or kids. Get their cooperation that on this day they will not hit you with problems that have been triggers for anger in the past. This is not the day to discuss your finances, your daughter's new boyfriend, or the incompetent way the contractor fixed the leaky roof.

What to Do When You Start to Feel Angry

1. *First, and most importantly, STOP.*

When situations arise (and they inevitably will) that stimulate annoyance, irritation, and anger, the first step is to *stop.*

Don't do or say anything. *Don't* try to push the feeling away, or ignore it. Just observe it. Notice its strength, how it pushes you toward action. But you do not have to act.

People describe feeling a "wave of anger" because the emotion tends to rise and fall. It crashes over you. It may knock you off your feet for a moment, but it will ebb and recede and you can get your bearings again. Watch how it grows and diminishes, building, cresting, and then receding. You are at a crossroad here. You have the choice of how to respond to your anger (pain) in a different way than you have in the past. This is the challenge, this is the moment of truth.

2. *Watch what you say to yourself.*

Your "self-talk" can help keep you calm, or feed the flames of angry rage.

Don't say things that intensify the anger. Things like:

"This is not fair."

"He always does this to me."

"I'm not going to take it anymore"

"Who do they think they are?"

"If I told them once, I told them a thousand times."

Don't review the events that led up to the emotions, or the past failings of the offending person. This type of thinking results in losing control. Remember, the goal this day is not to eliminate anger, but to act calmly, no matter what.

Do say things that will help you get over the wave of anger (pain). Things like:

"This is the challenge I have been preparing for. I can do something different this time."

"Remember, no raised voices, no threats."

"I don't have to take this personally."

"That's just how kids are (noisy, sloppy, forgetful)."

"That's how (my coworker, brother) always acts (pompous, conceited, lazy, controlling), but I have the ability to react differently."

3. *Act the opposite.*

One of the best ways to change a painful emotion is to act the opposite of the way you are feeling. During the next 24 hours you can test this out for yourself.

Did you ever watch a foreign language film without looking at the subtitles? You can tell when someone is angry without understanding a single word. The physical expression of anger is universal, and it functions *to intensify and prolong the emotion.* Glaring, balled up fists, attacking or threatening hand motions, raised voices, rigid muscles in the jaw, and rapid breathing, all result in increased anger and loss of control. Not to mention very negative reactions from others.

When you act calmly, even when you are feeling furious, you are more likely to avoid escalations. You also have much more control, and can make considered decisions away from the "heat of the moment." The result? You get cooperation and support instead of resentment and counterattacks. This is how you do it.

- Smile instead of frowning or glaring. Your smile may feel false, but do it anyway.

- Let your muscles relax, unclench your fists, loosen your jaw (you can do this by opening your mouth a bit), sit back in your chair, take a deep breath. Take two.

- Lower your voice. If you are dealing with someone who is speaking loudly, make your voice noticeably lower. That defuses the situation for everyone. Besides, when you talk quietly, the other person has to stop and listen.

- Talk slowly. The speed and cadence of your speech can have a big effect on the emotional temperature.

- Disengage rather than attack. You may literally want to get in someone's face. You may want to shake him or her. But on this day, do the opposite. Disengage, move away from that person. Open up some space between the two of you.

- Resolve to deal with the situation later, when you are calm, when you will have had time to figure out an effective response. The smart response: "I need some time to think about this." "Let's talk tomorrow, . . . after lunch, . . . at the next meeting, . . . after your parents are gone . . . etc."

- Say something slightly empathetic instead of judgmental and attacking. You don't have to *mean* it, and it may feel insincere, but just say it. See what kind of reaction you get. Notice how differently you may feel.

Try saying, "I hear that you worked hard getting the report in on time." Even while you are thinking, "It took you twice as long as anyone expected, and its still full of typos and misspellings!" Try saying, "You always make such a lovely salad." Even while you are thinking, "The rest of the meal is inedible, unrecognizable, and possibly toxic."

Keeping Track

Of course, the 24 hours will not go as planned. Of course, you will have stressors, people and situations that will provoke you, events you could not have predicted. You may not have kept your cool completely, but there are still many lessons and realizations you will take with you from this experience.

You may want to keep a notebook with you during this day and write down the people and situations that seemed to provoke you to anger, and how you coped with them. What contributed to the problem? Also record how others responded to you. Were you surprised by others' reactions?

Which coping strategies worked better for you, and which ones did not help at all? Did it help to "do the opposite?" What calming self-talk (things that you said to yourself when you felt your anger rising) was helpful in softening your anger? Did it help to plan for predictable stressors?

How did it feel when you were able to control your anger? Did you feel more powerful? Did you feel more empathetic with others? Were you aware of feeling more vulnerable without your angry shield? How did it feel when you were not able to control your anger? Did you feel defeated? Discouraged? Challenged? Embarrassed?

Hopefully, even if you lost your cool and lapsed into an angry outburst, you were able to get back on track and face the other situations during the day with new resolve.

If you were to repeat this experience, how would you have planned or prepared_differently?

Make the Commitment

It's time to sign a contract, a commitment to act in a calm manner for 24 hours. This is something real, a contract recorded with paper and ink. Be sure to have one close person sign as a witness.

Twenty-Four-Hour Commitment

I, _____ , between _____ o'clock

on _____ (date) and _____ o'clock

on _____ (date), promise to behave in a calm,

non-aggressive manner. I will act calmly no matter what stress or provocation may occur.

_____ (Your signature)

_____ (Witness signature)

Beyond the First 24 Hours

This 24-hour period may have given you some important insights, as well as a glimpse of a life without chronic anger and rage. Now you have a choice. You can make additional 24-hour commitments, and/or continue to monitor your anger as you work through the rest of this book. Whichever you choose, the commitment to control your anger—even for 24 hours—is an important beginning.

9

Combatting Trigger Thoughts

A young woman sank back into the chair in her therapist's office and began her story. "I can't control my anger at my children," she said. "I scream, I shake them sometimes. It's hurting our relationship, and down the line I think it will affect their self-esteem. I'm the worst with my eldest. Totally nuts at times. Sometimes, I feel like slapping and slapping him till he shuts up."

"What are you thinking when you get so angry at your son?" the therapist asked.

"What a brat, what a selfish brat. He's trying to get back at me because I want a little order in my life."

"Does it feel like he's doing something to you, something to hurt you?"

"In those moments I feel like he's trying to drive me to despair, like he wants to destroy me."

"So you're saying to yourself that he's a selfish brat, that he wants to get back at you, that he wants to destroy you, and drive you to despair. Let me ask you a question. Suppose, after his misbehaving, you said something like this to yourself: 'He's unhappy and he's trying to get my attention. His behavior is unpleasant, but he's just trying to take care of his needs.' "

"But I don't believe that, I think he's trying to . . ."

"I understand that, but we are speaking hypothetically. Suppose you were to say to yourself what I suggested. Would you feel as angry?"

"No, I don't think I would. I think I'd feel differently."

"Here is something very important, then, that we have to talk about. You see you do have control over your anger. What you think, what you say to yourself triggers your anger. You can gain control of your anger by changing your thoughts, beliefs, and assumptions about your boy's behavior."

In previous chapters, you learned that there is nothing automatic about getting angry. Pain does not make you angry. Thoughts make you angry; beliefs and assumptions make you angry. This chapter is an opportunity for you to examine the traditional beliefs and assumptions that are the cognitive foundations for anger and the necessary prerequisites for every angry outburst you have ever experienced.

You'll recall that the cognitive triggers for anger fall into one of two categories: shoulds and blamers. What follows is an exploration of how both shoulds and blamers create a distorted, anger-inciting picture of reality that leaves you feeling victimized and controlled by others. This chapter will help you to identify your trigger thoughts and replace them with new, more-forgiving perceptions.

Shoulds

If you listen carefully to the inner monologue with which you analyze and interpret your experience, you will notice that you judge the behavior of others many times each day. These judgments are based on a set of rules about how people should and should not act. People who behave according to the rules are right, and those who break the rules are wrong. You assume that people *know* and *accept* your rules. When they violate your shoulds, their behavior seems like a deliberate break with what is correct, intelligent, reasonable, or moral.

While waiting in line at the toll plaza, John deeply resents drivers who use the carpool lane to get ahead of the jam and then cut in front of him. He believes that people should wait their turn, and those who don't should be punished. Samantha has had a recent hysterectomy and is enormously angry that her husband rarely checks in about how she feels and even more rarely helps with any household jobs. Her should is that a spouse ought to show his concern by checking in and doing things to help. The problem with John and Samantha's shoulds is that the other people don't agree with them. This is almost always the case. Others don't see reality as you do. Their perception of a situation is colored by their own needs, feelings, and history.

The drivers who cut in think it's perfectly fine to do so, and Samantha's husband feels very righteous because he's given up golf and poker to stay home with her. It never occurs to him to be more helpful or inquiring.

So the first problem with shoulds is that the people with whom you feel angry rarely agree with you. Their perception of the situation leaves them blameless and justified. Their rules and beliefs always seem to exempt them from the judgments you think they deserve. And the more you try to convince them of their wrongness and their failure, the more indignant and defensive they become.

The second problem with shoulds is that people *never* do what they should do. They only do what is reinforcing and rewarding for them to do. Shoulds are your values and needs imposed on someone with different values and needs. The most complex human behavior can be looked at in terms of a very simple formula: strength of need minus strength of inhibition. If the strength of the inhibition is equal to or greater than the need, the person does not act. If the need surpasses the strength of the inhibition, some behavior will be activated. Consider the drivers who keep cutting in front of John. Their need to get ahead and save time is greater than the sum of all inhibiting factors—fear of disapproval or reprisal, fear of a traffic ticket, guilt for not waiting their turn, and so on. The same is true for Samantha's husband. His need to watch television, sleep, read, or do whatever else he does instead of helping Samantha, must be presumed greater than his inhibitions—fear of Samantha's disapproval, his self-rebuke for violating his own values of helpfulness and caring behavior, and so on.

When you demand that people behave according to your rules, you are violating reality in two ways. (1) In most cases others will not agree with your values and rules. Their unique history and needs shape their perceptions in ways that justify their behavior. Since you can rarely get others to agree that they are wrong, applying your shoulds to their behavior is an exercise in futility. (2) Because behavior is shaped by the formula of needs minus inhibitions, shoulds have almost nothing to do with it. Judging behavior according to your own arbitrary standard of right and wrong seems to miss the point. The real issue is how much does this person need to act this way and what inhibiting influences, if any, might stop him or her.

Exercise 1. Stand in their shoes.

When you're angry at someone, answer these four questions:

1. "What needs influence him or her to act this way?"

2. "What beliefs or values influence him or her to act this way?"

3. "What aspects of his or her history (hurts, losses, successes, failures, rewards) influence this behavior?"

4. "What limitations (fears, health problems, lack of skills) influence this behavior?"

Answer each question as completely as possible. If you don't have all the information, make up something that seems likely. The purpose of this exercise is to explain the behavior you don't like *from the other person's point of view.*

Exercise 2. Accurate empathy.

In his excellent book, *Feeling Good,* David Burns suggests an exercise to help you cope with shoulds. Imagine a dialogue between yourself and the person with whom you feel angry. Start out by accusing him or her of acting wrongly, of violating some basic rule of conduct. Clearly articulate your should. State it as persuasively as you can. Now imagine yourself as the other person, trying to answer your attack. Do your best to become this individual, to see the world from his or her point of view. After you've answered as the other person, go back to your original feeling of anger and expand on your accusations. Keep up the attack. Now go back again and answer as the other person, clearly explaining his or her viewpoint. Shuttle back and forth between your accusing voice and the other person's defense at least three times. Notice how your feelings begin to change as you acknowledge the other person's unique experience.

Although any kind of should can trigger anger, the five specific types of should statements covered below are extremely damaging in intimate relationships.

The Entitlement Fallacy

The entitlement fallacy is based on this simple belief: because I want something very much, I ought to have it. The basic idea is that the degree of your need justifies the demand that someone else provide it. The feeling is that there are certain things you are entitled to. Many people feel they are entitled to be sexually fulfilled, or feel emotionally and physically safe, or have a certain standard of living. Some people feel they are entitled to always rest when they are tired, or never be alone, or to have their work appreciated, or to have their needs known without asking. The list of possible entitlements is endless.

Sabrina was thirty-eight and very much wanted a child. Her husband remained ambivalent and was extremely fearful about losing a sense of spontaneity and freedom if they had children. Sabrina harbored the belief that if she wanted something this much, he should help her have it. Her anger with his ambivalence was so great that each discussion of the issue soon developed into an escalating series of accusations.

Sam wants his son to go on a fishing trip. After all, he pays for the boy's college education, he's his father, the boy can jolly well give up a few days chasing girls to keep his old man company. Sam flies into a rage when his son tells him that he'd rather make a demo tape with his band.

The entitlement fallacy confuses desire with obligation. It says, "When I want something this much, you have no right to say no." Strong feelings of entitlement deny others the freedom to choose. And this is how entitlement damages relationships. It demands that the other person give up his or her limits and boundaries for you. It says your need and your pain must come first, that the function of the relationship is to serve you.

Now, most of the time you would deny feeling that way and be quite offended if anyone were to accuse you of demanding that your needs come first. But the feeling of entitlement waxes and wanes. Sometimes you have no awareness of it. But when the needs are very strong, when the feeling of longing begins to engulf you, all you care about is getting what you want. And for a little while the other person may become only an instrument to provide for you. These painful feelings of need may periodically tempt you to forget the other person's equally important needs; his or her right to say no and set boundaries.

Exercise. Your right to say no.

Remember times you had to say no to another person's strong desire—a time when someone was in love with you, wanted to sleep with you, wanted your money, your support, your energy. His or her desire felt as real and vital and legitimate and necessary as yours does to you. Now try to remember why you said no. Remember the ways that your needs were different or conflicted. Remember how important it was for you to set your limits and clarify what you were and were not willing to do. You knew you had a right to your limits, you knew you had to say no because you needed something else.

Coping statements. These are things you can say to yourself when you find you are falling into the entitlement trap:

1. "I am free to want, but he or she is free to say no."

2. "I have my limits, and you have your limits."

3. "I have the right to say no, and so do you."

4. "My desire doesn't obligate you to meet it."

The Fallacy of Fairness

This belief hinges on the application of legal and contractual rules to the vagaries of interpersonal relationships. The idea is that there is some absolute standard of correct and fair behavior which people should know and live up to. The conviction that relationships must be fair reduces the complex give and take of friendship or marriage to a set of entries in privately kept books. Your books tell you whether you are in the red or in the black, whether you are getting as much as you give, whether you are owed something for all the sacrifices you have made. The difficulty is that no two people agree on what fairness is and in personal relationships there is no court or arbiter to help them. The measurement of what is fair is totally subjective and depends entirely on what you expect, need, or hope for from the other person. Fairness can be so conveniently defined, so temptingly self-serving that people can literally call anything fair or unfair. And as the debate rages, each person gets locked into his or her fortress of conviction. Each person is the victim, the bearer of injustice.

Joan was convinced that she had been victimized. "I supported him through grad school, and that was his dream. Now I want to buy a house—that's my dream—and he won't do it. It isn't fair." Anthony complains, "Ninety percent of the time we go to her place, ten percent to mine. She doesn't care if it's fair or not."

Joan and Anthony no doubt heard their parents appeal to the concept of fairness when they were children. "Be fair to your brother, let him play with the toys. . . . That's not fair, let her have some of the ice cream too. . . . I played with you now be fair and let Daddy read for a while." Fairness is sometimes a useful concept for controlling the behavior of children (after all, there is an adult present to be the final judge of all such matters). But as an adult, the concept is just too dangerous to use. The word "fair" turns out to be nothing more than a disguise for personal preferences and wants. What you want or do is *fair;* what the other person wants or does is unfair.

When you say, "This is fair," what you're really saying is, "My needs are more legitimate than yours." No one wants to hear this. People resist and defend against such assertions. A better approach is to throw out the concept of fairness altogether. Reframe the situation as one of competing needs or preferences. Each person's need is of equal importance and value. Each person's need is equally legitimate.

When you finally put away the idea of fairness, you can begin to negotiate as peers who have competing wants and somehow must resolve the problem. Joan wants a house, her husband doesn't. Instead of arguing about what's fair, they can negotiate from a position that each need has equal weight. Maybe they will buy a smaller house than Joan had originally envisioned, maybe they will put off buying till a specific date, maybe they'll buy a country place, maybe they'll continue to rent but invest in real estate. Anthony and his girlfriend can adjust the percentage of time spent in each house, or they may work out special compensations or accommodations and keep the current lopsided percentage. Once fairness is thrown out, real negotiation can begin.

Exercise. Equal needs.

If you are struggling with the issue of fairness, try reframing the problem as competing, but *equal* needs. Now try to make a clear, unbiased description of the other person's need. Don't try to evaluate whether it is more or less significant than yours. Now read chapter 16 on problem-solving communication and apply those skills to working through the conflict.

Coping statements. These are the things you can say to yourself when you find you are falling into the fairness trap:

1. "Our needs are equally important."

2. "Each need is legitimate, we can negotiate as peers."

The Fallacy of Change

The fallacy of change is based on the assumption that you really can have control over the behavior of others. Although people sometimes do change if you ask them, the fallacy of change reflects the belief that you can make people behave differently if you just apply sufficient pressure. Richard expects that if he criticizes and belittles his wife sufficiently, she will change into someone interested in discussing world affairs and political and social theories. Leanne thinks that if she complains enough and gets angry enough, she can change her husband's preoccupation with his job, his hobbies, and his personal experience (he keeps a detailed diary of his dreams and childhood memories).

The problem for both Richard and Leanne is that they are ignorant of one basic fact of human behavior: people change only when they are (1) reinforced to change and (2) capable of the change. In other words, people change when *they* want to, not when *you* want them to. Richard and Leanne find that their spouses are not changing, and the reason is that people do what is rewarding for them to do. Richard's wife finds it more rewarding to talk about her friends' psychology than the relationship between the United Arab League and the Islamists. Until Richard can make such discussions rewarding and fun for her, she will resist participating. Leanne has the same problem. Her husband is highly reinforced to keep doing the things he does. He won't change until she can make it more rewarding for him to spend time with her. Her current strategy of getting angry is having the opposite effect. He finds it more and more difficult to spend time with her and hence takes refuge in his hobbies and dream journal.

Expecting people to change leads to frustration and disillusion. If you can't find a way to make them *want* to change, you have undertaken a quixotic mission. You are tilting at windmills.

Exercise. You can't change others—only yourself.

Think about and answer the following questions:

1. How many times have you made a major change *and sustained* it because someone pressured you to do so?

2. What percentage of the people you have known have made a major metamorphosis to satisfy the needs of someone else?

3. How often have you succeeded in changing someone by pressuring him or her with anger?

Coping statements. Say these things to yourself when you find you are falling into the fallacy of change trap.

1. "The amount of support, help, and emotional nourishment I am getting now is all I can get, given the strategies I am using."

2. "People will change only when they are reinforced to change and capable of change."

3. "People change only when *they* want to."

Conditional Assumptions

Conditional assumptions are based on a syllogism like this:

"If you loved me, you'd pick me up at the subway station after work (or do the dishes, or show more sexual interest, or get home earlier, or help me when I'm tired, or help me with caring for the kids, or fix things in the house, or finish school so you could get a real job)."

Other variations include:

"If you were a real friend, you'd help me lay the bricks for my patio (or initiate more often, or just spend time with me rather than always being busy, or take more interest in my problems)."

And a last one:

"If they valued my work here, they'd get me a nicer desk (or give me a raise, or give me a better secretary, or ask what happened when I was sick last week)."

It's possible to love or care for someone and still not meet his or her needs. Disappointing others doesn't make one uncaring, and caring doesn't obligate one never to disappoint. No matter how much someone loves you, that person is still responsible for taking care of his or her own basic needs. That person is still responsible for saying no, setting boundaries, and protecting his or her own limits. "If they cared, if they loved me," is a setup to make you feel righteous and make the other person feel bad. Truthfully, it's a strategy for manipulation. But the result is rarely what you might hope. In the long run, making others feel bad doesn't reinforce them to do what you want. It makes them want to run away, to avoid you.

Exercise 1. How did you make your choices?

List the times you have disappointed someone you loved or cared for. Remember the times you had to make difficult choices, when you decided to take care of your needs over someone else's. As you think back, notice how little your choice had to do with how much you loved, but rather with how much you needed, or how much you were afraid, or how much energy you had.

Exercise 2. Equal needs.

As you did with the fallacy of fairness, reframe your conditional assumptions as a collision of equally legitimate needs. Define your need, and then carefully describe the needs, as you understand them, of the other person. See the problem as two peers working together to negotiate. Read chapter 16 and apply the assertive communication skills discussed there to a process of compromise and accommodation, so that each of you gets some of what you both need.

Coping statements. Say these things to yourself when you find you are falling into the conditional assumptions trap.

1. "Disappointing someone doesn't mean you don't care."

2. "Our biggest task, no matter how much we love, is to take care of ourselves."

3. "His or her needs are as legitimate as mine, and we can negotiate."

The Letting It Out Fallacy

This fallacy rests on the belief that people who hurt you or cause you pain *should* be punished. It often feels very good to express anger when you're frustrated and hurting. It helps to discharge the pain. And it functions as a kind of revenge for any perceived injustice.

The underlying belief is that you are not responsible for your pain. Someone else is. That person must have done wrong for you to feel so badly. Therefore, he or she deserves every bit of anger you feel like expressing. Maybe he or she will learn to do better in the future.

The problem with this whole line of reasoning is that *you* are responsible for your pain. And taking care of yourself is *always* your first responsibility. Pain and pleasure are essentially private experiences. You are the only one who really feels *your* hurt, you are the only one who experiences *your* joy. No one else can be held accountable or responsible for your private experience. You know it and you feel it. Therefore, you are the only one who can be responsible for it. If someone is frustrating or hurting you or causing you pain, your job is to either negotiate for your needs or let go of the relationship.

The second problem with letting it out is that anger destroys relationships. (This is particularly true for anger used as revenge.) When the object of your anger is to inflict the same degree of hurt that you are feeling on someone else, people begin to erect psychological barriers to protect themselves from you. The tissue of a relationship gets thickened and scarred. And finally you both become insensitive to pain and pleasure. This is how anger kills love: it makes you thick-skinned, untouchable. You no longer feel the warmth, the caress.

The last reason letting it out doesn't work is that anger rarely gets you what you want. What you want is to be listened to, appreciated, cared for. Anger gets you coldness, withdrawal, and anger in return. Letting it out feels good. But it's like smoking crack: a five-minute high, followed by depression, pain, and emotional bankruptcy.

Exercise 1. Think of the consequences.

When you are tempted to let it out, first review the positive and negative consequences of using anger with this particular person in the past. Draw four columns down a piece of paper. Over two of the columns write "short-term consequences" and over the other two write "long-term consequences." Label the two short-term consequences columns "positive" and "negative." Do the same with the long-term columns. Write down all the long- and short-term consequences of anger that you can think of, both positive and negative. At the end of the exercise, ask yourself this question: "Did anger get me what I wanted?"

Exercise 2. Be assertive.

Using the "I think, I feel, I want" structure discussed in chapter 16, make assertive statements to express the speaker's needs in the following situations.

1. "When she gets these stinking grades it makes me so depressed that I feel justified in letting her have it."

2. "I told him that I hate musicals, but off he goes to buy tickets to *The Producers*. I just blew up, it was so frustrating. He deserved it."

Coping statements. Say these things to yourself when you are falling into the letting it out trap.

1. "Anger won't get me what I want."

2. "I can protect my relationship by communicating assertively."

Blamers

They did it to you. You are lonely, hurt, frightened, and they did it. Blaming triggers anger by making your pain someone else's responsibility. In intimate relationships, blaming leads to the development of negative cognitive sets in which you begin to label, classify, and interpret a person's behavior in consistently negative ways. He is controlling or uncaring or selfish or insensitive. And as this negative cognitive set hardens, so do your assumptions about the other person. Even neutral or ambiguous behavior gets a negative label. More and more parts of the relationship are tainted by the consistently negative way that you interpret and evaluate the other person.

The problem with blaming is that it denies reality in two ways. First, blaming assumes that you are not responsible for your pain, someone else is. Chapter 7 on responsibility explains specific reasons why you should view yourself and only yourself as responsible for your experience. The second way that blaming denies reality is by constructing a world in which people are deliberately doing bad things. People do not do "bad" things. As Plato observed, people always choose the good. You and everyone else will always choose the action that seems most likely to meet your needs. The potential benefits of the action you choose, at least at the moment of choice, seem to outweigh the foreseeable disadvantages. Obviously, the action that seems best at the time depends on your awareness. Awareness is the degree of clarity with which you perceive and understand, consciously or unconsciously, all the factors relating to the need at hand. At any moment in time, your awareness is a product of your innate intelligence, your constitution, your physiological state, your emotional state, your beliefs, your needs, your total life experience and conditioning, and your skills and competencies. All of that goes into making a decision. And the decision you make is the very best one available *at that moment in time*. Good or bad is nothing more than a label you apply to decisions after you have observed their consequences for yourself and others. But at the moment the decision was made, those consequences were unknown. And it was therefore the best choice available.

Now you may be thinking that sometimes people know better but do the wrong thing anyway. "My son knows I'll be upset and that he diminishes his chances for college when he brings home C's and D's. He knows better, but he does it anyway." But "knowing better" is not sufficient to "do better" if the boy's awareness at the time is focused on stronger and opposing motivations. If his need to play football or go out with girls or rebel against the family rules is larger than his need to please you or his long-range goals about college, then grades will be a low priority. It all comes down to what *is most important at the time.*

So blaming doesn't make sense. It labels people and behavior as bad when in fact each person makes the best choice available. By blaming, you end up punishing people for actions *they could not help performing.*

Exercise. The components of awareness.

Think of someone you know well, someone you have at various times blamed. Think of a decision that person made that angered you. Now here's the hard part. Try to reconstruct the decision *from that person's point of view.* What do you know of his or her constitution or physiological state, emotional state, beliefs, needs, conditioning, competencies, or limitations? Try to see how these factors could combine so that his or her decision was the best choice available.

Good-Bad Dichotomizing

If you do a lot of blaming, you're beginning to repaint the world in black and white. People are good or bad, right or wrong. You don't see any shades of gray or any continuum between the polar opposites.

Once you start labeling people as bad, the problem with cognitive sets comes in. You develop a kind of tunnel vision that blocks out every behavior that doesn't fit your assumption of badness. You simply don't see the things that are kind or generous or loving. Jim very often sees Martha as selfish and uncaring. Even though she frequently gives him little hugs, does his laundry, and invites his friends to dinner, he fails to notice these as loving or generous acts. Jim is missing a big part of the relationship because his cognitive sets blind him to seeing the way Martha expresses her caring feelings.

Exercise. Finding shades of gray.

Write a complete description of someone you know well, someone you care for but with whom you also feel angry. Read over your description. How many of the items are judgments, implying that some aspect of his or her personality is either good or bad? How much of your description is either pejorative or praising? Now try rewriting the description without any hint of judgment. As best you can, make the descriptions neutral. Instead of saying that he's fat, say that he weighs 250 pounds. Instead of saying that she has a beautiful face, say that she has even features and smooth skin. Stick to the facts. Don't embellish with your value judgments. How does it feel to think about people without judgment? Does the description feel more accurate or less accurate when it is nonpejorative?

Coping statements. Say these things to yourself if you find yourself blaming.

1. "I make no judgments."

2. "People are coping with pain and stress in the best way they can, given their level of awareness."

3. "It is merely a problem that our needs conflict; he is not wrong, and I am not right."

Assumed Intent

The tendency to make inferences about how people feel and think is called mind reading. It is also called "assumed intent." It triggers anger when you conclude that your pain is a consequence of someone's deliberate effort to do you harm. Jill lost track of her nine-year-old son at the county fair. She assumed that he had deliberately disappeared to scare her. Joshua believed that the waitress was being deliberately slow and inattentive because he had asked for extra cream and wanted his eggs done a special way.

Notice that assumed intent must include two important concepts to make you angry. First, that you are in pain through the fault of someone else. Second, that you are being *deliberately* harmed. Few people would get angry if a pine cone fell and scratched their car. But a child throwing pine cones would be a different story. Now the two elements necessary for anger are present: harm and deliberate intent.

There are several problems with assuming intent. It is very difficult to accurately assess the true motives of another person. The word "assume" means that you think you know, but you never asked. Mind reading is so often dead wrong, yet it is probably the greatest source of anger. Claudette thought that a friend had deliberately excluded her from a luncheon "as a kind of slap." She was irate until she learned that the lunch had honored an unknown coworker of her friend's. Reese thought that his girlfriend was trying to hurt him by deciding to spend fewer nights together. After first withdrawing, then picking several fights, he discovered that her very deep feelings of love and dependence were frightening her. The motive that he had assumed was quite the opposite from the facts. It was her positive feelings rather than any attempt to harm that lay behind her decision.

Exercise. Don't assume anything.

Try this process for one day. Make a commitment to yourself that you will make absolutely no assumptions about the motivations of others unless you *check out* your assumption with the other person. In other words, you have to ask, "Is it true that you're being slow getting ready for the movie because I didn't wash the car today?" "I have a feeling you're being a little withdrawn because I spent the day with Rich. Is there anything to that?" "When you said the potatoes were overcooked, I felt like you were mad at me or something, is that true?" "You're driving so fast, I wonder if you're trying to scare me?" Your rule for yourself for this day will be that you either avoid assumptions or find out if they're true.

If you succeeded in doing the exercise for a day, try extending it to a week. The more you avoid mind reading, the healthier your communications will be.

Coping statements. Use these statements if you find yourself assuming an intention.

1. "Assume nothing or check it out."

2. "I don't guess at the motives of others."

3. "No mind reading."

Magnifying

When you magnify, you make things worse than they are. You use words like *terrible, awful, disgusting, horrendous.* You over-generalize by using words such as *always, all, every,* and *never.* Jill complains about her boss: "He's *always* handing me things at the last minute. He's *awful* with the whole support staff. *Never* a kind word, *never* a smile. He's just a *lousy* person to work for." Art complains about his neighbor: "He's *always* piling crap in my walkway. He *never* asks, he *never* even talks to me. It's *terrible* to live next to somebody who doesn't give a damn."

Both Jill and Art are magnifying. Jill's boss doesn't *always* give her things at the last minute. It isn't true that he *never* smiles. Art's neighbor isn't *always* piling things in the walkway. Nor does he *never* speak to Art. These magnifications crank up your sense of being victimized. By exaggerating the problematic behavior, you generate a feeling of being deeply wronged. They're bad and you're innocent.

Magnifying your trigger thoughts is like throwing gasoline on a fire. Your anger explodes because you feel so wronged, so righteous, so justified.

Exercise. Watch your language.

For one day, eliminate these words from your vocabulary: *all, always, every, never, terrible, awful, disgusting, horrible, sickening,* and so on. Commit yourself to describing people and events without magnifying. Strive for accuracy rather than exaggeration. Give the exact frequency: "Three times in the last two weeks . . ." "The second time this quarter . . ." "Once a month we chat for five minutes." Avoid using generalized pejoratives like *terrible* and *awful.* Instead, stick to simple conclusions like "I don't like it . . ." "I'd prefer he didn't hand things to me after four o'clock."

Coping statements. Say these things to yourself if you find yourself magnifying.

1. "No more 'always' and 'never.'"

2. "Accuracy, nonexaggeration."

3. "Let the facts speak for themselves."

Global Labeling

Your office mate is an *imbecile.* Your roommate's *neurotic.* Your father's *stupid.* The grocery checker is a *jerk.* Your lover's a selfish *asshole.* Your landlord is a *ripoff artist.* Your cousin is a *blabbermouth.* Global labels fuel your anger by turning the other person into someone who is totally bad and worthless. Instead of disliking specific behavior, you indict the entire person. Global labels are always false because they focus on a single characteristic or behavior, but imply that it's the whole picture.

It's much easier to get angry at an ogre, a despicable person, than it is to rage at one specific behavior. It's hard to really work yourself into a true feeling of victimization if you're only responding to one unfortunate event. But if you decide you've been mistreated by a selfish jerk, your anger comes to a quicker boil.

Exercise. Be specific.

The antidote for global labeling is specificity. The next time you catch yourself using pejorative labels, shift into a specific description of the offensive behavior. Leave the person out of it. Describe what he does, not who he is.

Coping statement. Say these sentences to yourself if you find yourself labeling.

"No labels. Be specific."

Changing Your Trigger Thoughts

Changing a long-standing pattern of thinking is no easy task. But it's absolutely necessary. If you don't find ways to combat your trigger thoughts, your shoulds and blamers, they will continue to ignite anger.

It'll take hard work and discipline to change what seems second nature now. But there is a way. Aaron Beck, one of the founders of cognitive behavioral therapy, devised an extremely effective process for confronting your distorted thoughts. It's called the three-column technique. Now take out your anger journal and divide a page into three columns. Whenever you feel angry, write down in Column A what you're saying to yourself. In Column B write down the kind of cognitive error you were using (some are listed below as a memory aid). In Column C, rewrite your original statement so that it no longer contains the distorted trigger thought.

Shoulds	*Blamers*
Entitlement fallacy	Good-bad dichotomizing
Fallacy of fairness	Assumed intent
Fallacy of change	Magnifying
Conditional assumptions	Global labeling
Letting it out fallacy	

Here's an example of how you can use the three-column technique.

Ann's Diary

Column A What I Say to Myself	Column B Cognitive Errors	Column C What I Could Say Instead
That jerk's keeping me waiting.	Assuming intention, Magnifying	I don't like waiting.
Yard duty again! The principal always does this to me.	Conditional assumptions	I assume he's doing the best he can, but it's quite inconvenient for me.
Why doesn't he learn to sit down and behave?	Fallacy of change	He'll learn to sit down when I figure out how to reinforce him to do so.

If she was any kind of a friend, she wouldn't stick me with the whole damn thing.	Conditional assumptions	It's a conflict of needs. I've got to negotiate this with her. Neither of us wants to do it.
Why do these people keep me waiting?	Shoulds	People never do what they should do, only what they're reinforced to do.
Why do I have to live in this closet when my ex-husband is still living in the house?	Entitlement fallacy	Just because I want that house doesn't mean I can afford it. He owns a plumbing business, I'm just a teacher. There is no reason why he should give up a house just because I want it.

As you can see, the third column is the most important. That's where you talk back to the trigger thoughts and begin to modify your anger. Here's another example.

Harold's Diary

Column A What I Say to Myself	Column B Cognitive Errors	Column C What I Could Say Instead
Now she's off to yoga and aerobics. We'll lose the whole morning, God damn her, she's avoiding me.	Letting it out fallacy, Assuming intention	Blowing up won't get me what I want. I'll stop assuming and find out what her needs are.
She consented to have breakfast. Big deal. I work all week so she can go to school, and I have to talk her into breakfast.	Fallacy of fairness	Okay, both our needs are important. She doesn't owe me anything. Her needs are as legitimate as mine.
Why do they always screw up my photos everytime I bring them here?	Good-bad dichotomizing, Magnifying, Global labeling	They're not that bad. They're doing the best they can. They don't always screw up. This is 4 out of 36 negatives

Why can't she wear something sexy to bed?	Entitlement fallacy	Just because I want it doesn't mean she has to do it. She has her own needs and limits. If I want to work on this, I can find out what her needs and fears are and negotiate some compromise.

Now it's time for you to try some on your own. In Column A you'll find a list of trigger thoughts. Name the distortion in Column B. In column C, rewrite or refute the distortion so it no longer triggers anger.

Column A What I Say to Myself	Column B Cognitive Errors	Column C What I Could Say Instead
1. Are you stupid? How can you forget your homework?		
2. He should stop the damned gambling. It's destroying our marriage.		
3. If she cared about me, she'd come home earlier.		
4. He never listens when I'm upset about something.		
5. He should have walked me to the car in this neighborhood.		
6. I took care of her when she had a cold last week. Now I have a toothache and she doesn't even ask how I am.		
7. He's walking this trail when he knows very well I'm afraid of heights.		

Suggested Answers:

1. *Global labeling.* "I don't like you forgetting your homework. How can we help you remember it? Perhaps you can stay up a half hour later if you remember your homework."

2. *Shoulds, fallacy of change.* "He'll only stop if he's reinforced to change and capable of changing. Pressure from me isn't working. I have to decide whether to live with this or let go."

3. *Conditional assumptions.* "Love has nothing to do with it. This is a conflict of needs. I have to find out what needs or fears keep her working late and negotiate some sort of compromise."

4. *Magnifying.* "Be specific. He listens maybe _____ percent of the time. How can I take responsibility to reinforce him to listen more?"

5. *Shoulds.* "That's my value and need, not his. He doesn't do what I think he should, only what his values and needs dictate."

6. *Fallacy of fairness.* "She has her own needs at this moment. Both our needs are equally legitimate. It is my responsibility to ask her for what I want."

7. *Assumed intent.* "I'm assuming things. I don't really know why he's walking here. Better check it out. I have to negotiate for my own needs."

Here are the main points to remember when you are writing your refutations to your trigger thoughts:

1. Be specific, not global.

2. Be nonpejorative, nonjudging.

3. Punishment and revenge won't get you what you want.

4. Check out all assumptions.

5. You, and only you, are responsible for your needs.

6. Recognize that people do the best they can given their level of awareness *at the moment of choice.*

7. Recognize that people do what is reinforcing for them to do. You can only get them to change by negotiating for and reinforcing new behavior.

Whenever you feel anger, continue to use the three-column technique to confront your trigger thoughts in your anger journal. It's essential that you make a commitment to keep at this. It is difficult, arduous work to keep examining your thoughts, to keep questioning and rebutting what seemed so natural, so reasonable. But getting control of your anger requires that you become more and more aware of how your trigger thoughts create upsetting feelings. It will take at least three months of consistent effort monitoring and confronting your angry cognitions before you begin to feel the tide turn. Gradually they will become less automatic. Gradually you will find yourself experiencing more and more *discomfort* when the old trigger thoughts pop up. They will no longer sound so right, so convincing. In fact, you will begin to recognize them for what they are—excuses to discharge pain, deceptions that trigger destructive aggression. As you keep talking back to the shoulds and blamers, you will find your new attitudes and beliefs beginning to take hold. As you accept more responsibility for your needs, you will move beyond anger to problem solving, negotiating, and exploring the needs of others.

10

Controlling Stress
Step by Step

Stress fuels anger. If anger is a problem in your life, it's essential that you learn a method for reducing stress that works for you. Read through the suggestions in this chapter and choose the techniques that seem most useful. You will find that you can learn alternative coping strategies that will help you regain control. You can deal successfully with stress, instead of being angry.

Aerobic Exercise

One of the best methods for controlling stress is to exercise. Exercise releases chemicals in your brain called *endorphins*. These act as natural tranquilizers and have tremendous stress-reducing properties. When you experience a state of arousal, exercising can return your body to normal equilibrium, leaving you feeling relaxed and refreshed. The simplest and easiest form of aerobic exercise is brisk walking or jogging. However, the principles discussed here apply equally to swimming, bicycling, cross-country skiing, or even jumping rope.

Aerobic exercise uses up oxygen. Your body's increased demand for oxygen is matched by an increased heart rate, fast breathing, and a relaxation of the small blood vessels. This allows more oxygen-rich blood to reach the muscles.

Caution: Do not start a strenuous program of aerobic exercise suddenly. Get a checkup from your doctor. If you are not used to physical exertion, start slowly by walking or doing easy calisthenics. Every winter at least one New Yorker has a fatal heart attack shoveling his car out of the snow, after a year of living a sedentary lifestyle.

If you develop heart palpitations, dizziness, or chest pain after beginning an exercise program, see a doctor as soon as possible.

In order to benefit from aerobic exercise, your heart must beat at 70 percent of its maximum rate for at least twenty minutes. The exercise must be repeated at least three times per week. By following this procedure you will place a moderate stress on your heart that will gradually improve its efficiency. The table below shows the estimated heart rates for different age groups.

Estimated Heartbeats per Minute for Average Man or Woman by Age Group

Age	Maximum Rate	80% Maximum Rate	70% Maximum Rate	60% Maximum Rate	50% Maximum Rate
18-29	203-191	162-153	142-134	122-115	101-95
30-39	190-181	152-145	133-127	113-108	95-90
40-49	180-171	144-137	126-120	107-102	90-85
50-59	170-161	136-129	119-113	101-96	85-80
60-69	160-151	128-121	112-106	95-90	80-75
70-79	150-141	120-113	105-99	89-84	75-70

In order to determine your heart rate, simply take your pulse for fifteen seconds. Then multiply this number by four to get your rate per minute. You can practice taking your pulse while sitting quietly. Wear a watch with a second hand (or a digital readout) on your left arm. Turn the palm of your right hand toward you. Put the fingertips of your left hand on your right wrist and locate the bone that comes down from your thumb. Move about 1/8-inch toward the inside of your arm and press firmly. The throbbing you feel is your pulse.

A normal resting pulse may vary from 40 to 100 beats per minute. Most healthy men have a resting pulse between 70 and 84 beats per minute. The resting pulse for most healthy women ranges between 75 and 85 beats per minute.

To determine how fast you should walk or jog to achieve the optimal 70 percent, follow these instructions:

1. Walk at a comfortable pace for five minutes. Take your pulse immediately (it will fall off fast). If the rate is about 50 percent of the maximum heart rate for your age group (see the table above), go to the next test. If it is already above the 70-percent level, continue to walk at this pace every other day until your heart rate falls below that level. When you have achieved that rate, continue

to the next test. If you have not had a recent physical exam, have one soon.

2. Walk at a vigorous pace for five minutes. Take your pulse immediately. If your heart rate is about 60 percent of the maximum, go on to the next test. If your pulse is over the 70-percent maximum, continue at this pace. Take five-minute walks every other day until your pulse falls below the 70-percent level. Then go on to the next test.

3. Alternate one minute of slow jogging with one minute of brisk walking for five minutes and then take your pulse. If your rate is above the 70-percent maximum heart rate for your age group, continue this regimen until your pulse falls below that level.

4. You are now ready to proceed on your own. A good rule of thumb is to continue to jog until you feel winded and then slow to a brisk walk for a minute. (You should be able to carry on a conversation while you are jogging. If you can't, you're going too fast!) Check your pulse frequently to find that pace which allows you to maintain the ideal 70-percent heart rate for at least twenty minutes.

5. When you're finished exercising, *cool down*. Always end your exercise sessions with five minutes of slow walking. Take long, stretching steps. Let your arms dangle loosely and shake your hands. Rotate your head around your neck a few times in one direction and then in the other direction.

Scanning Your Body for Stress

The first step in controlling stress is to recognize how and where tension is affecting your body. The following techniques and many of the others described in this chapter have been adapted from *The Relaxation & Stress Reduction Workbook* (Davis, Eshelman, and McKay 2000). Don't worry if you have trouble relaxing as you do this exercise. We'll teach you how to relax later. The important thing is to simply become aware of the existing tension.

1. Begin by paying attention to your feet and legs. Start by wiggling your toes, then rotate your feet and relax them. Note any tension in your calves. Let go of this tension.

2. Now focus on your lower torso. Become aware of any tension or pain in your lower back. Relax as fully as you can. Notice if you have tension in your hips, pelvic area, or buttocks. Relax these areas.

3. Move your focus to your diaphragm and stomach. Take a couple of deep breaths, breathing slowly in and out. Feel yourself relaxing, more and more deeply. Notice any tension that you are experiencing in this area.

4. Become aware of your lungs and chest cavity. Search for tension in this part of your body. Take a couple of slow, deep breaths and relax.

5. Next, pay attention to your shoulders, neck, and throat. Swallow a couple of times and notice any tension or soreness in your throat and neck. Roll your head around clockwise a few times. Now reverse and roll your head the other way. Shrug your shoulders and become aware of any tension in this area and then relax.

6. Begin at the top of your head and scan for tension. Feel for pain in your forehead. Perhaps there is a band of pain around the top of your head. Maybe there is pain or tension behind your eyes. Notice any tightness in your jaw. Check for locking or grinding of teeth and taut lips. Become aware of your ears. Go back over your head and tense and relax each part.

7. Now go back and scan your entire body for any remaining tension. Allow yourself to relax more and more deeply.

Do this exercise every day for a week and you'll have a much better understanding of where your body chronically holds tension. Each day record in your Anger Diary the location(s) where your tension seems to concentrate.

Stress Reduction Skills

The next step is to learn a relaxation strategy that works for you. Experiment with each of the techniques suggested below and find out for yourself what gives you the best results.

Breathing Away Stress

In order to live, you have to breathe; in order to live well, you have to breathe well. Proper breathing is a natural antidote to stress. The basic technique is called deep (diaphragmatic) breathing and may be practiced in a variety of postures. If you need a role model, watch a baby breathing; its little belly rises and falls with each breath.

1. Lie down on a blanket or rug on the floor. Bend your knees and place your feet about eight inches apart, with your toes turned slightly outward. Make sure that your spine is straight.

2. Scan your body for tension.

3. Place your left hand on your abdomen (belly) and your right hand on your chest.

4. Inhale slowly and deeply through your nose, filling your abdomen. Push the air way down to your belly. Notice your left hand being pushed up. Your chest should move only a little underneath your right hand and only with your abdomen.

5. Now inhale through your nose and exhale through your mouth, making a quiet, relaxing, "whooshing" sound as you gently blow out. Your mouth, tongue, and jaw will be relaxed. Take long, slow, deep breaths that raise and lower your abdomen. Focus on the sound and feeling of your breathing as you become more and more relaxed.

6. Continue this deep breathing exercise for about five or ten minutes. Do this once or twice a day for a couple of weeks. Then, if you like, you may extend this period to twenty minutes a day.

7. At the end of each deep-breathing session, take a little time to scan your body for tension. Compare the tension you feel at the conclusion of the exercise with what you were experiencing when you began.

When you have learned to breathe easily into your abdomen, you can practice this exercise whenever you feel stress during the day. It doesn't matter whether you are sitting or standing. Just concentrate on your abdomen moving up and down, as the air moves in and out of your lungs. Notice the feeling of relaxation that deep breathing gives you.

Progressive Muscle Relaxation

There is a reciprocal relationship between tension and anger. Physical tension creates stress, which predisposes you to anger. Anger then causes additional body tension, which escalates and exacerbates the anger response. When doing this exercise notice that we ask you to increase the tension first, then relax.

1. Get in a comfortable position and relax. Now clench your right fist, tighter and tighter, studying the tension as you do so. Keep it clenched and notice the tension in your fist, hand, and forearm. Now relax. Feel the looseness in your right hand and notice how it contrasts with the tension. Repeat this procedure with your right fist again. Tighten for about seven seconds. Always notice as you relax that this feeling is the opposite of tension. Relax and feel

the difference. Repeat this entire procedure with your left fist, then both fists at the same time.

2. Now bend your elbows and tense your biceps (in a Mr. Universe pose). Tense your biceps as hard as you can for seven seconds and observe the feeling of tautness. Relax and straighten out your arms. Let the relaxation develop. Feel the difference. Repeat this and each of the following procedures at least once.

3. Turn your attention to your head. Wrinkle your forehead (like a walnut) as tightly as you can for seven seconds. Now relax and smooth it out. Allow yourself to imagine your entire forehead and scalp becoming as smooth as silk. Now frown and notice the strain spreading throughout your forehead. Let go. Allow your brow to become smooth again. Close your eyes now. Squint them tighter. Look for tension. Relax your eyes. Let them remain gently and comfortably closed. Now clench your jaw, bite hard, and notice the tension throughout your jaw. Relax your jaw. When your jaw is relaxed, your lips will be slightly parted. Let yourself really appreciate the contrast between tension and relaxation. Now press your tongue against the roof of your mouth. Feel the ache in the back of your mouth. Relax. Compress your lips now, pursing, them into an O. Relax your lips and blow out forcefully, making a sound like a horse. Notice that your forehead, scalp, eyes, jaw, tongue, and lips are now all relaxed.

4. Press your head back as far as it can comfortably go and observe the tension in your neck. Roll your head to the right and feel the changing location of the stress. Roll your head to the left. Straighten your head and bring it forward, pressing your chin against your chest. Feel the tension in your throat and the back of your neck. Relax, allowing your head to return to a comfortable position. Let the relaxation deepen. Now shrug your shoulders. Keep the tension as you hunch your head down between your shoulders. Relax your shoulders. Drop them back and feel the relaxation spread through your neck, throat, and shoulders. Experience the pure relaxation, deeper and deeper.

5. Give your entire body a chance to relax. Feel the comfort and heaviness. Now breathe in and fill your lungs completely. Hold your breath and notice the tension. Now exhale, letting your chest become loose. Let the air hiss out. Continue relaxing, letting your breath move freely and gently. Repeat this several times, noticing the tension draining from your body as you exhale. Next, tighten your stomach and hold it. Note the tension, then relax. Now place your hand on your stomach. Breathe deeply into your stomach, pushing your hand up. Hold, and then relax. Feel the contrast of

the relaxation as the air rushes out. Now arch your back, without straining. Keep the rest of your body as relaxed as possible. Focus on the tension in your lower back. Now relax, deeper and deeper

6. Tighten your buttocks and thighs. Flex your thighs by pressing down on your heels as hard as you can. Relax and feel the difference. Now curl your toes downward (like a ballerina), making your calves tense. Study the tension. Relax. Now point your toes toward your face, creating tension in your shins. Relax again.

7. Feel the heaviness throughout your lower body as the relaxation deepens. Relax your feet, ankles, calves, shins, knees, thighs, and buttocks. Now let the relaxation spread to your stomach, lower back, and chest. Let go more and more. Experience the relaxation deepening in your shoulders, arms, and hands. Deeper and deeper. Notice the feeling of looseness and relaxation in your neck, jaw, and all your facial muscles.

A good way to do this exercise is to make a tape recording of the instructions for yourself. You can then play it back anytime you want, while you are relaxing. When you have followed this procedure daily for two weeks, you'll be ready to move on to the advanced, shorthand form of relaxation.

The following "short form" procedure can be used to achieve deep muscle relaxation quickly. Whole muscle groups are simultaneously tensed and then relaxed. As before, repeat each procedure at least once, tensing each muscle group for about seven seconds. Then relax for twenty to thirty seconds. Remember to notice the contrast between the sensations of tension and relaxation.

1. Curl both fists, tightening your biceps and forearms (like a Mr. Universe pose). Hold it. Relax.

2. Wrinkle up your forehead (like a walnut). At the same time, press you head as far back as possible. Roll it clockwise in a complete circle, then reverse. Now wrinkle up the muscles of your face: frowning, eyes squinting, lips pursed, tongue pressing to the roof of your mouth, and shoulders hunched. Hold it. Relax.

3. Arch your back (like a bow), and as you take a deep breath into your chest, hold it. Relax. Take a deep breath, expanding your stomach. Hold it. Relax.

4. Point your feet and toes back toward your face, tightening your shins. Hold it. Relax. Curl your toes (like a ballerina), simultaneously tightening your calves, thighs, and buttocks. Hold it. Relax.

Relaxation Without Tension

Up to now you've practiced progressive relaxation by *increasing* tension. Now it's time to eliminate that tension, as well. Once again, go through the relaxation sequence. But this time, as you scan each muscle group, simply notice any tension in that part of your body, take a deep breath, and as you exhale, relax away, and let go of all that tension.

1. This time you'll start at the bottom of your body. Begin by point-ing your toes, then gently reverse and pull your toes toward your head. Notice any tension, take a deep breath, and on the exhale, relax away the tension.

2. Now focus on your buttocks. Again, just notice tension (if you find any), then take a deep breath, and on the exhale, relax.

3. Next, focus on your chest and stomach muscles. Notice, breathe, exhale, and relax.

4. Arch your back, and, without straining, notice any tension. Then, take a deep breath, and relax away the stress.

5. Focusing on your arms and biceps, simply notice any tension you may feel there. Now, take a deep breath, and on the exhale, relax the tension. Just let it go.

6. Check out your neck and shoulders. Notice, breathe, exhale, relax away the tension.

7. Now turn your attention to your forehead and notice any tension you may find. Move your focus to the rest of your face and your mouth. Notice any tension there, take a deep breath, and relax on the exhale.

Cue-Controlled Relaxation

Now it's time to choose your personal cue word, a two-syllable word or phrase. This will enable you to enter into a state of deep, cue-controlled relaxation each time you repeat it. You don't have to say it out loud. Just saying it under your breath, or even think-ing it, will work just fine. Choose something like "relax," "let go," "release," or "okay." You might prefer a color, such as "deep blue," or a feeling, such as "true love." A phrase that evokes a personal memory of peace and contentment usually works best.

Keeping your cue word (or phrase) in mind, return your atten-tion once again to your deep, diaphragmatic breathing. Now, each time you exhale, say your cue word (or phrase) out loud or to your-self. Relax your entire body as you exhale, and think (or say) your cue word. Make your whole body feel as relaxed as it was when you had just finished the relaxation without tension exercise. Do this ten times in a row, to set up an automatic response pattern. Write your cue word (phrase) in the space below as a reminder.

_____

_____

Self-Hypnosis for Relaxation

You can achieve hypnosis by using an *induction*, which is a group of suggestions that can be repeated until you slip into a trance state. The induction described below is adapted from *Hypnosis for Change* (Hadely and Staudacher 1985). Your best approach to using it may be to make your own tape recording. To prepare for the recording, first read the induction aloud several times to become familiar and comfortable with the content. Say the words slowly. Keep your voice level and monotonous, as flat and expressionless as possible. (Helpful hint: Make sure that the tape you are using is long enough to handle the entire induction on one side.) When you are ready to use the tape you've made, prepare a special place, away from noise and distraction. Wear comfortable clothing and get in a comfortable position. You may want to lie down or sit in a rocking chair. Now allow yourself to experience the deep relaxation of a self-induced hypnotic procedure.

1. Take a nice deep breath, close your eyes, and begin to relax. Just think about relaxing every muscle in your body from the top of your head to the tips of your toes. Just begin to relax. And start observing how very comfortable your body is beginning to feel. You feel supported, so you can just let go and relax. Inhale and exhale. Notice your breathing; notice the rhythm of your breathing, and relax your breathing for a moment.

2. Be aware of the normal sounds around you. Whatever you hear from now on will only help you to relax. And as you exhale, release any tension, any stress, from any part of your body, from your mind and your thoughts. Just let that stress go. Just feel any stressful thoughts rushing through your mind, feel them beginning to wind down, wind down, wind down, and relax.

3. Begin by letting all the muscles in your face relax, especially your jaw. Let your teeth part just a little bit and relax this area. This is a place where tension and stress gather, so be sure to relax your jaw, and feel that relaxation move into your temples, and, as you think about relaxing these muscles, they will relax. Feel them

relax and, as you relax, you'll be able just to drift and float into a deeper and deeper level of total relaxation.

4. Continue to relax and now let all the muscles in your neck relax. Feel those muscles become smooth, smooth and relaxed. And your shoulders feel so heavy. Now you can feel a heavy weight being lifted off your shoulders and you feel relieved, lighter, and more relaxed. As all the muscles in the back of your neck and shoulders relax, you feel that soothing relaxation go down your back, down, down, down, to the lower part of your back.

5. And those muscles let go with every breath you exhale. Just feel your body drifting, floating, down deeper, down deeper, down deeper, into total relaxation. Let your muscles go, relaxing more and more. Let all of the muscles in your shoulders, running down your arms to your fingertips, relax. And let your arms feel heavy, so heavy, so heavy, so comfortable, so relaxed. You have tingling in your fingertips. That's perfectly fine. You may have warmth in the palms of your hands, and that's fine. And you may feel that you can barely lift your arms, they are so relaxed. They are so heavy, so heavy, so relaxed.

6. And now you inhale once again and relax your chest muscles. And now as you exhale, feel your stomach muscles relax. As you exhale, relax all of the muscles in your stomach, let them go and all of the muscles in your legs, feel them relax and all the muscles in your legs are so completely relaxed, right to the tips of your toes.

7. Notice how very comfortable your body feels, just drifting and floating, deeper and deeper, deeply relaxed. And just as you are relaxing deeper and deeper, imagine a beautiful staircase. There are ten steps, and the steps lead you to a special and peaceful and beautiful place.

8. In a moment you can begin to imagine taking a safe and gentle and easy step down, down, down, on the staircase, leading you to a very peaceful, a very special place. You can imagine any place you choose. Perhaps you would enjoy a beach near the ocean with clean fresh air, or the mountains, with a stream. Any place you like is perfectly fine.

9. In a moment you can begin to count backwards from ten to one, and you can imagine taking the steps down, and as you take each step, feel your body relax more and more, feel it just drift down, down each step, and relax even deeper. Ten, relax deeper, nine . . . eight . . . seven . . . six . . . five . . . four . . . three . . . two . . . one . . . deeper and deeper. More and more relaxed.

10. And now imagine a peaceful and special place. You can imagine this special place and perhaps you can even feel it. You are alone. There is no one to disturb you. This is the most peaceful place in the world for you. Imagine yourself there and feel that sense of peace flowing through you and the sense of well-being. And you enjoy these positive feelings. You can keep these good feelings with you long after this exercise is completed, for the rest of the day and evening, even tomorrow. Allow these positive feelings to grow stronger and stronger, feeling at peace with a sense of well-being (Pause.)

11. And each time and every time that you choose to do this, you go deeper. Regardless of the stress and tension that may surround your life, you may now remain more at peace, more calm, more relaxed, and allow the tension and stress to bounce off and away from you. And these positive feelings will stay with you and grow stronger and stronger throughout the day, as you continue to relax deeper and deeper.

12. Enjoy your special place for another moment and then you can begin to count from one to ten, and as you count from one to ten, you can begin coming back to full consciousness, and you will come back feeling refreshed, as if you just had a long rest. Come back feeling alert and relaxed. Begin to come back now. One . . . two . . . coming up, three . . . four . . . five . . . six . . . seven . . . eight . . . nine . . . begin to open your eyes, and come all the way back feeling relaxed and refreshed.

When you've listened to your tapes long enough to become familiar with the induction, you may wish to say the relaxing suggestions to yourself. You can hypnotize yourself and receive suggestions from yourself. After you hypnotize yourself and receive all the stress-reducing benefits by systematically relaxing your body, doing a countdown, repeating deepening suggestions ("I am drifting deeper and deeper. . . . I feel more and more drowsy, peaceful, and calm"), and visiting your special place. Then count back up to full alertness.

Brief Combination Techniques

These are techniques that literally combine two or more relaxation strategies. The net effect is synergistic, which means that one and one equals three. Combination techniques capitalize on a "piggyback" effect where each technique builds progressively on the other. And, as an extra bonus, they're designed to be quickies. You can easily do them during a coffee break. Many can be completed in two minutes or less.

Breathing with Imagery

This technique combines slow breathing with visualization. A mental picture of a sunny beach is good. But any image that you find relaxing will do as well.

1. Imagine that you're lying on a beach. A few clouds and an occasional seagull drift overhead. You hear the sound of the waves as they crash on the shore and then retreat silently. They ebb and flow in a rhythm that has been going on since time began. You're covered with sand. Your limbs feel warm and heavy. Really try to experience your body as warm and relaxed. Feel the weight of the sand.

2. Center your breathing in your abdomen, as described earlier, by putting your hand on your belly. Inhale slowly and deeply through your nose. Allow the air to escape easily through relaxed lips.

3. As you continue to visualize the beach and sand, breathe deeply and easily. Notice the warmth of the sand and repeat the word "warm" on your in-breath. Notice the weight of the sand, and repeat the word "heavy" on the out-breath. As you do this, switch off your muscles and allow the stress and tension to drain from your body. Continue doing this for at least five minutes.

Being in Control

1. Get comfortable and close your eyes. Loosen your tie, belt, or any other constrictions. Notice your breathing. Focus on each breath, one at a time. Each time you exhale, say the word "one." Continue saying "one" with each exhalation.

2. When you begin to feel yourself relaxing, allow your attention to drift to a situation that has been a problem for you. Now you can begin to visualize yourself handling that situation in a new and different way. Where you once felt stressed and uncomfortable, you now can see yourself as confident. You are smiling and smiling, and your lips say the right words automatically. Others around you lean forward, they smile, you're being a success.

3. Now you see yourself hesitating. A small mistake, a faux pas. You're uncertain for a moment. But you recover your poise and continue, confidently. You feel satisfied. You've done a good job. You remind yourself, " I can handle this, I'm in control."

Grateful Relaxation

1. Begin by using the short form of progressive relaxation outlined earlier in this chapter. Assume a Mr. Universe pose. Wrinkle your

forehead and hunch your shoulders. Arch your back and take a deep breath. Point and curl your toes and tighten your calves and thighs.

2. Let your mind wander and remember some good things that happened today. Find at least three things that you can be grateful for. These experiences don't have to be "biggies." Your good things may be something as simple as enjoying a sunset, getting a hug from a child, or a coworker offering to get you a cup of coffee. An unexpected smile from the boss, getting into the shortest line at the grocery store, or the soothing feeling of a warm shower. Life is full of small pleasures. Take a moment to relive and relish these experiences.

3. Continue to reflect on your day. Remember three things that you did that you feel good about. Again, don't look for Oscar-award level events. Simple, satisfying things like being supportive to a friend or paying a compliment to your spouse are ideal. Having the courage to say no to something you really didn't want to do or completing a difficult task are other good examples. Take a moment to re-experience these positive moments of your day.

Ultra Quickies

If all else fails, use one of these surefire strategies for guaranteed immediate (temporary) relief:

1. Spend ten seconds rubbing a tense part of your body.

2. Take ten slow deep breaths.

3. Change your posture and stretch.

4. Talk more slowly.

5. Get up and get a cold (nonalcoholic) drink.

6. Sit down and lean back.

Stopping Anger Before It Starts

Return now to your Anger Journal. We've included a blank page below to show you how to record every angry incident you experience. We've also included an example page.

These brief techniques are just the ticket for dealing with specific, anger-arousing situations. You should begin to track the physical signs and symptoms that you feel just *before* the anger hits. These are the pre-existing stressors that can act as early warning signals. These might include such physiological cues as an increased pulse rate or heavy or rapid breathing. Some people report feeling hot, some become sweaty. It is very important to pay attention to your body. Notice where and when you begin to feel tension. For some people it's a tightness in the gut that signals the beginning of frustration. For others, the tension might be located in the neck and shoulders. "Hunching" the shoulders might be an attempt to protect the neck, or even to cover the ears from hearing painful messages. Tension in the legs, calves, and thighs is often associated with the "fight or flight" syndrome. Tension in the jaw indicates an effort to stifle some response. A particularly telling sign is tension in the hands resulting in a clenching of the fists.

The early warning signs of stress are your signal to begin to cope. When you feel the first symptoms of anger arousal, you can decide which of the brief strategies will work best for your situation. Try different techniques and find the one that's most effective for you. Once you find the best solution for reducing your stress, be sure to use it consistently.

You now have two different ways to combat stress. The techniques for general stress reduction, such as progressive muscle relaxation or self-hypnosis, should be practiced daily. They will help you to reduce chronic states of tension and arousal. Remember, consistency is the key to mastery over your anger. The brief, focused techniques should be reserved for dealing with specific anger-evoking situations. They can be used as needed to manage acute problems successfully.

Substances that Increase Stress (A Cautionary Note)

Abusing any substance is a guaranteed way to increase your stress level. Drug-abuse problems involving opiates (heroin, Demerol, Darvon) and the major stimulants (speed and cocaine, particularly "crack") are beyond the scope of this book. If these substances are having an adverse effect on your life (i.e., causing problems at work or with your relationships, or affecting your health), then it is a good idea to see a therapist or drug abuse counselor.

More common legal substances, such as alcohol, nicotine, caffeine, and even sugar, are also potential stress inducers. All of these substances may feel good at first, but eventually they lead to irritability.

Alcohol is the most dangerous legal drug available. It affects (adversely) every major body system. Drinking one or two drinks will bring on euphoria and general good feelings. This deceptive "come-on" often tempts people into drinking more, which initiates the second stage. This is characterized by depression, fatigue, nausea, and general bad feelings.

Alcoholic hangovers are a major source of irritability, which often leads to rage and spousal abuse. Surprise attacks in the middle of the night by drunken partners make a kind of perverse sense in light of the irritation created by the second-stage alcoholic effect. Often, bad physical feelings may be combined with anxious self-talk about the other partner's negative reactions. This may set off an angry and violent response before the victim is even aware that a problem exists.

The body responds to sugar with a sense of fresh energy and well-being. All too soon (ten to thirty minutes at best) insulin is released to metabolize, for example, a candy bar (and all available blood sugars from previous meals). The overall blood sugar level therefore drops lower than before the candy was eaten, and an uncomfortable feeling of tiredness results. Because the brain cannot function well without a relatively high level of blood sugar, irritability is the inevitable result.

Nicotine and caffeine are both stimulants that raise the heart rate and provide a temporary "high" feeling. These substances also increase insulin secretion, which results in swings in blood sugar levels, resulting in irritable moods. These drugs cause other side effects that can increase stress, notably respiratory problems (due to heavy smoking) and stomach problems (caused by the caffeine in coffee and soft drinks).

Become aware of the effects that various substances have on your life. Stress and anger cannot be controlled if your life is ruled by drugs. If alcohol or drugs are taking over more and more of your life, we strongly suggest that you find a therapist or counselor to help resolve this problem.

11

Problem Solving

Life is stressful. It's just one damn thing after another. Probably the greatest source of stress in our lives is unresolved problems that result in chronic emotional pain. People who don't use effective problem-solving strategies usually end up feeling helpless. And anger is often the result.

Before we offer you an effective problem-solving program, it is useful to take a brief look at those strategies that are guaranteed *not* to work.

1. Trying to change other people's behavior is tops on the list. The problem is that people don't want to change. At least not because you want them to. The result is frustration and anger. The more you push, the more resistant they become. And the more helpless you feel. Which leads to more anger.

2. Avoiding the problem by numbing yourself out. This ineffective solution is an attempt to block out the pain by using alcohol, drugs, TV, or other compulsive behaviors. This strategy does work temporarily, but nothing gets solved. In fact the problem usually gets worse because it's not being attended to.

3. Short-terms solutions are tempting because they make you feel better immediately. Long-term solutions are more difficult and don't provide quick results. It's easy to give in to a child's noisy demands for candy in the supermarket. He gets the candy and you get a quiet child, for the moment. But this solution guarantees more tantrums in days and years to come. The long term solution requires you to set limits and endure the unpleasantness now, so there will be less problematic behavior in the future.

4. Doing nothing but waiting, hoping that things will get better. "Just wait until I get that raise ..."; "Things will really change when the kids leave for college ..."; "Once I get this idea patented ... " Perhaps things will get better in the future, but in the meantime, you're not doing anything to fix the problem. And your day-to-day life remains less than satisfying.

5. Letting things build up until disaster is imminent. This is the worst and, probably, most desperate strategy. The idea is that if you appear to be on the brink of devastation, totally overwhelmed, someone who cares about you will step in at the last minute to rescue you. The problem is that sometimes they don't, or they try, but it's just too late.

Now you're ready to look at a problem-solving program that really works. In fact, it's literally IDEAL, which means: Identify the problem; Develop alternatives; Explore the consequences; have an Action plan; and Look at the results. This IDEAL problem-solving program is adapted from *Successful Problem Solving* (McKay and Fanning 2002).

(I) Identify the problem.

Everyday life offers a broad spectrum of opportunities for experiencing problematic situations. Problems are normal and may appear in any area of life. It is often useful to examine your life, category by category, and make a checklist to pinpoint where to concentrate your attention. While reviewing the following list, pay particular attention to problems that seem associated with tension, emotional distress, or episodes of anger.

Health problems may involve eating (digestive, poor nutrition, weight), sleeping (insomnia, trouble getting up in the morning), or feeling chronically tired or run down.

Financial problems might include insufficient money for necessities or recreation, increasing debt, difficulty making ends meet, or unexpected or catastrophic expenses.

Work-related issues may include unemployment or underemployment, working conditions, boring work, trouble with a boss or coworker, fear of being fired, or desire for a career change.

Living situations may be unsatisfying (bad neighborhood, home too small or too far from work or school), a messy house, things always breaking down, or landlord hassles.

Interpersonal relationships may be a problem if you want more closeness but have few friends. You may feel vulnerable and shy. You might be ending a love affair, feeling a lack of affection or contact with your partner, or you just can't seem to find the right partner.

Recreational problems include not having enough fun, or an inability to think of anything to do to promote pleasure. You may need a vacation, or want to travel but don't have enough free time. Or you may simply lack skill at playing games.

Family troubles include fighting and arguing, or not getting along with parents or children. Other troubles include being worried or irritated with a family member, feeling rejected by the family, feeling trapped in an unhappy family situation, or feeling insecure about losing a mate. Maybe the problem arises from an inability to be open and honest with family members, different interests from your spouse, recurring rejection and criticism from your spouse, or children having problems at school. Perhaps it involves interfering in-laws, a sick family member, or a disintegrating marriage.

Psychological problems include feeling nervous or depressed, excessive worrying or trouble with bad habits, or problems with authority. Maybe you're feeling blocked from attaining goals, obsessed with unobtainable goals, or are suffering from a lack of motivation.

Now choose one category to start with, say, for example, your living situation. Begin by clearly stating your goal. In this case it might be, "making my home a nicer place to live in."

(D) Develop alternatives.

The next step in IDEAL problem-solving involves generating lots of ideas that could help to solve the problem. One useful approach for this is to use a process known as "brainstorming." There are four basic rules to observe to make the process work:

1. **Be uncritical.** Save evaluation or judgment for later. Write down whatever idea comes into your head, without considering whether it is good or bad.

2. **Be wild and crazy.** The more far-out your idea is, the better. Following this rule can help you get out of a mental rut and allow you to break free of old, limited views of the problem. Getting a new perspective will let you see the problem in an entirely different light.

3. **Be prolific.** The more the merrier. The more ideas you can generate, the better your chances of finding some really good solutions. Write them down, one after the other, without thinking about them. Don't stop until you have a good long list.

4. **Be creative.** Go back over your list and see how you can combine and improve the ideas you have generated. Sometimes, two fairly good ideas can be combined to make one excellent idea. Brainstorming at this point should focus on general strategies. The nuts and bolts, the details, will come later.

When brainstorming for ways to "make my home a nicer place to live in," the following ideas came up:

1. Remodel the kitchen.

2. Buy new carpeting.

3. Hang new artwork in the living room.

4. Put dirty laundry in hamper.

5. Paint the bedroom walls mauve.

6. Throw out all the dirty dishes in the kitchen sink.

7. Mop the kitchen floor and vacuum the rug in the living room.

8. Hire a maid.

9. Buy a new stereo.

10. Clean mold off the bathroom walls.

(E) Explore the consequences.

At this point you've chosen a problem to work on, defined a goal, and created a list of broad strategies for achieving that goal. The next step is to focus on the most promising approaches, and consider the consequences of putting each one into action. Some people can do this evaluation automatically; others need to take some time to figure it out step by step. Whichever way you do it, it really pays to do this step thoroughly and conscientiously.

Go over your list of strategies and rule out any obviously bad ideas. Whenever possible, combine strategies into one plan.

Now, get a separate piece of paper and, at the top, write down your best remaining strategy. Then make two columns below that. That is because any strategy will necessarily have both positive and negative consequences. In the column on the left, list all the possible positive outcomes. Negative outcomes go in the column on the right. Begin with personal consequences. How would putting this strategy into action affect what you feel, need, or want? Then think of social outcomes. What impact would this strategy have on other people? Or on their reaction to you? Next explore short-term consequences. How would it affect your life right now? And, finally, look at the long-term consequences—how you might be affected in a month or a year.

Remember to fill in both columns each time you think of a new consequence. Then, when you have listed the major consequences, it's time to evaluate the likely outcomes. Cross out any obviously unlikely outcomes. You can now score the remaining consequences using the following system.

- If the consequence is mainly personal in nature, give it 2 points.

- If the consequence is mainly social in nature, score 1 point.

- If the consequence is mainly long range, award it 2 points.

- If the consequence is mainly short term, give it 1 point.

Note that consequences can be both personal and long range at the same time (for a score of 4 points) or social and short term (for a score of 2 points), and so on.

Now add up your scores for your strategy to see whether the positive consequences outweigh the negative ones. Obviously, it pays to avoid strategies that have mainly negative outcomes. If the first strategy you chose to evaluate has satisfactory outcomes, move on to creating your action plan. If not, choose another strategy to evaluate. Repeat the process with the two-column list, until you arrive at an alternative that's heavily weighted with positive outcomes.

In exploring consequences, primarily the financial consequences, it was decided to focus on the kitchen first. Remodeling the kitchen and hiring a maid were economically prohibitive. So was throwing out all the dirty dishes. However, mopping the kitchen floor and agreeing to keep the kitchen sink clean seemed doable. Nobody wanted to clean the mold off the bathroom walls so they drew straws.

(A) Action plan.

The key to making a successful action plan is to create a "Do List." Like any successful business plan, the Do List summarizes what you have to do, and in what order tasks must be done to accomplish your goal.

To be most effective, a Do List should be action-oriented. When writing a Do List it's best to use action verbs that describe specific activities or behaviors. For example, instead of writing, "keep kitchen sink clean" (too vague) write, "do dishes daily." And, more specifically, an effective Do List spells out what needs to be done in detail. In fact, the more detailed the better. For example, instead of just writing, "do dishes daily," consider writing, "rinse and put dishes in dishwasher after every meal."

A good Do List lists activities in a logical order, first things first. For example, if you want to cook a gourmet meal you must first go shopping. A good Do List breaks down steps into their incremental elements. That means starting with basic simple tasks and building to more complex ones. In cooking a gourmet meal, for example, you'll first need to read the recipe, then check to make sure you have the necessary ingredients, and finally make a shopping list. Then, and only then, do you go shopping. Cooking the actual meal is the final step.

Here are step by step instructions for making a Do List:

1. **List every step.** Start by writing down everything you'll have to do to achieve your goal. At this point the order doesn't matter, just write down everything that occurs to you. One helpful technique is to work backwards. Begin by sitting in a comfortable chair, closing your eyes, and relaxing with some diaphragmatic breathing. Then, picture yourself at a time in the future when your goal has already been accomplished. From this vantage point use the "retrospectroscope" to look backwards and see yourself doing everything necessary to achieve your goal. When new steps occur to you, open your eyes and write them down. Then close your eyes again and keep "remembering" all the steps you used to get to your goal.

2. **Rewrite the steps in a timed sequence.** Now, get a fresh sheet of paper and rewrite your list in a strict time sequence. First things first, then the second, then third, etc. If you find a step that seems too big to accomplish all at once, break it down into smaller, more manageable steps.

3. **Put easy tasks or those that are not time-sensitive first.** When you are working out the time sequences, you will find that some things can be done in any order. Choose the simplest, easiest, and smallest items first. That way you'll start to feel a sense of accomplishment, and gain some momentum to do the more difficult tasks on your list.

4. **Use multiple task columns for parallel tasks.** If your strategy involves doing several things that can be done at the same time, set up a time line with a separate column for each task. This is called multitasking and is used by successful business people. Remember to check off items on each parallel column as you finish them.

5. **Add dates.** When you've gotten all your steps in order, including parallel columns, you need to commit to a time frame. Working backwards, start by assigning a fixed date to the last

step you want to accomplish. Then come back to the first step and write "today." Now, go through the list and put down dates for all the intervening steps. Use terms like "tomorrow, next week, in a month" to mark every step, until you come to the target date for completing your goal. Go back and fill in exact dates for each step, if possible. Sometimes it's necessary to juggle deadlines. Sometimes you even have to extend the final date a bit in order to accomplish all the intervening steps. It's okay to be realistic.

(L) Look at the results.

The last step in the IDEAL problem-solving process is to look at how you're doing, evaluate the results, and make any necessary changes. At this point, you've already **I**dentified the problem, **D**eveloped a list of alternative strategies, **E**xplored the results, and created an **A**ction plan. Or maybe not. Maybe you've gotten stuck in one of the steps. Most people are able to breeze through the first three steps pretty easily, but some get stuck, frustrated, and angry when it comes down to implementing their action plan. For example, if your goal is to have a nice-looking backyard instead of an eyesore, it takes proper planning.

Perhaps you're stymied because you didn't list the necessary actions in a logical order. If you want to plant a garden, the first step is not to simply buy some seeds and put them into the ground. The first step is to prepare the soil by (a) removing all the rocks and debris from the area, (b) rototilling the ground, and (c) adding soil enrichments such as fertilizer. Then you can plant the seeds.

Perhaps you haven't broken down your action plan into small enough pieces. For example, if you want to plant a garden, step (a) can be broken down even further: that is, buy a rake, shovel, and gardening gloves; set aside large rocks for the rock garden (if you plan to have one); if there's too much debris, consider renting a dumpster. For step (b) you will have to check the yellow pages for companies that rent rototillers, and reserve one for the weekend. Arrange to borrow a friend's pickup truck to transport the rototiller. For step (c) you will have to go to a garden shop, get advice from a local expert, and buy the appropriate soil enrichments.

Perhaps procrastination is a real issue for you, and you just can't seem to get started. Set a definite date for the first step. Then get a friend to commit to working with you. That will make it harder to back out.

When you've completed or finished much of your action plan, you can use the Reality Checklist below to evaluate outcomes.

My Reality Checklist		
Do List Steps	Predicted Consequences	Actual Consequences
General Consequences		

A True Example

April was miserable; she felt angry all the time. She began the IDEAL problem-solving process by *identifying* several major problem areas, and she decided to focus on work-related issues first.

Work really was the biggest problem in April's life. She was a high school graduate and had some good secretarial skills, but she was stuck in a two-person office with Madge who had been there forever and considered April her personal assistant (read personal slave). Madge would talk on the phone all day, schmoozing with the buyers, while April did all the word processing, filing, and general drudge work. Even worse, instead of being appreciated, April was the daily butt of Madge's critical tongue. She would sometimes cry at night on the bus going home.

In *developing alternatives* April came up with a very short list. (1) Getting someone to bump off Madge (a very satisfying fantasy). (2)

Confronting Madge in the hope of being treated better. (3) Going to the boss to complain about Madge. (4) Just quitting. (5) Upgrading her skills and secretly searching for a better job.

When April *explored the consequences* of these strategies she realized that (1) She didn't know any "hit men", and she couldn't afford one anyway. (2) Confronting Madge would only make things worse, if that was possible. (3) The boss thought Madge (who routinely stroked his ego) was the greatest employee he had ever hired. If April complained, she was likely to be fired, after a receiving a humiliating and dismissive dressing down. (4) With her meager savings account, and some credit-card debt, she couldn't "just quit." That would be financial suicide. (5) Upgrading her skills and looking for a better job seemed like the most promising option.

Using the two-column system, assigning positive and negative points, confirmed her analysis that upgrading her skills would be her best strategy.

In creating her *action plan*, the first item on her Do List was to research options for upgrading her skills. She quickly discovered that upgrading her computer skills was the key to getting a better job. The next item on the Do List was to make a list of places offering computer classes. But that's where she got bogged down. Her little brother got sick and she was sidetracked from her goal by having to take care of him.

When April used the Reality Checklist to look at the results, she saw some progress but she was still way short of her goal. She realized that she needed to revise her Do List and set smaller steps with exact time lines. She got back on track quickly by finding some computer training classes at the local community college. Then she invested some of her meager savings to enroll in the classes. And, in a great stroke of luck she found a girlfriend who was willing to attend classes with her.

This story has a happy, but surprising, ending. Just as April was finishing up her computer course and getting ready to look for another job, her boss decided to "modernize" the firm. He was all set to underwrite a crash course in computers for Madge, when she received a small inheritance and promptly quit her job. When the boss realized that April was already trained in computers, he gave her a raise and made her office manager.

An ideal ending for the IDEAL problem-solving system. Results may vary, but we guarantee that if you follow this system your life will improve. And you'll be less frustrated and angry.

Once you set a goal and choose the strategies that you believe have the greatest chance of getting you what you want, it's time to put your decision into action.

Now take a deep breath, and DO IT!

12

Stopping Escalation

This chapter is designed to give you specific tools to help control the two major contributors to anger escalation: aversive chains and mind reading. You can stop escalation by understanding exactly how conflicts start and learning how to modify your behavior so that a simple discussion doesn't turn into a thermonuclear war.

Aversive Chains

Gerald Patterson of the Oregon Social Learning Center has pioneered the systematic examination and analysis of social interaction sequences. According to Patterson (1982), escalating anger depends on chains of aversive behavior in which two people attempt to influence each other through a rapid exchange of punishing communications. Escalating aversive chains are most likely to occur between two people with approximately equal power: husbands and wives, coworkers, and (remarkably) parents and children. Aversive chains build over time. They usually begin with a common innocuous event and develop along predictable lines. Patterns of reactions and counterreactions can grow to incredible complexity.

Irritable exchanges often appear to be relatively trivial in the early stages. In fact, the beginnings of an aversive chain are often overlooked because they seem so unimportant. They are, however, the basic building blocks of family anger and violence.

The vast majority of aversive chains never proceed past the first link. For example, someone in the family will tease or insult another and then stop. Since no one reacts aversively to the provocation, it lasts only a few seconds. Three- or four-step sequences last less than half a minute and occur even in "normal" families. But when aversive chains last longer than half a minute, yelling, threatening, or hitting may occur. Sequences like these are frequently observed in dysfunctional families. The longer the chain lasts, the more likely it is that violence will occur.

The last link in a chain is often called a *trigger behavior*. These behaviors usually precede and precipitate a violent outburst. Triggers are often verbal or nonverbal behaviors that bring up feelings of abandonment or rejection. The following list offers a representative sample of possible "links" that may be used to build an aversive chain.

Verbal Behaviors

1. Giving advice ("Ask your boss for a raise, you know we need more money.")

2. Global labeling ("All you women are alike . . .")

3. Criticism ("That's not a good parking job, you almost hit that car.")

4. Blaming ("If it weren't for you, we'd be on easy street right now.")

5. Abrupt limit setting ("That's it, I've had it." "Forget it." "Stop this instant!")

6. Threatening ("If you don't shut up right now . . .")

7. Using expletives ("Dammit!" "Shit!")

8. Complaining ("My life is empty." "All I do is work." "You never help me with the laundry.")

9. Stonewalling ("There is nothing to talk about.")

10. Mind reading or assuming ("I know what you're really trying to do: drive me crazy.")

11. "Innocent" observations ("I notice that the dishes haven't been done for the past two days.")

12. Teasing ("Those slacks must have shrunk in the wash, you're having a hard time closing that zipper.")

13. Humiliating statements ("You used to look good, now I'm embarrassed to be seen with you.")

14. Dismissing comments ("Get out of my life." "I'm tired of looking at your ugly face.")

15. Put downs ("Is this what you call a meal? I've had better grub at the greasy spoon on Market Street.")

16. Profanity ("You son of a . . .")

17. Sarcasm ("Sure you're going to fix it. Like last time when we had to call the plumber after you . . .")

18. Accusations ("You went out and did _____ again, didn't you?")

19. Guilt ("You should know better . . .")

20. Ultimatums ("This is your last chance. If you don't shape up, I'm leaving.")

Nonverbal Sounds

1. Groaning ("Oh no, not that again.")

2. Sighing ("I'm tired of this crap.")

3. Clucking sound ("Do you have to bring that up right now?")

4. "Tsk, tsk" ("You've done it again.")

Voice Quality, Tone, and Volume

1. Whining (trying to irritate)

2. Flatness (suggesting "I'm not here.")

3. Cold, frosty tone (suggesting "I'm here, but you'll never be able to reach me.")

4. Throaty, constricted (suggesting controlled fury)

5. Loud, harsh quality (attempting to intimidate)

6. Mocking, contemptuous tone (trying to get your goat)

7. Mumbling under your breath (making him guess what you said)

8. Snickering (demeaning, putting down)

9. Snarling ("Back off!")

Gestures Using Hands and Arms

1. Pointing a finger (accusation)

2. Shaking a fist (intimidation)

3. "Flipping the bird" (obscenity)

4. Folded arms ("You can't get to me.")

5. Waving away (dismissal)

6. Chopping motion (cutting off)

Facial Expressions

1. Looking away, looking at the floor (abandonment)

2. Rolling eyes ("Not that again.")

3. Narrowing eyes (threatening)

4. Eyes wide (incredulous disbelief)

5. Grimacing ("I don't like that.")

6. Sneering (disparaging)

7. Frowning (disapproving)

8. Tightening lips (suppressed anger)

9. Raising an eyebrow ("Watch it, buster.")

10. Scowling (annoyance)

Body Movements

1. Shaking head ("No, no, no!")

2. Shrugging shoulders ("I give up.")

3. Tapping a foot or a finger (annoyance)

4. Moving or leaning toward (intimidating)

5. Moving or turning away (abandonment)

6. Hands on hips (exasperation)

7. Quick movements or pacing (increased agitation)

8. Kicking or throwing objects (anger getting out of control)

9. Pushing or grabbing (angry physical contact)

Examples of Aversive Chains

Husband and Wife

1. *(Husband comes home, silent, eyes down.)*

2. *Wife (frowns, sighs):* "What's the matter now?"

3. *Husband (with folded arms, complaining, tightening lips):* "My boss is an asshole."

4. *Wife (in a cold tone, giving advice and using guilt):* "Well, you'll just have to stick it out. You should know we can't afford you quitting your job now."

5. *Husband (using an expletive and global labeling in a loud voice):* "Dammit, you give zilch support, you know that? I can't take much more of this!"

6. *Wife (abrupt limit setting, guilt, flatness):* "Stop shouting right now! The children will hear you."

7. *Husband (in a constricted voice, using global labeling, finger-pointing, and an expletive):* "Yeah, all you ever think of is the children. You don't give a damn about me."

8. *Wife (sneering, sarcastic, accusation):* "Oh yeah! I didn't know you had feelings. You haven't talked to me in weeks."

9. *Husband (with tight lips and narrowing eyes, complaining and using profanity):* "You never have time for me anyway. You're always on the phone with your goddamn mother. I wish she would keep the fuck out of our life."

10. *Wife (loudly and harshly with narrowing eyes, using profanity and a dismissing comment, leaning toward her husband):* "Shut up, asshole! You get out of my life." *(She throws her wedding ring at him.)*

11. *Husband (loudly and harshly, using profanity, threatening):* "All right, bitch, I've had it from you. I'll leave, but I'm going to shut you up first!" *(He makes a threatening gesture with his fist.)*

Coworkers from a Repair Crew

1. *(Matt comes to work five minutes late scowling.)*

2. *Jeff (frowning):* "Where you been? The truck's ready to leave."

3. *Matt (waving him away):* "Leave me alone. I've had a bad night."

4. *Jeff (accusing, using profanity):* "Hung over again! Fuck!"

5. *Matt (in a harsh voice, using profanity):* "Back off. What I drink is none of your fucking business."

6. *Jeff (turning away, in a cold tone):* "All right, buddy, let's get on the truck and get to work."

Later:

7. *Jeff (in a cold tone):* "Hand me a wrench."

8. *Matt (turning away):* "Get it yourself. I'm not your slave."

9. *Jeff (groaning, accusing):* "Come on, willya. We're supposed to be partners. And you haven't done a damn thing all morning."

10. *Matt (snarling, throwing tool, using profanity):* "Here's your goddamn wrench. And you know where to shove it!"

11. *Jeff (threatening, in a loud voice):* "Listen buster, I've had enough of this. Cut the shit or I'll get me another partner."

12. *Matt (sneering, moving away, using profanity):* "Big deal, who wants to work with a jerk like you anyway?"

After Lunch:

13. *Jeff (in a flat tone):* "All right, give me a hand with this cable, it's heavy."

14. *Matt (mumbling under his breath, sarcastic):* "Yes, master."

15. *Jeff (sniffing, rolling his eyes, using an expletive and global labeling, dismissing):* "Jee-sus! You smell like a brewery. You're a goddamn lush. Get out of here before you cause an accident."

16. *Matt (in a loud, harsh voice, using an expletive):* "Shit, you're as bad as my wife. Get the fuck off my back."

17. *Jeff (in a contemptuous tone, moving away, putting down):* "I feel sorry for her, having to put up with a bum like you. You used to be a man. But now you ain't worth shit, boy."

18. *Matt (moving forward, pushing, using a loud, harsh voice, threatening):* "You can't talk to me like that. I'll kick your ass."

19. *(Jeff moves to one side, Matt stumbles and falls.) Jeff (in a flat voice):* "Get out of here now."

Parent and Teenage Child

1. *(Child slams the door. Silence.)*

2. *Parent (frowning):* "Hi, darling. How was school?"

3. *Child (looking away):* "Okay."

4. *Parent (sighing):* "What's the matter?"

5. *Child (rolling eyes):* "Nothing."

6. *Parent (hands on hips):* "Come on. Tell me what's going on."

7. *Child (groaning, turning away):* "Nothing, just leave me alone. Okay?"

8. *Parent (moving toward, narrowing eyes):* "Listen, I have a right to know what's going on. You're not just a boarder here, you know."

9. *Child (moving away, scowling, mumbling):* "You're always hassling me."

10. *Parent (shrugging shoulders, sighing, making an "innocent" observation):* "I notice that the dishes weren't done last night, and there's a pile of your clothes in the living room."

11. *Child (rolling eyes, shaking head):* "I'll do 'em later, okay?"

12. *Parent (moving toward, setting an abrupt limit, threatening):* "No! You'll do it right now or you're grounded for a week."

13. *Child (grimacing, speaking in a loud, harsh voice, using an expletive):* "I'll do it later, now just leave me alone, dammit!"

14. *Parent (shaking head, constricted voice, dismissing comment, humiliating):* "I've had it with you. Go to your room right now. And clean it up, it looks like a pigsty in there."

15. *Child (turning away, "flipping the bird," using a loud voice and profanity):* "Fuck you. It's my room—and stay out of it!"

16. *Parent (shaking a fist, leaning forward, using a loud voice, dismissing, threatening):* "You can't talk to me like that. Get to your room right now. And no dinner until your room is clean!"

17. *Child (leaving, sneering, putting down):* "Big deal. You're not the world's greatest cook, you know."

18. *Parent (in a loud voice):* "You come back here!"

19. *(Child slams the door. Silence.)*

We will return to these examples several times in this chapter and give concrete suggestions for breaking the chains.

Anger Diary

It is now time to return to your Anger Diary and start a new section. While you are working with this part of the book, you can begin to jot down your observations about your own patterns of escalation. Make a point to spend some time each evening reviewing the events of the day. Fully explore each step in an aversive chain—particularly your verbal and nonverbal behavior. Over time you will be able to recognize repeating patterns.

Coping with Aversive Chains

Here are four important methods for altering your aversive chains to begin to set yourself free from a sequence of escalating attacks.

Time-Out

Perhaps the single most useful strategy in controlling the escalation of anger is the "time-out" technique. Part of its effectiveness undoubtedly stems from the fact that the time-out is a familiar and acceptable metaphor in sports. It is also a guaranteed method for stopping violence. It has been used successfully by many men who have attended male "batterer" treatment programs.

Anger is not something that happens "in a flash." Even people who are "quick to anger," or have a "short fuse" go through progressive stages. Beginning with irritation, anger is "kindled" and the body begins to tense. Destructive self-statements "fan the flames," and trigger behaviors ignite the "explosive" rage. As you will see, this sequence is not inevitable.

"T" Time

When either person in an interaction notices the early warning signs, he or she may decide that a time-out is needed. This strategy could have been used effectively at any point in the husband and wife aversive chain scenario. Either person could have initiated the time-out, even as late in the chain as the "trigger event," which occurred when the wife threw her wedding ring.

The need for a time-out is communicated simply and efficiently by using the same gesture the referees use. The "T" sign is made with your hands. Nothing need or should be said at this point, except perhaps the announcement "Time-out!" The other person is then obligated to return the gesture and stop talking. It is permissible to say "Okay, time-out."

DO NOT say "You are making me angry" or "You're getting out of control." These kinds of statements will inevitably lead to a defensive posture and escalation rather than the hoped-for cooling off and safety of temporary separation. Some people suggest using the statement, "I'm beginning to feel angry and I need (or want) to take a time-out." This version has the advantage of being a nonblaming "I" statement that talks about how the person feels. However, there is some evidence that merely using the word "angry" will trigger an automatic aggression sequence. Therefore it is recommended that you stick with the neutral term, time-out.

Using this procedure has several benefits. First, the T sign makes it less likely that you will indulge in hostile or threatening gestures. Second, the T sign can provide a protective shield for a person feeling threatened if the sign is held directly in front of the face. Last, the procedure stops the tendency on both sides to try to "get in the last word."

Leaving and Returning

The T sign is a signal that it is time to separate for a while. (This works best if you have both discussed ahead of time what will happen next.) Ideally, the person who is "beginning to get angry" will take the cue and leave for an agreed-upon period of time. Agreeing ahead of time will prevent any misconception that this necessary separation is a form of running away or a means of punishing the other person with abandonment.

A good rule of thumb is to separate for one hour (plus or minus five minutes). It is important to allow yourself an adequate amount of time to cool off. It is even more important to return when the time is up. This is hard to do. It takes real courage to return to a painful situation without the protective shield of anger. Similarly, it is of the utmost importance that the person who was left is there again when the leaver returns. Trust will grow as each partner becomes more experienced in this method.

While You're Gone

A few do's and don'ts are important to follow while you are away from the stressful situation.

DO something physically challenging that will help to reduce the tension in your body. Taking a long walk or going for a run are two of the best methods. If angry thoughts come to your mind, let them come. And then let them go. Use a relaxation or arousal-reduction technique that works for you. Picture a river that flows down to the sea. Put your angry thoughts on the river and allow them to float away from you.

DON'T hang on to angry thoughts or waste time building a case. The more you focus on proving how wrong and awful the offender is, the angrier you get. Resist getting stuck in rehearsing what you should say. If you do, you may return more upset than when you left. Don't drink or use drugs while you're away. Please don't drive. Angry drivers are a real danger to themselves and others.

When You Get Back

When you come back be sure to check-in. More than anything else, this will help to build trust in the relationship. The check-in involves a willingness on both sides to communicate. See if you're ready to talk about the issue. If not, set a specific time when you'll be ready to do so. Talking about what made you angry will help you both to reduce the possibility of escalating anger in the future.

Practice Time-Outs

The best way to get into the swing of taking time-outs is to practice when you are not angry. You might take a practice time out at the first sign of mild irritation, or just for the hell of it. A practice time-out works just like a regular one, except that you say, "Practice time-out!"

and the time away is cut in half. Go through all the steps, including the check-in. It is very important to do this. The more you practice taking time-outs, the easier it will be when the real thing happens.

Abuses of Time-Out

In order to build trust and reestablish a good relationship, it is critical that the time-out process not be abused. If time-out is called simply to avoid contact or to forestall any form of disagreeable discussion, it is bound to fail. Similarly, if time-out is used to hurt or punish the other person, it won't work.

Be particularly careful about scenarios like this one. An unpleasant scene is beginning to shape up. A time-out is agreed-upon. One person takes this as an opportunity to skip down to the bar or over to a friend's house. Watching football, drinking a couple of six-packs, and not calling or coming back for several hours makes matters worse. Although it's understandable to seek support and solace, this kind of behavior undermines the trust you need to use the time-out as an effective strategy for anger control.

Making a Contract

When two people want to make a commitment to change patterns of anger that occur when they are together, a contract is in order. The following suggested outline (adapted from Deschner 1984) provides a framework for making the kind of changes that will benefit you both.

Time-Out Contract

When I realize that my (or my partner's) anger is rising, I will give a "T" signal for a time-out and leave at once. I will not hit or kick anything and I will not slam the door.

I will return no later than one hour. I will take a walk to use up the anger energy and will not drink or use drugs while I am away. I will try not to focus on resentments.

When I return, I will set a time with my partner—when we both feel calm—to resume discussion of the issue.

If my partner gives a "T" signal and leaves, I will return the sign and let my partner go without a hassle, no matter what is going on. I will not drink or use drugs while my partner is away and will avoid focusing on resentments.

Name _____ Date _____

Name _____ Date _____

Rechanneling

So far you've learned how an escalating pattern of behavior can be stopped dead in its tracks by using time-out. A more subtle approach is to *rechannel* or redirect the sequence at critical junctions. This is analogous to the shunting system used by railroads. When the engineer is warned of trouble ahead, he may avail himself of the opportunity to switch to another set of tracks.

The first step in this process is to identify a sequence of behaviors and then find the weak links in the chain. A "weak link" is that piece of behavior which is most easily changed and which will make a difference in the outcome. As a rule of thumb, earlier interventions are best. It's easier to stop a car that has just begun to roll than one that is speeding downhill, out of control.

A review of the husband and wife aversive chain, described earlier in this chapter, shows several opportunities for rechanneling. The earliest is response 4, when the wife is coldly unsympathetic to her husband's complaint about his boss. This chain is probably a familiar one, where behaviors like response 4 inevitably lead to escalation. A small behavioral change here can alter the whole course of the interaction. If the wife answers response 3 with understanding or compassion ("Is he giving you a bad time again?"), the aversive chain is stopped and a healthier pattern may emerge.

The next opportunity to rechannel occurs in response 7, where the husband discounts his wife's concern about the kids hearing their argument. The husband could instead reply by validating his wife's concern or by saying, "We're both getting upset; let's talk about it later when we're not so tired."

For another example, look back to the parent and teenage child aversive chain. In this familiar chain, the first opportunity occurs at response 8. In reply to response 7, when the teen wants to be left alone, the parent can say, "I know that you need your own space, but I really want to feel a part of your life. Maybe we can talk later?"

The child has a powerful opportunity to rechannel in reply to response 14, when the parent sends him to his room. Instead of response 15, he can say "Okay, okay, I'll go. Let's both cool out for a few minutes. Can we talk in half an hour?"

If you want to use the rechanneling technique successfully, it is necessary to plan ahead. After laying out a typical sequence and locating the weak links, decide what you can do differently. What behavior can you substitute for that link in the chain? Whatever new behavior you decide on, it has to be something that you know from experience will relax and defuse the situation. Simple acknowledgment or murmuring a few sympathic words may be enough in some cases. Just keeping quiet may be the best thing in others. Remember that your verbal behavior is only part of the aversive sequence. You may also need to change threatening or accusatory gestures, expressions, tone of voice, and so on. Read Chapter 15 on response choice rehearsal and chapter 16 on problem-solving communication to get more ideas.

When you've made your decision, you will have to wait for an opportunity to practice it. Usually this won't take too long. When you see your chance, say to yourself, "Time to rechannel," and do it. The next day, review the sequence and notice the difference it has made. Or notice what didn't work about your new response and decide how to modify it. Continue practicing until your response becomes automatic.

Inquiry

Another subtle way to short-circuit an escalating pattern is to use the technique of inquiry. Remember, the basic assumption is that anger is a response to personal pain. It follows that when someone is beginning to get angry it makes sense to ask, "What hurts?" As with all of these intervention strategies, the sooner in the sequence this is done, the more effective it will be.

Let's return to Matt and Jeff, the repair crew. The first good opportunity to use inquiry in their aversive chain occurs in reply to response 3. Matt probably is hung over, but his drinking is an attempt to self-medicate his personal pain. Jeff can choose to respond to the "symptom" (being late for work and feeling ill) or to the underlying pain. If Jeff changes response 4 to "Having more trouble with your wife?" the whole rest of the day might go differently.

Another opportunity for Jeff occurs in reply to response 8, where Matt refuses to hand him the wrench. He can either escalate, as he does with his accusation (probably accurate), or choose the inquiry method. If Jeff changes response 9 to "You've been on a bummer all morning. Tell me what's really bugging you," this aversive chain can still be stopped before it gets worse.

Calling Process

This technique is probably most effective with people who have sophisticated verbal skills and tend to intellectualize. Instead of getting enmeshed in a hopelessly escalating argument about something (the *content*), you can choose to comment on how the discussion is progressing (the *process*).

For example, Pat and Mike were having a pleasant conversation about football. As disagreements started to pile up, the discussion became more heated. When they got to arguing about the relative merits of Joe Montana and Steve Young, tempers began to flair. A potential disaster was neatly averted (they were already at the name-calling stage) when Mike said, "Hey Pat, we're both getting pretty excited." Instead of continuing with the *content* of the discussion (a losing cause), they could both agree about the *process*—how they are feeling or acting at that moment.

Other examples can be found in the husband and wife scenario. When the husband starts raising his voice in response 5, the wife can reply with "I can hear that you're getting angry, let's talk about this more quietly." Or later in the sequence at response 10, she could say, "I'm really getting upset. I don't even know what we're talking about anymore."

In the parent and teenage child chain, the first chance occurs at response 10. The parent can say, "I feel that you're always making distance between us, and I keep trying to get closer." The last opportunity for a process comment occurs at response 18. Here the parent can interject, "We seem to be caught up in more and more accusations. Let's stop now and talk some more when we've both cooled off."

Mind-Reading

A major hidden factor in anger escalation is the tendency to mind-read. This process starts with an ambiguous interpersonal communication. Your lover looks up at the ceiling and sighs. Then she says that you got a call from work, they expect you to attend a conference Saturday morning. There's something incongruent about the communication. Her glance upward and the sigh indicate that something may be bothering her. But her voice is flat and expressionless.

You now have to figure out what's really going on. You start to mind-read. She's angry, you decide, because you'll be abandoning her on Saturday. So you get huffy: "Well, it's my job, what can I do about it?" (spoken in a loud voice, with a shrugging gesture). What you don't know is that her sigh had nothing to do with anger. She's just been assigned an overwhelming project at work and arrived home to find the toilet clogged.

Your assumption about her anger may trigger a process that Richard Bandler and John Grinder (founders of Neurolinguistic Programming) call *calibrated communication* (Bander, Grinder, and Satir 1976). It works like this: An incongruent or ambiguous message creates uncertainty about the true meaning being conveyed. To deal with the uncertainty, you mind-read. You make assumptions about the feelings, intentions, motives, or attitudes of the other person. Since mind-reading is almost never totally accurate, your assumptions about the other person are always a little bit off.

Now the trouble starts. You respond as if your mind-reading were accurate, as if your assumptions were absolutely true. You get defensive or critical. You withdraw or pout. However you express your negative reaction—by a shrug, a grimace, or a blaming attack— the other person is put on guard and begins to act defensively. Now you take the defensive reaction as a confirmation of your original assumption. He or she really was angry or judging, or selfishly uncaring. Your anger grows. You step up the attack, and in turn you find yourself attacked.

With each exchange, you have gotten further and further from the original experience; further from the truth. Consider again your argument with your lover. You've interpreted her sigh as anger when in fact she felt overwhelmed. You've responded defensively. Now, in calibrated steps, the two of you will move away from the real experience. She hears your loud voice and notices your shrug. She reads the shrug as suppressed anger. (Her father did that when he was mad, and now her lover seems to do it also.) "You give too much to that job," she says coldly. You tell her that it pays the bills. "You're sucked dry at work," she says. "You're just a yes-man. You say yes to them, but no to me. You've shown zero commitment to making this relationship work." By the time the dust settles, the room will have a radiation half-life of fifty years.

Pathologically calibrated communication patterns are very similar to a well-choreographed ballet. Each member of the family moves in and out on cue, executing their steps with exquisite timing. As the ballet moves to an exciting crescendo, so too does the family's communication pattern lead to an inevitably tragic and painful finale.

Your Old Files

When you are confronted with ambiguous or incongruent messages, the uncertainty creates anxiety. One way to handle this situation is to go through your old memory files to see if you've ever experienced anything remotely similar before. Is the tone of the voice familiar? The gesture? The facial expression, the body posture? Who in your past looked or sounded this way? What were they conveying with that look or tone? Comparing the present situation to past experience is largely an unconscious process. Most of the time you'll have no idea you're doing it, or what it reminds you of.

Personality theorist Harry Stack Sullivan called this process *parataxic distortion:* the tendency to superimpose the experiences and meanings of an old relationship over a current one. It's as if you were no longer really seeing and reacting to the person in front of you. You are instead responding to your father or sister or your first boyfriend.

Mind-reading is greatly influenced by parataxic distortion. Your assumptions about the thoughts, feelings, and motives of the person in front of you are very often based on repeated painful experiences during your earlier years.

Danny's childhood was full of angry exchanges with his father. At a certain point in their battles his father would always raise one eyebrow. Danny knew that meant his father was getting *really* angry, and was on the verge of "blowing it."

Now when he is interacting with someone who raises an eyebrow while giving ambiguous or incongruent messages, Danny assumes that that person is angry.

Sara's older brother was deeply involved in a fundamentalist church. She was an admitted hell-raiser during her late teens, and her brother frequently expressed disapproval. He'd stare at the floor or the wall behind her, but never make eye contact. He would pinch his lips together just before a lecture on her "affront to God." Now Sara finds herself inexplicably enraged when someone won't look her in the eye. Her husband tends to pinch his lips when his arthritic knee gets inflamed, and Sara's first reflex is to read disapproval in his expression. The residue from her painful sibling relationship still distorts her perceptions. And when Sara acts on assumptions pulled from her old files, she bewilders and then angers her husband.

Now consider Brenda's experience with her first lover. She was seventeen and very unsure of herself. He praised her, called her beautiful. He said she was the only girl worth knowing in the school. His mouth was always held in a broad, rather fixed smile. But the smile switched off instantly if Brenda disappointed him. Then, in a monotone, he'd describe with excruciating detail her physical and psychological flaws. Brenda spent her senior year slamming back and forth between total love and total rejection. Twenty years later, Brenda's new boyfriend tends to smile when he's embarrassed or threatened. If things are the least bit ambiguous, she reads this nervous reaction as a dangerous prelude to attack.

There are several examples of parataxic distortion in the aversive chains described earlier. Remember Matt and Jeff? Notice that Matt mumbles "Yes, master" in response 14. He does the same thing when his wife asks him to take out the garbage. As a boy, Matt used this very same phrase when his rather controlling mother told him to do his chores. He now responds to a simple request from his partner with feelings of annoyance that have their roots in his childhood and are echoed in his marriage.

In the parent and child scenario, response 8 seems like an overreaction. The child's turning away and unwillingness to talk has brought up old feelings of abandonment experienced in the mother's own childhood. In fact, the mom felt like a boarder in her own home, due to her parents' emotional unavailability.

Coping with Mind-Reading

The following two techniques will be helpful in the battle against calibrated communication and parataxic distortion. The more you practice them, the better control you will achieve.

Checking It Out

This technique is especially valuable for use in situations where mind-reading is contributing to the escalation process. As noted earlier, mind-reading occurs when someone makes assumptions about another person's thoughts or feelings, based on minimal or ambiguous cues. Remember Danny's mistaken assumption that a raised eyebrow means that someone is getting really angry.

The antidote for this poisonous problem is simply to "check it out." Couples can use a helpful exercise to undercut the problem. When something confusing is happening in an interaction, one person can say, "I observe _____ (*making an observation*), and I imagine _____ (*making an assumption or interpretation*)." It's now the other person's turn to give feedback. "Yes, I am doing _____ , but I'm thinking (or feeling)."

To see the process spelled out more clearly, return for a moment to Matt and Jeff. Instead of response 4, Jeff could have said, "You look pretty bad this morning, are you hung over?" The reply to that might have been "Yeah I do look pretty bad. My son was sick and kept me up all night." Notice how that exchange would have changed the whole complexion of the situation.

Another example can be found in the parent and teenage child aversive chain. Instead of response 8, the parent might have said, "You seem kind of tired or unhappy or something. Am I guessing right?" To which the child might have responded, "Yeah, I just need to cool out." These two responses would undoubtedly have moved the interaction in an entirely different direction.

Hearing Voices from the Past

How do you know when you are using parataxic distortion? It's often difficult to tell, but there are four helpful cues. First, watch out for responses with a fast reaction time. Sudden anger or instant distrust suggests the presence of an habitual knee-jerk reflex. Ask yourself, "What past situation am I reminded of, what scene or relationship does it feel like I'm replaying?"

All-or-none, either-or, and black-or-white responses should also be suspected, since reality is rarely that clear-cut. If someone seems all bad to you, if you're using global labels like *stupid, selfish, worthless, lazy,* and so on, check your old files to see who you're being reminded of.

A third thing to watch out for is a familiar physical feeling. Do you always feel a warm glow when someone with blonde hair smiles at you? Or a lump in your throat when the boss says something critical?

Finally, parataxic distortion is often present when a one-foot stimulus triggers a ten-foot response. If it feels like your reaction greatly exceeds the provocation, the situation may be charged with old pain and old conflict.

If you experience any of these four cues during an interaction, try the exercise of assuming that your present relationship is in some way being contaminated by a voice *from the past.* Start by writing down the salient elements of the current situation:

1. Describe the provoking person's physical characteristics.

2. Describe the tone of voice, gestures, body language, and facial expressions.

3. Describe the nature of the conflict. Is it a struggle for control? Do you feel devalued?

4. Describe your feelings in the conflict.

Do any of your descriptions ring a bell? What aspect of this experience have you lived through before? When you have an answer to these questions, you may choose to share what you've learned with the provoking person (especially if he or she is an intimate). Or you may privately use the knowledge to recognize the process and improve control over your responses.

This chapter has presented various ways of examining and understanding the process of escalation in angry interactions. More importantly, it has offered a variety of strategies and techniques that can be used to effectively stop escalation from occurring. The main thing to remember is that escalation is *not* inevitable. You can make choices all along the line that will enable you to prevent the escalation from reaching a tragic culmination.

13

Coping Through Healthy Self-Talk

Now it's time to begin practicing some of the basic skills of anger control. In this chapter you'll select or develop coping thoughts that can help you respond effectively at the moment of provocation.

Effective Coping Thoughts

Coping thoughts have proven effective at helping to manage anger (Novaco 1975). That's because they keep you focused on a set of pre-planned strategies that calm you down and lead you away from aggressive reactions. Let's begin by becoming familiar with how a coping thought is worded, and the various categories of such thoughts you might choose from. The following list includes coping thoughts that have been found to promote better anger management. Read them over and imagine yourself using them during typical provocations. Put a star next to the thoughts that sound like they might be helpful to you.

Relaxation Reminders

- Take a deep breath and relax.
- It's time to relax and slow things down.
- Relax the hot spots.
- I can stay calm and relaxed.

- Relax and let go.

- Shrug my shoulders and relax.

- Anger means it's time to relax and cope.

- Keep the jaw loose and relaxed.

Sticking to the Task

- I can deal with this.

- I'll state my needs clearly and simply.

- Acknowledge what the other person wants.

- Acknowledge the other person's point of view.

- Ask the other person for a solution. Work for compromise.

- How can I negotiate for what I want?

- Try to reason it out. Treat each other with respect.

- No point in blaming. Try a new strategy.

- Stick to the facts, no putdowns or attacks.

- Use "I" statements only.

- Let's try a cooperative approach. Maybe we're both right.

- What do I want to get out of this?

- We have to find a solution that works for both of us.

- I can take care of myself without blowing up.

Coping with Arousal

- Getting upset won't help.

- Just as long as I keep my cool, I'm in control.

- Easy does it—there's nothing to be gained by getting mad.

- I'm not going to let him/her get to me.

- Stay calm—no sarcasm, no attacks.

- Stay cool, make no judgments.

- I'll stay rational—anger won't solve anything.

- Take a time-out. Cool off, then come back and deal with it.

- I can manage this; I'm in control.

- I don't have to take this so seriously.

- Don't escalate it. Cool it.

- I'm annoyed. But I can keep a lid on it.

- If I start to get mad, I'll just be banging my head against the wall, so I might as well relax.

- Getting mad will cost me (*insert the negative consequences of anger in the situation*).

- Just roll with the punches. Don't get bent out of shape.

- Neutral words only.

- Voice calm and flat.

Coping with the Angry Person

- I'll let him make a fool of himself.

- She'd probably like me to get real angry. Well, I'm going to disappoint her.

- I don't need to prove myself to him.

- Let her look all foolish and upset I can stay cool and calm.

- No one is right, no one is wrong. We just have different needs.

- I can't change him/her with anger; I'll just upset myself.

- It's really a shame that he has to act like this.

- There's no need to doubt myself. What she says doesn't matter.

- I can't hurt him with anger. I'll just make things worse.

- I've acted this way in the past myself. I can cut him some slack.

- I won't be manipulated into blowing up or losing my cool.

- Blowing up only gives her what she wants.

- It's just a hassle. Nothing more, nothing less. I can cope with hassles.

- Some situations don't have good solutions. Looks like this is one of them. No use getting all bent out of shape about it.

The Best of the Lot

Reread the coping thoughts that you noted as possibly useful in anger situations. Now write down the four best coping thoughts from this list. These are the ones you're going to start using—and testing—when you're upset. Some of them may work well; some may not. You'll find out. If a coping thought proves ineffective, go back to the list above and select another one to replace it.

You'll need lots of reminders to use your coping thoughts, so it's helpful to put them up in places where you'll see them often. For example, you could tape them to the mirror where you shave or do your makeup. Or tape them onto the refrigerator, or the dashboard of your car. You should have them in your wallet and somewhere on your desk. Some people prop up their anger-coping thoughts in front of the TV, and they make a discipline of reading them over each time they turn the tube on. The point is to make your coping thoughts a part of your everyday life, so they become familiar and easy to remember. And when you need them, they'll easily come to mind.

Coping with Trigger Thoughts

Sometimes general coping thoughts are insufficient. The anger is too raw and you're entangled in trigger thoughts that inflame you. Controlling anger in these cases requires a higher level of planning. You'll need coping thoughts tailored to particular anger triggers. So let's start with a quick refresher for the countermeasures you might use for each category of trigger thoughts.

Trigger Thought Countermeasures

Shoulds. (1) People rarely do what they should do, only what they need or want to do. What needs, beliefs, or fears are influencing the other person in this situation? (2) Stay with your wants, desires, and preferences—not shoulds. Think, "I prefer," not "You ought to."

The Entitlement Fallacy. (1) Remember times when someone wanted or expected something of you, and you couldn't give it or had to say no. Assume, in the situation where you now feel entitled, that the other person needs to say no as badly as you once did. (2)

Everyone has the right to say no and to set limits. Affirm how important that right is, even though you are very disappointed by the other person's refusal.

The Fallacy of Fairness. (1) Identify the other person's underlying need in the situation. (2) Focus on the fact that you have different needs from that person. And there's no way to prove that your need has more weight or validity.

The Fallacy of Change. (1) Count how many times people really changed because you pressured them to; how many times did you try to change someone and he or she resisted? (2) People change because they want to, not because you want them to. Assume that most changes will have to be made by you. (3) Make a plan to solve the problem yourself.

Conditional Assumptions. (1) Avoid the kind of logic where you draw a big conclusion from a single event. Instead, make limited conclusions from a single case (i.e., your husband rarely does dishes; assume he dislikes doing dishes [*limited conclusion*] not that he doesn't love you). (2) Recall the times you disappointed someone you care for. Understand that disappointing someone doesn't always mean you don't love, respect, or care for that person. (3) Negotiate for what you want. How can you reward the other person for giving it to you?

The Letting It Out Fallacy. (1) Describe problem behavior in neutral terms; make "I" statements about how it affects you emotionally. (2) Count the number of times anger/punishment made you hurt less or got you what you wanted. Is it likely to make you feel better or create a positive outcome in this situation?

Blaming. (1) Make a coping plan to solve the problem yourself. (2) Recognize that people are mostly doing the best they can—what they think will best meet their needs.

Good-Bad Dichotomizing. (1) Describe the person or situation without evaluative labels. Just state the facts. (2) Eliminate good-bad, right-wrong distinctions in favor of a specific, accurate description that includes a balance of some positive and some negative attributes.

Assumed Intent. (1) Check out your assumptions by asking directly about other people's motives and feelings. (2) If you haven't done that, assume that you don't know their motives and feelings. (3) Find alternative explanations for the problem behavior.

Magnifying. (1) Be realistically negative (i.e., the situation is "disappointing" or "frustrating," not "terrible" or "awful"). Ask, "How bad is it really?" Then answer honestly. (2) Use only accurate language that doesn't exaggerate. (3) Look at the whole picture. Try to find evidence that the opposite is also true.

Global Labeling. (1) Be specific: focus on behavior, not on the person as a whole. (2) Look for exceptions to the label.

Revising Trigger Thoughts—Examples

Let's take a look at three examples of how you can use the counterresponses we've just reviewed to change anger-evoking trigger thoughts. Each example includes a problem situation, trigger thoughts (the specific thought is in quotes while the category of cognitive error—blaming, magnifying, etc.—is in parentheses), the counterresponse plan, and revised trigger thoughts.

1. **Situation:** Your son tells you he has finished a homework assignment that was never even started.

Trigger thoughts (specific thought + category): "He's a liar." (Global labeling) "He's destroying all the trust in our relationship." (Magnifying) "If I ask him a straight question, he should always give me a straight answer." (Shoulds)

Counterresponse plan: For *global labeling*, be specific, focus on behavior, look for exceptions. For *magnifying*, look at the whole picture. For *shoulds*, look at needs and fears that might be influencing the other person.

Revised trigger thoughts: "He has said something untrue only once in the past year, and during the same period he has owned up to several things he was embarrassed or scared to tell me . . . the trust is diminished, but not destroyed because he's risked telling me lots of things that I know were hard to talk about . . . he was afraid I'd blow up and there would be a breach in our relationship."

2. **Situation:** Your husband seems distracted and uninterested as you discuss a health problem that worries you.

Trigger thoughts (specific thought + category): "Why aren't you focusing on this problem and supporting me?" (Entitlement Fallacy) "You don't care about me." (Conditional Assumptions) "You're selfish." (Global Labeling)

Counterresponse plan: For *entitlement fallacy*, think of the times you couldn't give what others wanted. For *conditional assumptions*, don't draw big conclusions from a single instance. For *global labeling*, be specific and focus on exceptions.

Revised trigger thoughts: "A lot of times I'm distracted when my husband is upset and complaining about work ... I can't conclude he doesn't care just because he's sometimes distracted. More likely he's tired or upset about his own problems ... he often seems focused on his own difficulties, but he does usually listen to me if I make a big deal out of something—like the time when I lost my watch."

3. Situation: Doing more than your share of house-maintenance tasks.

Trigger thoughts (specific thought + category): "You're wearing me out, dumping all this stuff on me." (Blaming) "It's time you learned to take responsibility." (Fallacy of Change) "You're not doing anything around here because you're mad at me for going back to work." (Assumed Intent)

Counterresponse plan: For *blaming*, solve the problem yourself. For the *fallacy of change*, think of how many times the other person has been successfully pressured to change. For *assumed intent*, check out your assumptions and find alternative explanations for the problem behavior.

Revised trigger thoughts: "I'm hiring a once-a-week housecleaner and we can share the costs ... I've never been able to make him do anything, change anything; that's a lie I'm telling myself. He won't change just because I demand it ... I've asked him whether he's angry that I returned to work—he says no. Maybe a better explanation for his lack of help is all the overtime he's been working lately."

Exercise: Creating coping thoughts.

Now that you've identified four potentially helpful types of coping thoughts (relaxation reminders, sticking to the task, coping with arousal, and coping with the angry person), and learned a process that will allow you to rewrite your angry trigger thoughts, it's time to actually get to work applying these skills to your real life situations. The worksheet that follows will help you prepare for typical anger situations that you encounter.

Right now, make three copies of the worksheet, and fill one out for each of the three most recent anger situations you've experienced. Be sure to include both the specific trigger thought (exactly what you said to yourself that ignited anger) and the trigger thought category (blaming, the fallacy of change, assumed intent, etc.). Make a counterresponse plan for each trigger thought category. Then use that plan to revise the trigger thought. Finally, go back to the list of effective coping thoughts earlier in this chapter to identify three or four coping thoughts that might be useful in this particular anger situation.

Worksheet: Creating Coping Thoughts

Complete the following for each significant trigger thought in an anger situation.

1. Trigger thoughts (specific thought + category of cognitive error):

   a.

   b.

   c.

2. Counterresponse plan for each of my trigger thoughts (e.g., looking for exceptions, alternative explanations, preferences instead of shoulds, etc.). Revise trigger thought based on each counterresponse plan.

   a. Counter-response plan:

   Revised trigger thought:

   b. Counterresponse plan:

   Revised trigger thought:

   c. Counterresponse plan:

   Revised trigger thought:

3. Helpful coping thoughts (see Effective Coping Thoughts List)

   a.

   b.

   c.

   d.

Here's an example of a Worksheet for Coping Thoughts filled-out by a man who had become increasingly angry with a coworker named Jane. Jane had offered to take over parts of his job. She had even passed on some of her suggestions to the division manager.

Worksheet: Creating Coping Thoughts

Complete the following for each significant trigger thought in an anger situation.

1. Trigger thoughts (specific thought + category of cognitive error):

   a. Jane's trying to screw me out of a job. (Assumed Intent)

   b. She's making me look bad, like I don't know what I'm doing. (Magnifying)

   c. It's not fair. (Fallacy of Fairness)

2. Counterresponse plan for each of my trigger thoughts (e.g., looking for exceptions, alternative explanations, preferences instead of shoulds, etc.). Revise trigger thought based on each counter-response plan.

   a. Counter-response plan: Assumed Intent

   If you haven't asked, assume you don't know what's going on. Find alternative explanations.

   Revised trigger thought:

   I don't really know what Jane's up to, maybe she's insecure and trying to prove her worth to the boss.

   b. Counterresponse plan: Magnifying

   Use accurate language, look at the whole picture.

   Revised trigger thought:

   Jane's offering to do parts of my job. I guess I'm just worried that the boss might think, if she can do the job, that I'm expendable. Truth is, I know a lot about the job that she doesn't.

   c. Counterresponse plan: Fallacy of Fairness

   Focus on the other person's need in the situation; assume her need is equal to yours.

   Revised trigger thought:

   I suppose she might be scared of losing her job, and she's trying to make herself indispensable. I can understand how big that fear can be.

3. Helpful coping thoughts (see Effective Coping Thoughts List)

   a. I'm not going to let her get to me.

   b. Take a deep breath and relax.

   c. It's just not worth it to get so angry.

   d. I can't expect people to act the way I want them to.

We're aware that using a worksheet to develop alternatives for your trigger thoughts will take effort, and commitment. But we promise you that your work will pay off. Situations where you chronically react with anger can finally change—because you've developed new ways of thinking and responding. The more you use this worksheet the more skilled you'll become at modulating your anger.

14

Anger Inoculation

It's now time to learn about a process known as anger inoculation. Don't worry—it has nothing to do with needles! This technique was pioneered by Raymond Novaco, building on the work of Donald Meichenbaum. It is basically a structured way to rehearse your coping thoughts and new relaxation coping skills, in the context of visualized anger scenes.

The visualized anger scenes are graduated, starting in the mild to moderate range and climbing to situations where you feel extreme anger. This step-wise practice, using a hierarchy of anger-evoking situations, allows you to rehearse and perfect your coping skills with mildly upsetting events, before progressing to more challenging provocations. In a little while, you will be asked to write out descriptions of anger situations that arise in all the affected areas of your life—work, family and children, daily responsibilities, social and sexual relationships, and so on. Then you'll learn how to visualize these scenes while practicing relaxation and using anger-cooling coping thoughts.

Before we begin, you first need to understand the concept of SUDs in creating a hierarchy of anger-producing situations. Subjective Units of Distress, otherwise known as SUDs, is not a new laundry detergent. It is a scale designed to assign scores to a variety of distressing situations. You can create your unique SUDs scale, keyed to your own behavior, by assigning scores to various anger-provoking situations, from 0 (no anger at all) to 100 (totally enraged).

Anger inoculation focuses on five different levels of anger-provoking situations. The SUDs level is scored as follows:

1. Mild to moderate: 40–50 SUDs

2. Moderate: 50–60 SUDs

3. Moderate to high: 60–75 SUDs

4. High: 75–85 SUDs

5. Extreme: 85–100 SUDs

Now you are now ready to begin anger inoculation by working step by step through the sequence described below. First, read the entire sequence through to familiarize yourself with the process. Then, we'll walk you through each step in the next section.

1. Create two mild to moderate anger scenes and describe them thoroughly. Include feelings and physical reactions. There is a blank worksheet for Creating Anger Scenes on the next page. It would be a good idea to make several photocopies so you can reuse the form.

2. Next, identify the trigger thoughts and anger distortions in each scene and record them on the worksheet, "Creating Coping Thoughts" in this chapter. It would be a good idea to photocopy this blank form as well.

3. Still using the worksheet, "Creating Coping Thoughts," develop two or three coping thoughts for each scene. Transfer the trigger thoughts and coping thoughts to the worksheet "Creating Anger Scenes."

4. Then relax using whichever brief method works best for you. Try relaxation imagery, cue-controlled relaxation, and perhaps relaxation without tension, as described in chapter 10, "Controlling Stress Step by Step."

5. Once you feel relaxed, start to visualize your first mild to moderate anger scene. See all the details, hear what's said, and carefully observe your feelings and any bodily sensations. Crank up your anger with a few juicy trigger thoughts. Stay with it. Allow your anger to intensify as much as possible. Maintain the scene for thirty seconds.

6. Then mentally erase the scene and begin doing relaxation imagery, cue-controlled relaxation, and perhaps relaxation without tension (focus on a particular muscle area). Also, rehearse two or three coping thoughts until you feel completely calm again.

7. Repeat the entire sequence again, using a second anger scenario.

8. Keep alternating the two scenes for four to six repetitions of each. Practice this step on two separate occasions.

Worksheet: Creating Anger Scenes

Instructions: In the spaces provided below, fill in the details of a situation in which you have experienced anger. Include details about he physical environment, and what other people are saying and doing. Next, describe your thoughts and physiological reactions. Pay particular attention to your trigger thoughts and list them in the space provided. Finally, list some new coping thoughts.

1. Describe the scene in detail:

2. Feelings and physiological reactions:

3. Trigger thoughts:

4. New coping thoughts:

Anger Inoculation: Mild to Moderate Anger

Start right now to create the two mild-to-moderate anger scenes (40–50 on the SUDs scale) that you will use to practice anger inoculation. This technique works best when the images in the scenes are clear and strong. That's why it's essential to get as much detail into your scenarios as possible. The scenes should be based on something that really happened and is fresh enough to recall easily.

To develop a scene fully, begin by closing your eyes. Mentally look around and notice the environment. What time of day is it? Be aware of the temperature. Listen to the sounds around you. What are people saying? Notice the feelings inside your body. Is there tension somewhere in your body? Do you feel hot or cold? Are there any odors?

Once you've recalled some of the details of your anger scene, fill out the Creating Anger Scenes worksheet to help you put your ideas in order.

The next step is to identify some trigger thoughts and anger distortions associated with the scene. Visualize the scene you've created and notice what you're thinking. Once the trigger thoughts become clear, try to identify which cognitive error they represent.

For the last step, generate some new coping thoughts. Use the blank "Creating Coping Thoughts" worksheet on the next page to work through this process, and then transfer your notes to the "Creating Anger Scenes" worksheet (sections 3 and 4) in this chapter. Remember, you will need to make some photocopies of the blank forms so they can be reused.

For an example of how this process works, consider Tom's story. Tom is a fifty-three-year-old middle manager who works for a large printing firm. He has a teenage daughter, Lisa, who's driving him nuts.

Using the "Creating Anger Scenes" worksheet, Tom developed the following mild anger scenario: "It's Friday night, after a long, difficult week, and my daughter Lisa has decided to invite some friends over for a hot-tub party. The kids are loud and boisterous. It's after nine o'clock and I'm concerned that the neighbors will get upset. There are wet towels, fast-food wrappers, candles, and assorted junk strewn all over the place. I ask Lisa to ask her friends to help clean up, and she says, 'Stop worrying, and just let us have fun for once.' My throat is getting tight as I choke back a retort. I feel anger rising in me."

On the "Creating Coping Thoughts" worksheet, Tom records his trigger thoughts; "*She's so self-centered. She never cares about anyone but herself.*" The cognitive error is "*Global labeling.*" Under counter-responses he writes, "*They're just kids having fun. And Lisa was really thoughtful last Sunday, making me tea in the morning.*" Under "Helpful Coping Thoughts he writes, "*Just take a deep breath. I'm in control.*" And, "*I'm not going to do anything to hurt my relationship with Lisa.*"

Tom repeats this same process with his second mild-to-moderate anger scene (40-50 SUDs). This one has to do with a lunchtime altercation with some coworkers.

Worksheet: Creating Coping Thoughts

Complete the following for each significant trigger thought in an anger situation.

1. Trigger thoughts (specific thought + category of cognitive error)

    a.

    b.

    c.

2. Counterresponse plan for each of my trigger thoughts (e.g., looking for exceptions, alternative explanations, preferences instead of shoulds, etc.) Revise trigger thoughts based on each counterresponse plan.

    a. Counterresponse plan:

    Revised trigger thought:

    b. Counterresponse plan:

    Revised trigger thought:

    c. Counterresponse plan:

    Revised trigger thought:

3. Helpful coping thoughts (see Effective Coping Thoughts lists in chapter 13).

    a.

    b.

    c.

    d.

Now let's follow along as Tom goes through the anger inoculation sequence, step by step from the very beginning.

First, he begins the relaxation process by doing some deep breathing. Then he closes his eyes and calls up his relaxation image, which for him is a deserted beach on the island of Molokai. He can feel the gentle breeze and the warm sun, and he can hear the ocean waves breaking on the shore. He does some cue-controlled relaxation, and feels himself let go completely.

Then he switches to his mild-to-moderate anger scene. He sees himself going outside and watching the hot-tub scene. Noisy kids, a mess all over the place, and Lisa just shining him on. He remembers his trigger thought: *"She's so self-centered."* Tom holds this mental picture for thirty seconds, and his throat starts to tighten.

Then, he mentally erases the anger scene. He pictures a slow fade-out like in the movies. He tries to get back to the beach on Molokai, but it won't come. He switches to cue-controlled relaxation. It doesn't work. Then he tries the relaxation without tension exercise, and that helps him to focus on the knot in his throat. That's it. He's feeling more relaxed. At this point he rehearses two of his favorite coping thoughts. "Just take a deep breath and relax," and "I'm in control, just keep cool." After several minutes, he feels completely calm again.

Switching to his second scene, Tom imagines that it's lunchtime at the plant. He hears himself being dissed by the other employees. He starts feeling tension in his gut. He holds a mental picture of this scene for thirty seconds.

The scene does a slow fade-out. Tom focuses on his stomach and again uses relaxation without tension. That's it, just let go. Now, some deep breathing with his cue word, and here comes the beach on Molokai. All right! Now some coping thoughts: "I can stay calm, I'm in control." "Their opinions don't affect me." Within a short time Tom feels completely calm again, and he thinks to himself, "Yes. This is really working."

Tom keeps alternating the two scenes for a total of four to six times each. Then, a few days later, he repeats the anger inoculation sequence for the same two scenes. After his second session, Tom observes that he's becoming more skilled at relaxing and using coping thoughts when he's upset.

Anger Inoculation—Moderate Anger

Now you're going to begin practicing anger inoculation with two moderate (50–60 SUDs) anger scenes. Just as you did last time, imagine an anger-producing scenario and then manage your anger by using relaxation and coping thoughts.

It's very important to make a real effort to create anger scenarios that are as vivid as possible. That means including lots of specifics: what you see and hear, even smells associated with the scene, kinesthetic aspects like temperature and texture can help too. It's also good to include details about the emotional and physical reactions that take place during each scene. Be sure to identify the trigger thoughts that go with each scene. These are important to include in your visualization because they crank up your anger.

Time to get started. Using the "Creating Anger Scenes" worksheet, write out your two moderate anger scenes. To give you an idea of what this could look like, you'll find one of Tom's moderate anger scenes, *The Parking Space* (60 SUDs), below:

"This nitwit is trying to park his SUV in a space that's way too small for his car. And because it's a narrow street, he's blocking traffic. He's going back and forth, back and forth with the car sticking out into the road. Nobody can move. And he doesn't care. Everybody can just screw off while he's doing this stupid, incompetent parking job. I honk my horn and he ignores me. I feel a flush in my face, and my chest is getting tight. I shout 'Fucking nitwit' inside my car."

Next, Tom identified his trigger thought: "He doesn't care," and added some new coping thoughts: "He's doing the best he can." "I'm not in a hurry, just relax."

When you feel completely prepared, go to a quiet, comfortable place and start the relaxation process. It usually works best to begin with relaxation imagery, then segue into cue-controlled relaxation, or relaxation without tension.

Once you feel relaxed, you can start the moderate anger scene. It's like pushing the "Play" button on your VCR remote control. Allow your anger to intensify by focusing on the images and trigger thoughts that really outrage you. Stay in the scene for thirty seconds.

Now erase the scene, like pushing the "Stop" button on the VCR, and go back to the relaxation process again. Be sure, at the very least, to use cue-controlled relaxation. As you feel yourself begin to relax physically, repeat some of your coping thoughts. Continue until you feel completely calm.

Repeat the entire sequence again using a second anger scene. Keep alternating the two scenes four to six times each. Do the entire series (four to six alternating repetitions) one more time.

Anger Inoculation—Moderate to High Anger

When you feel comfortable managing moderate anger scenes, it's time to move up a notch to moderate-to-high (60–75 SUDs) anger.

This time, using a new format, you will not erase the scene as you did previously. This time, we want you to continue visualizing the provocative scene while simultaneously using a variety of coping strategies to reduce your anger. In other words, you'll cope with your anger during the scene, not after it.

Begin by writing two moderate-to-high anger scenes, using lots of detail, on the "Creating Anger Scenes" worksheet. Next, identify the trigger thoughts in each scene. Then, develop coping thoughts for each scene. (Use the "Creating Coping Thoughts" worksheet.) Once you've finished all the preparatory work, relax, and then start to visualize the first scene.

Important Note: Don't start any coping strategies until the scene is fully developed.

Now, here's the important part. You need to *maintain* the image of the provocation, while simultaneously practicing your coping skills. Hold on to your mental picture of the scene while using cue-controlled relaxation, and perhaps releasing tension in a tight area of your body. Stay locked on to the image, while reminding yourself of your coping thoughts. Repeat your coping thoughts until they take effect. Then go back to cue-controlled relaxation, more coping thoughts, and so on. It's not easy to do several things at the same time, but, with practice, you will be able to balance your visualizations with your coping strategies. Only when you feel completely calm during the anger scene should you erase it and take a break using relaxation imagery..

Here's an example of someone working her way through this process. Sarah begins by developing two anger scenes in the 60-75 SUDs range. She calls her first situation *The Tree in the Backyard.*

Sarah describes the scene as follows: "My husband, Ian, never liked the tree in our backyard. He thinks it makes the area too dark and shady. But I loved it. I told him that it makes for a beautiful view. I come home on Saturday afternoon, after the Brownie Bake Sale. And . . . IT'S GONE! The Goddamn tree is gone! He's cut it down! There's a big stack of firewood, and next to it, Ian is beaming like Paul Bunyan. He says, 'Now we can all enjoy the sun back here. I know that you'll agree with me eventually.' I have this sick, heavy feeling in my stomach. And I'm thinking, what a bastard—he just does what he wants. He doesn't respect me one bit. My opinion counts for nothing. He gets in his tank and runs all over me and anybody else who gets in his way. I feel a huge surge of anger."

Using the "Creating Anger Scenes" and "Creating Coping Thoughts" worksheets Sarah adds trigger thoughts and new coping thoughts. Now she's ready to begin. She goes into the bedroom, sits in the rocking chair, and begins to relax. She pictures a meadow in the Catskill mountain range. Filtered sunlight, shadows floating across the sky. Cue-controlled relaxation.

Click. Now to work. Sarah pictures the scene in the backyard, her shock on coming home, the feeling in her stomach, a sense of emptiness and the surge of anger. With the scene firmly established, and feeling quite angry, she's ready to start coping. Cue-controlled relaxation, that's better. Still visualizing the scene, she uses new coping thoughts, "I can adjust to this, just breathe, and relax." "Ian does a lot of nice things for the family and he thinks this is nice, too." Now Sarah focuses on relaxing her tight stomach, allowing each deep breath to loosen the knot she feels. Some more coping thoughts and she starts to feels herself calming down. When she feels completely relaxed, she turns the scene off.

She takes a break by returning to her meadow in the Catskills, and then she starts on her second scene, repeating the process outlined above. Sarah alternates the scenes for four to six repetitions and then calls it a day. Then she repeats the process two days later.

Anger Inoculation—High Anger

Before you move on to the highest levels of anger inoculation, it will probably be useful to spend a moment reviewing the information you have accumulated in your Anger Diary. In particular, look back on the times when you felt angry, but somehow you weren't able to mobilize and use your new skills.

On the checklist below, mark the categories of anger situations where you either forgot to use your new skills, or they didn't seem to work.

☐ Anger with people you supervise

☐ Anger with authority figures

☐ Anger with spouse/partner/lover

☐ Anger with children

☐ Anger with close friends

☐ Anger with strangers (i.e., road rage, anger at store clerks, receptionists, etc.)

☐ Anger with parents

☐ Anger when you feel criticized

☐ Anger when you feel disrespected

☐ Anger when you feel hurt

☐ Anger when you feel pressured to do something

☐ Anger when you feel humiliated/shamed

☐ Anger when you feel disappointed

☐ Anger when you feel frustrated

☐ Anger when you feel threatened

☐ Anger when you feel guilty or wrong

☐ Anger when you're scared something bad will happen

☐ Anger when you're tired/overwhelmed/pushed to your limit/running on empty

☐ Anger when people don't live up to your expectations

☐ Anger when people don't listen to you

The categories that you've marked represent ongoing problems. Now, go back over the list and <u>underline</u> the four items that evoke the most anger in terms of their impact on you. These are the items that should be used to create the remaining anger scenes.

Now it's time to move on to anger inoculation with high (75–85 SUDs) anger situations. Use the "Creating Anger Scenes" worksheet to develop two scenes that are rich in detail. Next, identify the trigger thoughts in the scene. Then, using the "Creating Coping Thoughts" worksheet, develop some appropriate coping thoughts.

Here's an example of a high anger scene written by Chuck. He called it, *The Parent-Teacher Conference.* It's worth 80 SUDs.

"After a long day at work I have to go to this parent-teacher conference. Next thing I know, this communications teacher starts talking all this shit about my daughter, Vicki. He's dissing her motivation and says that she doesn't care about anything. He says, all Vicki does in class is sit there with her friends, laughing and making fun of some of the weirder kids in the class. I know for a fact that he doesn't like her, and is always putting her down in class. I think, 'What a fucking asshole. He's on a power trip, just trying to cut her down to be as small as he is.' I'm really angry. Really hot. And I tell him that from what I hear, he's a total loser as a teacher."

The process for this anger inoculation scene is the same as the one used with moderate-to-high anger scenes. Begin by relaxing, then visualize the scene and let the anger build. Once you've achieved a high level of anger, remember to stay in the scene and use your coping strategies. Do the entire series (four to six alternating repetitions of each scene) on two separate occasions.

Anger Inoculation—Extreme Anger

This is the last, and perhaps the most important, phase of the anger inoculation process—the one that may save your life. Develop two scenes where provocation can lead to anger scores in the 85–100 SUDs range. Use the "Creating Anger Scenes" worksheet to fully flesh out the details. As before, identify potential trigger thoughts and then use the "Creating Coping Thoughts" worksheet to prepare your coping strategy.

Here's an example of a scene developed by Laura called, *The Critical Boss,* rated at 95 points SUDs.

> "It's Friday afternoon. My boss comes bursting into my office and says loudly, 'Laura, this report is completely unacceptable. There's not enough detail, and these tables make no sense at all. What made you think this crap was going to fly? Were you just trying to sneak it through thinking nobody would care what kind of half-baked shit you turn in? This isn't high school where you can turn in some gobbledy gook to fill up a page.' His breath smells of cigarettes. His gut looks like he swallowed a washtub. I hate all his stupid bean-counting, his whole 'little Hitler' act. I'm so angry I'm getting dizzy. I'm sickened by his breath. I want to shove his nicotine-stained teeth down his throat."

When you feel fully prepared, follow the same sequence that you used in the last set. Begin by relaxing completely. Then visualize the scene. Use your trigger thoughts and let your anger build up as much as possible. Immerse yourself in the situation. Only when you are fully immersed should you start to implement your coping strategies. Maintain the scene until you've managed to fully relax; then click off the image. Return briefly to relaxation—take a few deep breaths, and move on to the second scene.

Do the entire series (four to six alternating repetitions of each scene) on two occasions.

We know that these exercises are not easy to do. However, we ask you to consider the painful alternatives. When your anger has the potential to hurt the ones you love, the effort required is well worth it.

Anger inoculation is a proven technique. Dozens of studies have established its effectiveness. As you work through the hierarchy of anger scenes you will get vital practice in using your coping skills. That will make it far more likely that you'll remember to use your skills in real-life provocations. The success of your anger management program—and the long-term health of your relationships depends on your commitment to learning new ways of coping. We believe that anger inoculation is the most effective technique available to help you change your behavior when you are angry.

15

Response Choice Rehearsal

So far you've been working on changing how you think during provocations. That's half the battle. In this chapter you will learn a way to structure your behavior in confrontational situations so that you get better results. What you're about to learn is a series of specific responses to provocation that will (1) keep the conversation focused on resolving the problem, or (2) cut off a discussion that's starting to escalate.

The Key Attitude

Behavior is enormously influenced by attitude. How you act when you're angry has a lot to do with your attitude toward conflict. Some people respond to conflict by becoming *avengers*. They want to injure and punish the offending party to the same degree that they've been hurt. Pain must be paid back. They believe in retribution; an eye for an eye. Avengers make their point. They're loud. They're cutting. But relationships are damaged, and very often the conflict continues.

The key attitude for successful conflict resolution is *problem solving*. You're not trying to get the other person to feel bad. You're not trying to prove them wrong. You're trying to *fix* what's wrong. The problem-solving attitude assumes that conflict has no moral dimensions. Instead, conflict is a matter of opposing needs. Disagreements are more easily resolved when each person's needs are assumed to be legitimate and important. That way you don't have to argue about whose needs are bigger, whose more justified. Since everyone has an equal right to want it their way, problem solving becomes a matter of acknowledging and factoring these needs into an agreement.

Response Choice Rehearsal

This method for handling conflict has the advantage of requiring very little thought or preparation. You can do it when you're stressed, when you don't have time to plan a response. You can do it when your buttons have been pushed and the automatic rage starts to well up inside you. Even when all your instincts say, "Smash the bastard," you can still use response choice rehearsal (or RCR) to keep things from exploding.

Response choice rehearsal consists of six prelearned responses to provocation. Each one is designed to de-escalate conflict *while making room for real problem solving.* When one response doesn't work (because you're feeling too angry or the exchange heats up), you simply choose another one. Eventually you will find a response that breaks the tension and gives you the emotional safety to start searching for agreement.

Response choice rehearsal is divided into active and passive responses. Either one may be effective, depending on the situation. The key to understanding and using RCR is to remember that no single response is likely to be the answer. The first thing you try may not have much impact on your anger or the anger of the provoking person. Your second response may still not be effective. Or the third. But taken together, a series of adaptive responses is very likely to both cool you down and de-escalate the conflict.

In RCR, you use your anger as a red flag that signals you to switch to a new coping response. Rather than fueling aggression, anger is a sign to change tack, to shift strategies. Anger lets you know that you're stuck. Your current method of coping isn't solving the problem. Something still hurts, and you need to try a new response.

Active Responses

1. **Express a specific need.** Anger starts with pain. You need to do something about it. One of the healthiest responses you can make is to ask for what you need to reduce the pain.

   Opening line: "I'm feeling (what's bothering me is) _____ . And what I think I need (want, would like) in this situation is _____ ."

   Try to memorize this opening line. The less you have to think when you're angry, the better. The first sentence, where you describe your feeling or what's bothering you, is optional. Include this if you think it's important information, if you think it would help the other person be more responsive, or if the other person is an intimate who deserves to know your reactions. Don't include it if you're going to end up sounding judgmental and blaming. Don't include it if there's no need on either side for your feelings to be part of the discussion. Telling your garage mechanic that you feel betrayed by the size of his bill probably isn't appropriate. A salesclerk doesn't need to know that you're hurt by her brusqueness.

When stating your need, make sure you're asking for something that's behavioral, not attitudinal. Asking for someone to be more sensitive, more loving, or more responsible sets you up for a lot of disappointment. Research shows that people don't know how to respond to nonbehavioral requests. First of all, asking someone to be more caring or more responsible is pejorative. It implies that he or she is generally uncaring or irresponsible. Second, it's hard to know what is meant by value-laden words such as "caring" or "responsible." What kind of responsibility are you requesting? Do you want your partner to do the dishes more often? Or be more active in birth-control decisions?

Your requests should be specific, preferably limited to one thing. The more you ask for, the less likely you are to get it. If you stick to one specific behavioral request, you're much more likely to reach agreement or negotiate a compromise.

While clarifying your request in your own mind, it's extremely helpful to develop a fallback position. This is the minimum change that would be acceptable to you. For example, if your husband is unwilling to help with the kids immediately after work, you might suggest a half-hour decompression time, after which he'll do some child care.

John was angry because his girlfriend kept arranging that they visit certain friends of hers he didn't like. He decided to ask her to check with him *before* making any dates. As a fallback position, he was willing for her to make dates as long as she told people that he might not be able to come. Here's how John phrased his request: "What bothers me is you're making dates with people I'm not sure I want to see. What I'd like is for you to check with me first before making any arrangements."

2. **Negotiate.** Here your effort is to engage the other person in problem solving. You're both feeling stuck; the battle lines are drawn. Getting the other person to propose a solution, no matter how inadequate or self-serving, is the first step toward a negotiated agreement.

   Opening line: "What would you propose to solve this problem?"

   If you get resistance or a worthless proposal in return, you can offer your fallback position at this point. On the other hand, if the proposal has possibilities, you can start to negotiate.

The section on negotiation in chapter 16, "Effective Communication," has more specific suggestions.

- "My way this time, your way next time."

- "Part of what I want with part of what you want."

- "If you do _____ for me, I'll do _____ for you."

- "Let's meet halfway or split the difference."

- "Try it my way for a week and see. If you don't like it, we'll go back to the old way."

- "We'll do this one my way, but we'll do _____ your way."

- "My way when I'm doing it, your way when you're doing it."

When working toward compromise, remember that each person's needs must be taken into account. Don't expect to reach agreement unless the solution in some way addresses the conflicting needs you both feel.

Audrey wants her brother to participate more in the care of their housebound mother. She's angry because he contributes nothing to the day-to-day work but gets a lot of strokes from Mom for his occasional visits. Here's how their dialogue went:

Audrey: I'm feeling overwhelmed by the responsibility and upset that you don't help more. What I think I'd like is for you to visit Mom twice a week, bring her a meal, straighten the place up, and stay long enough so that she feels she really got to talk to you.

Edward: I've got a full life, Audrey. A law practice, two kids, I can't do that!

Audrey: Okay. What would you propose to solve this problem?

Edward: Audrey, I just don't have time. You're asking too damned much of me.

Audrey: (*presenting her fallback proposal*): How about at least visiting twice a week, forget bringing dinner?

Edward: It adds more than an hour to my commute coming home. Plus it'll take at least an hour to get out the door once I show up. I don't see my kids enough as it is.

Audrey: Come on, Ed. Let's put our heads together on this thing. Do you have some ideas?

Edward: Okay, okay. If you can find somebody, I'll pay for them to come in and cook and help out three evenings a week. How's that?

Audrey: *(looking for compromise):* That's a big help. But, Ed, she needs to see you. How about you pay for someone two nights a week, and you visit once a week?

Edward: You're relentless, Audrey. All right, I'll do it.

3. **Self-care.** This is where you deliver an ultimatum. You let the other person know your plan to take care of your own needs if he or she fails to cooperate with problem solving.

> *Opening line:* "If _____ (the problem)
> goes on, I'll have to _____ (your self-
> care solution) in order to take care of myself."

It's important to say it exactly as it's written above. By framing it as taking care of yourself, the ultimatum doesn't sound so much like punishment or revenge. What you're really doing is letting the other person know the sanctions for ignoring you. But you're doing it in a nonattacking way, so that you're less likely to trigger an angry response.

Self-care is not something you're going to do *to* the other person. It is something you do *for* yourself. It emphasizes your commitment to meeting your own needs and finding alternative solutions to your problem if the other person won't help. Typical self-care solutions include paying someone else to do it (good if you have a penny-pinching spouse), doing it yourself (but using time that otherwise would have been devoted to the needs of the other person), getting the help of an authority (police, lawyer, principal, theater manager), withdrawing from the relationship, (temporarily or permanently) or getting your need met elsewhere.

Jarret's friend won't take no for an answer. All through dinner Jim badgers him about a fishing trip Jarrett's already declined. Jarrett tries several other responses, but now he feels pushed to make a clear self-care statement. "Jim, if you press me again about the fishing trip, I'm going to just pay the bill and leave. We'll go bowling like we planned tomorrow, but I'll pack it in for tonight." Jim got the message and gave it up.

Passive Responses

1. **Get information.** Many conflicts stay unresolved because one or both parties harbor unexpressed feelings or needs. If things feel stuck, one of the best things you can do is probe to understand more about the feelings and needs of the other person.

Salespeople know this. When a customer says no, they immediately begin a line of questions to uncover the feelings and needs that lie behind the resistance.

Opening line:

1. "What do you need in this situation?"

2. "What concerns (worries) you in this situation?"

3. "What's hurting (bothering) you in this situation?"

Choose whichever of the three lines seems most appropriate. If your husband won't talk about his needs, perhaps he'll talk about his feelings, or vice versa. Camille was a nurse. One of her coworkers in the hospital repeatedly criticized her for various forms of inefficiency. After the fifth or sixth such encounter, Camille was frothing. Here's how she handled the problem:

Camille: I understand your point, but what bothers you about my being slow?

Sandra: It's just not right, these people should have been bathed three hours ago.

Camille: I understand, but what bothers you about that?

Sandra: Well, whenever we get late admissions you can't take them. You're too behind. And then when you have special problems, you don't have time to solve them. The admissions and the problems often end up in my lap.

Sandra's tone is hard-edged, but at least Camille understands her concern. From here, they can begin negotiating what to do about it.

2. **Acknowledge.** This is important for de-escalating conflict. People want to know that you understand what's bugging them. They need to feel heard. All you have to do is say in your own words what you understand their feelings or needs to be.

Opening line:

1. "So what you want is _____."

2. "So what concerns (worries) you is _____."

3. "So what hurts (bothers) you is _____."

Be certain that you describe the other person's position in a neutral, nonpejorative way. Your statement doesn't have to be sympathetic, just accurate. If there's any hint of sarcasm, exasperation, or judgment in your voice, the effort you made to acknowledge will be wasted.

Lennie's been taking a lot of flack from his father about his lousy computer science grades.

Father: I'm afraid you're not going to be able to compete. It's a technological world. A lot of jobs will depend on knowing this stuff. You're going to be stuck at the low end of the pay scale because you didn't learn it while you had a chance.

Lennie: What's worrying you about my grades is that I'll be stuck in a pretty low-level job. I won't be able to compete.

Lennie almost said, "You think a C makes me a computer nitwit." But he realized that this interpretation would sound mocking and derisive. The point was to let his father know that he heard him, not stir up more conflict with sarcasm.

3. **Withdrawal.** This is basically a time-out. If things are continuing to escalate despite a series of adaptive responses, it's time for damage control.

> *Opening line:* "It feels like we're starting to get upset. I want to stop and cool off for a while."

Just keep repeating this statement like a broken record until you can get disengaged. With intimates, give a specific time when you'll return. Or set a time when you'll be willing to resume discussion of the issue. Don't get caught in any further discussion; don't get suckered by another provocation. The key is to say the line verbatim, and then physically exit the situation as soon as possible.

Rules for RCR

The rules for RCR are very simple:

1. **Memorize all six opening lines.** This is a must. These opening sentences have to be so well learned that you can say them without effort, without thinking. See the chart of opening sentences at the end of the chapter. Test yourself daily for a week to verify your retention.

2. **Whenever possible, rehearse in advance active responses 1 and 3.** Decide if you wish to include your feelings about the situation. Then formulate your request and your fallback position. Make sure that your request is behavioral and specific. Also try to generate a self-care response. Ask yourself how you can take care of the problem *without* the other person's cooperation.

3. **Continued anger or escalation are your signals to switch responses.** Don't get stuck if a response isn't working. Move on to what you feel intuitively is the next best option.

4. **Don't be afraid to repeat responses.** You may wish to return several times to questions that get more information. You may wish to acknowledge what you're learning about the other person's experience. And as the discussion progresses, you may wish to invite another round of negotiation.

5. **If you don't know what to do next, try shifting from active to passive responses (or vice versa).** If you've been focusing on getting information, try expressing your own needs now. If you're stuck in fruitless negotiation, consider asking for information.

6. **Keep shifting among responses until the problem feels resolved or further communication appears pointless.** If you're still angry and stuck, go to one of the exit responses (either self-care or withdrawal). Stop talking and physically leave the situation.

Practicing with Imagery

In 1971, Joseph Cautela suggested that you can practice new, desirable behaviors by *imagining* yourself successfully performing the new behavioral sequence. He named his technique *covert modeling*. Here's how you can practice response choice rehearsal using imagery.

1. Go back to the hierarchy of anger-producing situations that you developed in chapter 14. Select a scene from the midrange of your hierarchy. Make sure it's one that you can visualize well and that it contains a considerable amount of angry dialogue. You'll probably find it easier if the scene is something that happens frequently and involves someone you know fairly well.

2. Choose several (two to four) of the coping statements that you used to reduce anger while visualizing your hierarchy. Make sure that at least one of the coping statements helps you relax your physiological arousal, and that another deals with trigger thoughts that occur during the scene.

3. Plan your RCR responses. Identify your feeling in the situation, if you wish to express it. Identify your need and your fallback position. Create a self-care option.

4. Now visualize the provocative scene. At the point where you are starting to get angry, imagine yourself using your coping statements to relax and neutralize your trigger thoughts. Now imagine

yourself choosing the first response from RCR. Imagine the other person resisting this first effort. Hear him or her escalating and provoking you. Use your coping instructions again: remind yourself to relax, deal with the arousal. Feel yourself struggling to keep control and stay focused on the task. Remind yourself that the goal is problem solving, not revenge. Use your anger as a signal to switch to your next RCR response. Imagine that your second response is poorly received. See yourself starting to lash out, then hold back. Again instruct yourself to relax, to stay focused on the task. Use your continued anger as a signal to shift to yet another response.

5. For your first scene, imagine a negotiated compromise. Hear yourself suggesting your fallback position, and imagine the final agreement. Be sure not to give the resolution a Pollyannaish flavor. Imagine reluctance on the part of the other person. See yourself starting to attack, then pushing back the anger to work toward a compromise.

6. Continue the covert modeling process with at least five scenes from the upper end of your hierarchy. Note that you may need to change your coping statements to make them more appropriate with new scenes. You will also need to plan different need and self-care responses with each new scene. Let some scenes resolve in agreement and imagine that others require exit responses. You may even wish to rehearse the same scene with various endings.

Example of Covert Modeling

Jill was a law student who'd had several blowups with a colleague during a summer internship. The scene from her anger-evoking hierarchy went like this:

> Rebecca drops a case on my desk. It hits with a loud bang. She says it's almost past the statute for filing, and the paperwork has got to be done like yesterday. Otherwise, the statute's blown, and the firm can be sued. She uses sort of a blaming "shame on you" kind of voice. I've never even seen the case before, but I feel put down because I didn't know about it. I'm starting to get steamed. "Leave it over there," I say coldly. "Well, it's your case," she says. "Blow it if you want to." I'm out of my mind. That prim, goody-two-shoes. Then I start getting loud—"Leave me the fuck alone," etc.

Jill chose four coping thoughts to help her deal with the anger generated by the scene.

1. "Take a deep breath and relax."

2. "Look for the right response."

3. "I won't give her the satisfaction of upsetting me."

4. "That's how she copes with her anxiety."

Now Jill prepared her need and self-care responses. She decided that she didn't want to express her feelings to Rebecca. She wanted to stick with a simple request.

"Rebecca, what I'd like is if you wouldn't bring any cases to my attention. To not warn me about anything."

Jill also decided on a fallback request. She'd ask Rebecca to leave cases in her box with the statute dates written on them.

For her self-care ultimatum, she decided she would have to appeal to authority.

"If you keep warning me about cases, I'm going to ask the head paralegal to clarify for both of us that we have separate duties and don't need to be involved in each other's cases."

Jill scripted the scene like this. First, she'd express her need. Rebecca would stay very prim, keeping an "I know better than you" tone in her voice. Jill would control her anger with coping thoughts. She'd use the anger as a cue to try another response. Moving from active to passive responses, she'd next try to get information. She'd ask Rebecca what bothered her about the situation with her cases. She imagined Rebecca saying, "If you blow it, it'll look bad for me." Jill imagined her anger surging again and saw herself having to take a deep breath and remind herself to look for the right response. She'd try shifting to negotiation: "Rebecca, what would you propose to solve this problem?" "I guess for you to keep on top of your cases," Rebecca says primly. Jill pushes the anger down, reminding herself not to give Rebecca the satisfaction of upsetting her. "That's how she copes with *her* anxiety." Jill sticks with negotiation and offers her fallback suggestion. She imagines Rebecca awkwardly accepting it and leaving her office. She congratulates herself for getting what she wanted without blowing up.

Jill ran the scene through several more times, with different endings. She imagined the negotiations breaking down and pictured herself having to announce her self-care solution. She imagined her anger escalating so quickly that she had to withdraw before exploding. Each time Jill went through the scene, she found it easier to remember the opening lines of her responses. She was able to use anger as her cue to shift responses and a signal to use her coping statements.

Jill practiced with four additional scenes from her hierarchy. Before visualizing each scene, she prepared coping reminders, as well as need and self-care statements. She scripted the scene, deciding in advance which responses she would try, and establishing how Rebecca would act at each point in the scene.

Role-Playing RCR

The ultimate goal is to use RCR in real-life situations. But you may need additional practice as you make the transition between visualized scenes and provocative encounters. There are three ways you can role-play RCR. First, you can rehearse in front of a mirror while imagining the other person's part in the dialogue. Second, you can act out both parts of a dialogue by saying your lines while sitting in one chair and moving to another chair to take the part of the provocative person. You keep shifting chairs as you alternately play the role of each person in the dialogue. A third method is to role-play with a close friend. Have your friend play the provocative role. Describe the scene and how he or she should generally respond. As always, you need to prepare for the scene by deciding on your coping reminders and your need and self-care statements. Then go ahead and play the scene, using your anger as a cue for shifting to a new response.

Doing It

You've practiced RCR, visualized scenes, and perhaps done some role-playing. Now it's time to incorporate the six response choices into your real-life repertoire of anger-coping strategies.

1. Choose a provocative situation that occurs with some frequency or predictability (ideally, one you've already practiced in imagination). Make sure it's a situation where you tend to *act* angry, not just *feel* angry. If it's a scene from your hierarchy, make sure that it falls in the midrange. Don't select a scene where your buttons are pushed so badly that you flash into instantaneous rage.

2. Prepare your coping statements, including ones that remind you to relax and neutralize trigger thoughts.

3. Plan your need, fallback, and self-care statements.

4. Commit yourself to using RCR. Remind yourself that anger is a signal to make your first RCR response or to shift responses.

5. If the first situation doesn't occur within a few days, prepare for a second situation that you're certain to encounter soon. When you're in the presence of a provocative person from one of your

target situations, mentally rehearse the opening line of an RCR response.

6. When the target situation occurs, congratulate yourself if you were able to make even one RCR response. If you are dissatisfied with the outcome (either because you forgot RCR or got derailed very early in the process), rehearse the scene again in imagination. See yourself struggling for control, but finally switching to an RCR response that either helps you reach agreement or disengages you without a major blowup.

Don't be discouraged when you have trouble implementing RCR at first. Remember that your old way of reacting is a well-learned, habitual response. It takes time to change habits, particularly ones that help you cope with pain. The key is to keep rehearsing RCR in imagination each time you get derailed in a real-life scene. It takes time. It takes patience. But gradually you'll find yourself using RCR more and more naturally. The responses will come without thinking. You'll get better at remembering your coping thoughts as anger starts to rise.

Motivating Yourself

You need a lot of motivation to change deeply ingrained habits. The best way to do it is to use both a carrot and a stick.

The Carrot

1. Plan specific rewards in advance. Reward yourself both for practicing RCR through imagery and for using your new coping responses during real provocations. Set it up so that you'll go to that movie you've wanted to see or treat yourself to a terrific dinner out. Arrange things so that you'll play tennis or call your friend or pick up your book *after* doing your covert modeling rehearsal.

2. Celebrate your success. Let people know that you've been working toward anger control in new ways. Tell them about situations where you're now able to stay cool and really focus on problem solving.

3. Put up signs. Stick reminders on your bathroom mirror, inside your front door, or in your briefcase. Remind yourself: "Use RCR with Nancy . . . express your need, negotiate . . . anger is a sign to cope," and so on.

The Stick

1. On your way to work each day, spend five minutes reviewing what your anger costs. Explore its toll on you emotionally and physically and reflect on how it has affected your relationships. Think about how your anger is affecting your career, your children, and your marriage.

2. Review in detail the consequences of your last anger episode.

3. Make a contract to use RCR with a friend or a support person or even with the provocateur him- or herself. Specify in your contract the target person with whom you plan to use RCR. Include in your contract the understanding that you will report the outcome of any interaction with the target person.

RCR is hard work. It costs you time and energy to learn these new ways of coping. Sometimes the process feels foreign, artificial. Sometimes you want to chuck it all and go back to handling things "naturally." But the natural way is the angry way. And the anger, as good as it makes you feel at the moment, has torn and damaged some of your important relationships. There is no other way to change except the hard way. You already know that. RCR and other techniques in this book will help you change the way you cope with pain. It is your decision now whether you are ready to implement them.

RCR Opening Lines

ACTIVE

1. *Express specific need*

I'm feeling (what's bothering me is) _____ ."

"And what I think I need (want/would like) in this situation is _____ ."

PASSIVE

1. *Get information*

"What do you need in this situation?"

"What concerns (worries) you in this situation?"

"What's hurting (bothering) you in this situation?

2. *Negotiate*

"What would *you* propose to solve this problem?"

2. *Acknowledge*

"So what you *want* is _____ ."

"So what concerns (worries) *you* is _____ ."

"So what hurts (bothers) *you* is _____ ."

3. *Self-Care*

"If (the problem) goes on, I'll have to (your self-care solution) in order to take care of myself."

3. *Withdraw*

"It feels like we're starting to get upset. I want to stop and cool off for a while."

16

Effective Communication

Your parents probably never sat you down and explained how to get your needs met. You learned those skills from observing them and other adults in your life. You saw how they settled the inevitable problems that arose when people had differing needs. You heard how they expressed their disapproval and how they set limits. You learned through example the tone of voice and body language that they used when they were on the warpath. If they used violence, tantrums, intimidation, or withdrawal, you learned that too. You saw the results when one person was unable to ask for what he or she wanted. You saw the results when people failed to set limits or couldn't say no to expectations or demands. You saw long-standing bitterness that set in when problems were not resolved but pushed under the rug.

You also learned what it felt like to have someone angry at you. To a child, anger is terrifying. Adults are all-powerful, and children depend on them for every aspect of their lives. Children cannot feel safe without adult acceptance and approval. It's vital, therefore, for them to find some way to cope with anger from their parents.

Some children learn to avoid anger by being compliant. Then, as adults, they deny their feelings and needs in order to feel safe. Other children find that the best defense is a good offense. As adults, they tend to act aggressively, using threats of violence or other means of intimidation to avoid conflict and escape criticism.

Neither the passive nor the aggressive styles of coping work for meeting your needs in the long run. Although they may have helped you survive as a child, adult relationships are seldom improved by these strategies.

The Passive Coping Style

The essence of the passive style is to say nothing that would offend. At best, your needs are expressed indirectly. It feels too frightening to push for what you want if it conflicts in any way with the needs of others. And it's hard to say no. You set limits by going along grudgingly, by dragging your feet, or by being less than competent.

Outwardly you're good, you're sweet, you're compliant. Inside you feel the pain of helplessness and unmet needs. The pain builds. Sometimes you feel suffocated by the demands of others. Sometimes you blame them for not seeing or acknowledging what's important to you.

The passive style leaves you invisible. Others are forced to guess about your feelings and wants. Usually they end up guessing wrong. For example, Ralph's sister has asked him to help her move three times in the past year. Lugging boxes isn't his favorite recreation (particularly since she rarely has things packed when he arrives). But what really burns him is that his sister never initiates contact other than to ask for his help. She never calls to say hello, never invites him to dinner. Ralph misses her and he resents her. Always indirect, he expresses his feelings by being curt and complaining about his back.

The Aggressive Coping Style

The aggressive style lets people know how bad and wrong they are for not giving you what you want. The impulse is to punish, to climb into a tank and blow away the opposition. But as you've learned, this strategy costs a lot. When you're loud, others get loud. When you blame, others go on the attack. When you psychologically punch someone, that person punches back. People resist you. What is achieved through anger must be defended that way as well. The intimidated, frightened people you push around will find other ways of defeating and getting back at you. You are never sure if even those close to you are cooperating out of love or fear.

You pay for anger in the coin of guilt. Angry people often regret their outbursts. And they feel compelled to make it up in other ways—favors, gifts, concessions. Then in the process of compensating for the recent outburst, new resentments grow. You sit on all your needs and feelings for a week so that the pain can subside from the last explosion. But the nice-guy act wears thin, and soon enough you're attacking and blaming again.

Cheryl was chronically annoyed by some of her boyfriend's habits. He always left the milk out, he wore his stinky undershirts to bed, he never made any salad when it was his turn to cook, and he

often cooked pork (her least favorite meat). Cheryl periodically triggered her anger with the thought: "He never listens to me about my
needs." Then the donnybrook. Cheryl's boyfriend would get so
defensive that he simply stopped listening. Afterwards, Cheryl felt
guilty and resolved to keep her mouth shut about "such petty stuff."
Until the next time.

Passive, then Aggressive

When you're afraid to ask directly for what you want, the pain
builds. Your passive response leaves you feeling stuck and helpless.
And the helplessness adds to already high levels of stress. When the
pain reaches a critical threshold, you seize on a convenient trigger
thought to ignite rage. Usually the angry outburst is still not direct,
still not about the real issue that bothers you.

Coming home after a long day and an hour's commute, Jim
needs time to decompress before addressing the problems and
pleasures of a noisy household. A half hour of peace and quiet with
the paper would significantly reduce his stress. But he has trouble
asking for what he wants. He picks up the living room, he sets the
table, he reads a story to the kids. He sighs, he smiles weakly to his
wife. During dinner, his four-year-old chatters with her mouth full.
Jim blows up.

The Assertive Style

Assertive communication allows you to express feelings, thoughts,
and wishes, and to stand up for your rights and limits without
violating the rights of others. Assertiveness is the antidote for anger.
You can say, "I want more attention" instead of accusing your
husband of being a "cold fish." You can say, "I want help with the
shopping" instead of complaining that your children are "hopeless,
lazy bums like their father." You can write a proposal requesting a
raise instead of complaining that you are not valued at work.

The most important thing to remember about assertiveness is
that you have every right to express your needs. Other people have
that same right, and their needs are every bit as important to them as
yours are to you. By using assertiveness, you can work toward a
settlement without anger and seek a solution where both parties get
at least some of what they want. You can protect yourself without
blame. You can set limits without turning other people off. Assertive
communication works for nearly every interpersonal problem: sex,
money, power struggles, conflicts at work or in school. The key is
being direct, clear, and nonattacking.

How to Make an Assertive Statement

An assertive statement has three parts: I think, I feel, I want. The "I think" component is an objective description of what you see, hear, or notice. "The facts, and nothing but the facts," as you perceive them. An assertive statement presents the facts without judgment, blaming, or guessing the intentions of the other person. "The clothes are still on the floor." "When I called the office, the secretary said you had been out all afternoon." "When I got into the car this morning, there was no gas."

Sometimes it's hard to separate the facts from the feelings, but it is the first step in reducing the anger spiral. Stating the facts lays the issue on the table for discussion. You'll be more likely to get the other person's cooperation if you start with an objective statement than if you start with an insult ("What a lazy slob you are. Don't think that I'm going to pick up after you!") or a challenge ("Where the hell were you when I called this afternoon?") or sarcasm ("Thanks a lot for all the gas you left me this morning.") Statements like these fuel your own anger and make the other person defensive and angry as well. Nothing is solved, nothing changes.

The "I feel" statement acknowledges your honest reaction. It lets the other person become aware of how his or her behavior affects you without using tactics that blame, scare, or intimidate—and without making the other person defensive. At first, you may want to use a structure like this to state your feelings: "When _____ happens, I feel _____ ." "When I come home and find dishes in the sink, I feel angry." "When you promise me a dinner out and then cancel it because you have to work late, I feel resentful." "When you ignore me at a party and talk to other men, I feel abandoned and humiliated."

It's important to look for and acknowledge other feelings that may underlie your anger. Often anger is the *overriding* emotion and the only one of which you are aware. Worry, fear, disappointment, guilt, and embarrassment are some emotions that can lead to anger. Bobby couldn't understand why he felt angry every time Ralph discussed his new girlfriend, Judy. When he really thought about it, he realized that his anger was made up of two other feelings. When Ralph and Judy started seeing so much of each other, Bobby was *worried* that he'd lose a friendship and *jealous* of the time they spent together. The pain of worry and jealousy made him angry.

When Meg got drunk at the company party, Paul realized that his anger at her was caused by his feeling *discouraged* that she would ever be able to stay on the wagon and *disappointed* that she had broken her promise not to drink. He was also *embarrassed* by her loud, inappropriate laughter.

Anyone with teenagers knows how often fear and worry will trigger anger. One teenager candidly said, "My parents were so mad when I got home late that I almost wish I had been in an accident and could call them from the hospital. At least they'd feel sorry for me." When you acknowledge the different feelings that make up your anger, the other person gets to understand you better. And they are more likely to cooperate with you in problem solving.

Notice that the emphasis is on the "I." "I think," "I feel." Take responsibility for your own experience. She doesn't "make you jealous." He doesn't "make you feel stupid." When you blame others for how you are feeling, you end up feeling helpless. When you take responsibility for what you feel, you give yourself the power to change the situation.

Sometimes people think they are using "I" messages when they are really using "you" messages, and blaming the other person. For instance, "*I think you* are being controlling," or "*I feel you* are taking advantage of this situation." The "facts" should be as objective and fair as a photograph—a statement or a picture of what is there. The "feelings" are a statement of your emotional reaction, not a judgment or attack. Compare the blaming "you" message above with assertive statements. "When you make decisions without consulting me, I feel discounted and frustrated that I don't have any input about important issues." The *facts* are there, the *feelings* are there, and the other person knows what's bothering you without feeling accused of being "controlling." You say, "When you bring the children here for me to watch them without calling or giving me notice, I feel a bit resentful." The *facts* are there, the *feelings* are there, and the other person gets to understand your limits without being accused of being "inconsiderate" or "selfish."

The "I want" part of an assertive statement is the most important. Here are the guidelines for making a request: (1) Be sure to deal with only one area at a time. (2) Make your request specific. (3) Make your request behavioral.

Deal with one area at a time. You're bound to overwhelm your wife if you ask her to be more supportive of your job, spend less money on the kids, give you a hand with the yard work, and wear sexy nighties! All of these issues might be important to you, but if you bring them all up at the same time, the other person may feel attacked and overwhelmed.

Be specific. Instead of saying, "I want you to help out more with the child care," describe exactly what you want. "I'd like you to get the girls ready for school while I fix lunches and make breakfast." Instead of saying, "I want you to do more around the house," specify your needs. "I want you to clean the downstairs bathroom and vacuum the rugs." And you can be even *more* specific. Try describing when, how often, in what way you want things done. Instead of saying, "I'll need the budget finished by the end of the week," try "I need four copies of the budget by 2:00 P.M. Friday." If you want your child home by 10:00 P.M., don't say, "Be back soon, remember you have school tomorrow." You're likely to have a long night of worry ahead when the request is vague. Say the exact time limit and there's a good chance you'll avert a crisis.

Ask for behavior change. You can't demand that people change their attitudes, values, priorities, or feelings. You can only ask that they change behavior. For example, you can ask your husband to accompany you to your office party, but you can't ask him to *want* to go to the office party. Requesting that your partner be "more loving" or "more considerate" results in frustration and disappointment. At the particular moment when it's most important to you, he may not feel loving or considerate. Moreover, he may have only the haziest idea of what you mean by these words. Your best strategy is first to define for yourself and then for him exactly what loving *behavior* you're looking for. Does it mean making the tea after dinner, helping sort the bills, giving you a shoulder rub, cuddling with you in front of the TV, taking a shower together? It may not be romantic to define love behaviorally, but it is effective.

Even though you can't demand a change in attitude, when behavioral changes do occur, attitudes and feelings often change as well. John was a near-fanatical baseball fan. His family could simply forget any activity that included him during the season (six months of the year). Marilyn could put up with the daily radio broadcasts and the occasional TV games, but she really wanted him to be a part of their weekend plans during the summer. She tried sarcasm: "I see it's going to be another exciting weekend of beer and pretzels." And she threatened him: "One of these days you'll look up from that TV and find us gone." She wanted him to *want* to spend the weekend with them—a change in attitude. But she decided to settle for a change in his behavior. They worked out this agreement. He would spend every Saturday from the hours of 10:00 A.M. to 2:00 P.M. with their eight-year-old twins so that she could take an art class. They would arrange a daylong family outing one Sunday each month. He could pick which Sunday, but no baseball that day. At first, John agreed because he hated the nagging and complaining. At least she would be off his back about baseball during the other times. Later, John was surprised to learn that he tremendously enjoyed time spent with the twins. He taught them how to play ball. He made friends with the other dads at the park and started a little neighborhood softball team on Saturdays. The kids learned to enjoy the sport and looked forward to going to the games together on Saturdays. They loved being included in their father's favorite activity and were developing into precocious little ball players. By pushing to change behavior rather than attitude, Marilyn got much of what she wanted.

Saying what you think (the facts), feel, and want adds up to a complete assertive statement. Using this format will make it easier to organize your thoughts, avoid anger-evoking attacks, and get attention for your needs.

Anna May's best friend is always borrowing money. A dollar for the bus. Three dollars for burgers and fries at McDonald's. Fifty cents for a package of gum. Half the time she forgets to pay it back. Using the *I think, I feel, I want* protocol, Anna May developed this assertive response.

> *I think:* "Two or three times a week you borrow money for the bus or to buy a snack. Some of the time you forget to pay it back."

> *I feel:* "I feel angry and frustrated sometimes when I don't get the money back."

> *I want:* "Would you keep track of the tab in your civics notebook or somewhere and try to pay me back by the end of each week?"

Kate's first year teaching second grade was tough. There were times when she felt that she was doing creative and exciting work with her students. But there were times when she had a hard time keeping control of the noise and energy in her class. The teacher who worked next door would make sarcastic comments in front of the other teachers in the teacher's lounge. Kate felt criticized and embarrassed. Finally she stopped the teacher in the hall and was assertive.

> *I think:* "You've been making comments in the lounge about how I manage my class."

> *I feel:* "When you do that in front of the other teachers, it's embarrassing."

> *I want:* "I'd like to talk to you privately sometime about what I am trying to do in my classroom and hear some of your suggestions. Maybe we can have lunch together next Monday."

Joanna provided afterschool child care for six children. She was constantly frustrated by the fact that some parents would come to pick their child up late and would never call to let her know. One parent in particular was often between thirty and sixty minutes late because she would stop to shop or do errands. Then she would casually say, "Oops, I guess I'm running a little behind. You don't mind do you? You're home anyway."

Joanna worked on an assertive response using the *I think, I feel, I want* structure.

I think: "In the last two weeks, you have been over thirty minutes late four times without calling and letting me know you would be late. When you're late, it means that I can't start my own evening activities. My work day isn't over until all the children are picked up."

I feel: "I feel a bit taken advantage of."

I want: "I would like you to be here at 6 o'clock promptly, and if you must be late please call and let me know."

Jeff and Bill were partners in a small design business. They operated on a very tight budget and tried to get along without hiring a secretary or office manager. That meant that there were many little tasks that needed to be done, and they tried to share the work. Jeff would ask Bill to buy stamps, make airline reservations, or call to check on the status of the loan that they had applied for. Bill would agree to do it, but when he got busy he would forget or put it off. When Jeff later found out that it wasn't done, he got really steamed. Jeff was finally able to put out what he wanted in an assertive way.

I think: "There are a lot of time-consuming tasks that just have to get done in order to run this business. Often when I ask you to take care of something, you don't get to it or forget. Meanwhile I've put it out of my mind because I assumed it had been done."

I feel: "I feel really frustrated when I look for a stamp and there are none. I felt angry when I found out that we had no plane reservations for that trip last month."

I want: "I want us to keep a list of all the tasks that need doing and put our initials on the ones that we agree to do. If you can't get to it, I want you to tell me. You can cross them off the list once it has been done."

Paul hired his friend's nephew to paint the front of his house. They had agreed in writing what the cost would be. When the job was done, the nephew added $150 in labor to the price, claiming that the wood was cracked and needed filling and sealing. Paul felt like he was being manipulated, but was able to put together an assertive statement.

I think: "We had an agreement in writing of what this painting job would cost. You did extra filling and sealing without asking me."

I feel: "I feel very unhappy about the price change."

I want: "I'm willing to pay you the amount that we agreed upon, plus the cost of the wood putty and sealer."

Cassie loaned a friend her suede suit. When she returned it, it was soiled. Cassie was shocked. She had just assumed that her friend would return the suit in good condition, although they had never discussed it. Instead of suppressing her resentment, she expressed what she wanted assertively.

I think: "When I loaned you the suit, it was clean and pressed. Now it's soiled."

I feel: "I feel a bit hurt and taken advantage of."

I want: "I want you to pay me the amount it costs to have it cleaned."

Being assertive means that you get your needs met because other people know about them. Being assertive means that others listen to you because they are not afraid of your anger. Being assertive establishes you as a person who can take care of yourself, who can be cooperative, but who is honest and open about what you want and what you expect from others.

Sanctions

Some people are already motivated to go along with what you want. They might value your friendship or want a favor from you in the future. They might see the fairness of your position or just want to make you happy. But when people aren't motivated to meet your needs, you'll need to provide some form of reinforcement. Whenever possible, use positive reinforcement to motivate people to cooperate. It generally works better than punishment (if they don't go along with you, something bad will happen). Punishment creates resistance and resentment. Typical positive reinforcers include:

"If you'll do the dishes, I'll hang out with you and dry."

"If you handle the checkbook, I'll give you a foot massage."

"If you take Bill to school, I'll be able to start on the painting earlier. I'd really appreciate it."

"If we meet at the restaurant near my house, I could spend more time with you at lunch."

There are times, alas, when positive rewards don't work. No amount of praise or promised benefits gets you anywhere. One solution is to develop sanctions. Sanctions are the consequences or costs of not going along with what you want. "If _____ happens, then I will do _____ ." Their purpose is to motivate the other person to cooperate with you or respect your limits. Used appropriately, sanctions can help you get your needs met without anger. In using sanctions, remember these four rules.

1. **Sanctions should be specific.** Be precise about what behavior will trigger the sanction and what specifically will happen. Vague threats like, "If I can't reach you, we'll have a real problem," don't give the other person enough information. Say instead, "If you refuse to accept my calls, I will find another lawyer."

2. **Sanctions should be reasonable.** There's no sense going after a mosquito with a shotgun. You'll probably blow a hole in the wall and miss the mosquito anyway. Reasonable sanctions help you feel in control. Reasonable sanctions are respectful of other people and their right to make their own decisions. Using public humiliation, betraying a confidence, threats of violence, or other unreasonable sanctions make people angry and less likely to cooperate with what you want. Sanctions such as, "If you are not here on time, I'll leave without you," or, "If you bring up that subject again, I'll leave the room," are appropriate for minor irritating behavior. Bring out the big guns only for the big battles, not the little skirmishes.

3. **Be sure you can live with the results.** The sanctions you impose shouldn't hurt you more than the other person. Peggy, a Catholic, was marrying a Jewish man. Peggy's mother said she wouldn't attend the wedding unless it was in a church with a priest. Peggy and her fiancé chose to have a nonsectarian wedding officiated by both a priest and a rabbi and include traditions from both religions. Just as she threatened, Peggy's mother skipped the ceremony. Peggy felt hurt, but it was her mother who was the real loser. She missed seeing her daughter marry, she was in none of the wedding pictures, and her relationship with her daughter and their family was damaged. Be careful when you threaten to divorce, quit, call the FBI, or kill yourself. Dramatic ultimatums might seem appropriate in the heat of battle, but usually end up hurting you more. When you create sanctions that you can live with, you make it possible to follow the next rule.

4. **Sanctions should be consistent.** Be prepared to carry out what you said you would do. If you said that under certain circumstances you would hang up the phone, call the manager, or refuse to pay, then do it. Do it every time the situation arises. If you don't, you are *training* the other person not to take you seriously. Being consistent makes the other person respect you and your

limits, and lets them know where you stand. Being consistent means that others will be less likely to take advantage of you in the future.

Negotiation

Negotiation doesn't take place only between labor and management or between nations. You can use negotiation any time you have a conflict of needs and want to work out a solution for mutual benefit. "I give you what you need, you give me what I need." "I give you a pound of apples, you give me a dozen eggs." "I give you several hundred dollars, and you give me a ride on your airplane."

People often hesitate to negotiate when they have conflicting needs because it requires that they listen and understand the other person's position. They have an easier time being assertive if they see the other person as wrong, stupid, selfish, inconsiderate, or unfair. Instead of negotiating, they try to convince the other person of the rightness and fairness of their own position. They expect others to do all the changing.

Negotiation requires a different attitude. It starts with the premise that the other person's needs are just as important to him or her as your needs are to you. Nagging, shouting, or being angry or coldly rational usually won't get others to change their view. If you have a conflict of needs, negotiation allows you to find a middle ground where you both can get some of what you want. Here's how it works.

1. **Know exactly what it is that you want.** State it in behavioral terms—what you want the other person to do or not do.

   "I want you to return the children by 6:30 Sunday night."

   "I want to be in charge when you go on vacation."

   "I don't want you to use our driveway."

2. **Listen to the other person's objections.** The purpose of this step is to understand his position; not to argue or try to convince him to give up his needs. Be an active listener by asking questions, clarifying, and paraphrasing what you understand the other position to be. Don't be afraid to hear or even empathize with the other person's view. Just because you understand it doesn't mean that you have to agree with the point or accept the opposing position. From the information you have gathered, you can take the next step.

3. **Make a proposal.** Your proposal should take into consideration what the other person needs or wants in this situation. If she accommodates you, is there something in it for her? You may have to be creative and flexible, breaking through the constraints of rules or traditions

Marge, who worked as an accountant in a large urban highrise, really wanted to have the office with the window instead of a partitioned work space. She appealed to her manager in terms that took into account his interests as well as her own. "If I can have this office, I'll be willing to store the overflow files. I'll also make the office available for the weekly meetings. And I'd be willing to share the space with the other nonsmoker in the office. That way, she'll be off your back about the new no-smoking policy. How about it?"

4. **Make a counterproposal.** If the other person won't accept your proposal, encourage him to come up with a different solution. People unfamiliar with negotiation may need some help getting started. Remind them that your objective is to understand their position and to find a compromise that both of you can live with. Here are some typical compromise solutions.

   - "My way this time, your way next time."

   - "My way when I'm doing it, your way when you're doing it."

   - "If you do _____ for me, I'll do _____ for you."

   - "Part of what I want with part of what you want."

   - "Try it my way for a week and see. If you don't like it, we'll go back to the old way."

   - "Split the difference."

You might even say, "I really want _____ . This is really important to me. What would you need me to do to make it worth your while to go along this time?"

Switch back and forth, listening, clarifying, and proposing until you both can agree on a solution.

The hardest part in negotiation may be getting started. You may first need to negotiate about negotiating. If you've had a long history of painful fights, or you have been angry and intimidating in the past, the other person may hesitate even to talk about the conflict. Try to determine why they resist an open discussion. Maybe they need reassurance that you will listen. They may feel safer if you set ground rules, such as a time limit, make a prior agreement about not fighting or shouting, or decide to negotiate in the presence of a neutral third party.

Setting Limits

Think of the many requests made of you each day. Sometimes you agree to do things that are enjoyable to you. But some of the time you say yes when you want to say no.

The ability to say no is a crucial skill. It says to the world, "I am a person. I have needs, tastes, and preferences that are just as valid as yours. I can take care of myself." Saying no is a statement of your boundaries. Outside you are the needs and demands of all the people in your world. Inside are your own needs and desires. Being able to say no establishes that boundary. "No" is one of the first words you learned as a child, and one that first allowed you to make your needs known. "No, I won't eat my spinach." "No, I want to stay up." "No, I won't use the potty."

If saying no is such a basic and simple way of being assertive, why is it that many people have such a hard time doing it? Your early religious and moral training might have taught you to put others first. Those who give selflessly are admired. Those who look out for themselves are considered selfish. In some dysfunctional families, the children become the peacemakers and caregivers. Only by putting the needs of others first and denying their own needs can they survive. These lessons in survival stay with you long after they are useful or appropriate.

People with damaged self-esteem have special difficulty saying no. They feel unworthy. They have no right to their limits. They fear that saying no could mean losing a job or being abandoned by friends. By just going along, they hope to avoid disappointing or angering others.

But people who can't set limits may become chronically angry. They feel taken advantage of. Anyone can take their time, space, or money. They feel overrun and overwhelmed. An intimate relationship becomes a prison of limitless demands. They spend their time and energy on people and activities that don't give them pleasure and they end up having little time for things in life that bring real joy.

Shirley joined a carpool even though she preferred to take the train. Joan plays cards with her old friends every Tuesday even though she would prefer to take a quilting class. Tom accepts the job of United Fund organizer even though he hates dealing with office collections and doesn't have the time. Jill agreed to sew all the costumes for her daughter's dance recital because she doesn't "work" like the other mothers. All these people have difficulty setting limits and it makes their lives less productive, creative, and enjoyable.

Just Say No

In many circumstances, a simple "no" or "no thanks" is all that's appropriate or necessary. You don't owe the other person an explanation. You need not apologize. Keeping it simple will get the job done assertively. "No, I don't want a drink." "No, I don't need a vacation home in the Bahamas." "No, I don't want to contribute to the baby-shower present." Your pleasant but confident refusal conveys the feeling that you are not rejecting the person, just the request.

In other circumstances, you might want to give the other person more information. Complete limit setting has three components: it acknowledges the other person, states your position, and sets the limit. When you use the three-part statement, you don't have to get angry at demands ("What do you mean asking me for more money?"). You don't have to give advice ("If you kept your car maintained, you wouldn't be in this situation."). You don't have to blame ("If she'd plan ahead, she wouldn't keep me waiting for an hour."). You don't have to fix or solve the problem ("How will you get home now? I'll ask around and see if I can find someone else who can give you a ride.").

1. **Acknowledge the other person's needs.** If you are not sure exactly what is being asked of you, probe and get more details. What exactly is meant when the other person asks you to "help him move" or "support his program?" Acknowledging the other person's request assures him that you hear him correctly.

2. **State your position (your preference, feelings, or perception of the circumstances).** Be as confident and assertive as you can be. Do this without apologizing. Don't put yourself down. Just describe what is so for you. "I'm too tired tonight." "I have a previous engagement." "I decided that I'd rather drive my own car."

3. **Say no.** Say "No thanks . . . I don't want to . . . I'd rather not . . . This is not right for me . . . I've changed my mind . . . I won't be there."

Here are some examples of saying no.

- "I hear you need someone to watch your baby this afternoon while you go to the dentist. (*Acknowledgment*.) I wanted to spend this afternoon working in the yard while my boy is in school. (*Your position*.) I won't be available to help. (*Saying no*.) I sure hope you can find someone else."

- "I understand you need someone from our unit to go to that meeting. (*Acknowledgment*.) It can't be me. (*Saying no*.) I'm pretty busy with my own projects now, and I don't want to take the time off. (*Your position*.)"

- "I'm aware that you are sexually attracted to me. (*Acknowledgment*.) I enjoy the time we spend together, but the chemistry is just not there for me. (*Your position*.) A sexual relationship with you now wouldn't feel right for me. (*Saying no*.)"

- "I'm sorry that you feel that I'm being unfair. (*Acknowledgment*.) But I have to consider the needs of the business at this time and we just can't afford to lose you now. (*Your position*.) I won't okay your transfer. (*Saying no*.)"

You can't always plan ahead, but it might be useful to think of recurrent situations in your life where you need to set limits or say no. You might try to rehearse an assertive response using the three-part statement. You can practice saying no to a friend who often asks you for money or to your supervisor who expects you to work late or take work home. You can practice saying no to a relative or neighbor who drops in without notice, to committee work that takes up too much of your time, to telephone solicitors, and so on. When you are able to set limits, you can do more of the things you really enjoy.

Here are some more suggestions about saying no and setting limits.

1. **Take your time.** If you are someone who has had trouble setting limits and who automatically says yes, try delaying your response. You'll probably be able to think more clearly without the pressure of another person waiting for your answer. "I'll call you by the end of the week." "I'll let you know this afternoon." "Can I give you a call back in five minutes?"

2. **Don't over-apologize.** When you apologize for setting limits or saying no, you communicate to the other person and *to yourself* that you don't have the right to take care of yourself. You are saying, "Forgive me for putting my needs before yours." Excessive apologies invite the other person to put more pressure on you to change your mind. Apologizing also inspires people to impose on you about other things so you can make it up to them.

3. **Don't put yourself down.** Some people can set limits only if they put themselves down. "I'm too weak, stupid, clumsy, poor, afraid." In the long run, saying "I won't" is better than saying "I can't." When you say "I can't," the other person will try to

convince you that you *can do it*. You are then stuck trying to prove that you can't. When you say "No, I won't," the other person is less likely to argue.

4. **Be specific.** State exactly what you are and are not willing to do. "I am willing to help you move the furniture, but not pack or clean." "I am willing to drive you to work, but only if you can be ready by 8:15."

5. **Be aware of voice and body language.** Stand, or sit comfortably. Look the other person in the eye. Speak with confidence, your voice strong. Let your body and tone of voice match your assertive words.

6. **Beware of guilt.** After you say no, you might be willing to do something *else* for the other person. But take your time before offering. Be sure you are not acting from guilt. You don't want to obligate yourself to do something you will be sorry for later.

Dealing with Criticism

Criticism is painful. You can end up feeling wrong, judged, guilty, or afraid. And each of these painful emotions has the potential for triggering anger. "How dare she?" "He has no right."

For people sensitive to criticism, it doesn't matter if the issue is minor. It doesn't matter if the critic is someone whose opinion is unimportant. It doesn't even matter if the criticism is inaccurate. Just feeling criticized sets off a chain reaction—like a row of falling dominos, your self-esteem tumbles, your confidence drops, and you begin feeling extremely defensive.

Being criticized reminds you of what it felt like when you were a child, when you were corrected and judged by angry parents. As an adult, you don't want to reexperience the old feelings of being wrong, bad, even worthless. And you resent being made to feel like a child.

Being criticized makes it hard to feel perfect. Many people irrationally expect that they can do it all, do it right, and please everyone. So criticism is scary. If, as you imagine, others expect you to be perfect, you have to fear the slightest mistake. Any flaw, it seems, could lose you a job, a friend, and so on.

You may use anger to avoid and cover over the many painful emotions triggered by criticism. This was the case with Linda, a newly graduated RN. The occasion was her first three-month evaluation by her Head Nurse. Most of the evaluation was full of praise for her energy, her potential leadership ability, and her warm, professional interactions with patients. The evaluation also included this line: "When Linda gets behind in her work, she sometimes becomes rushed and careless. She needs to develop time management skills."

After the evaluation, Linda was depressed for a few days. Then she was so angry that she almost quit her new career. How did that happen to her?

First, she disregarded the majority of the evaluation (which was positive and praised her skills and strengths). She read the critical line over and over, focusing on the words "rushed and careless." Her internal monologue went like this: "Oh, God, this is awful. If I'm rushed and careless, I'll probably kill someone. How can I do this job if I'm afraid that I'll bump someone off? Good nurses don't rush patients. I rush around in a careless way. I must be a bad nurse."

Her self-deprecation spread well beyond the evaluation. "I'm not only a bad nurse, but a bad person as well. Imagine being sick and in pain and having someone rush you. How cruel to rush helpless sick people. Other people get their work done on time without rushing. Their patients are well taken care of and they finish on time. I'll never get it right. I'm a failure."

After several painful hours, Linda began covering her guilt and depression with anger. "Good God, this is an impossible job. I do my best but it just isn't good enough. What do they expect? They give me too many patients who are too seriously ill, and then complain if I can't breeze through the day. What does the Head Nurse know? All she does is pencil pushing. This job is impossible. I don't have to take it anymore!"

There is a way of hearing even hostile criticism that allows you to assess it, benefit from what is appropriate, and disregard what is not. Here are the steps you need to take.

1. **Limit the damage.** First, you can limit damage by stopping abusive, angry attacks from others. Even if you feel guilty about the situation, don't allow yourself to be verbally battered. Even if you're wrong, you don't deserve to be called names, threatened, or violated. Take a time-out, or simply refuse to go on with the discussion if the attack continues.

   Next, remind yourself that you are hearing one man or woman's opinion about a specific aspect of your behavior. The criticism is about what you do, not about who you are. Even if the other person is attacking and rejecting you, you don't have to join in. "This paper is not acceptable" does *not* mean that *you* are unacceptable. It does not mean that you are incapable of doing acceptable work. It does not mean that all of your past papers have been unacceptable.

   Finally, you can limit the damage by accepting that perfection is impossible. There is no way you can do it all, do it right, all the time. Accept that mistakes are inevitable. There are times when you will be tired, distracted, misinformed, unmotivated, or rushed. By accepting that about yourself (and others), you will be less angry and less damaged by criticism. When faced with an angry attack, repeat to yourself the mantra "I am a good person, doing the best I can." Just keep saying it, over and over. For other coping mantras that might be useful, see chapter 13 on coping through healthy self-talk.

2. **Probe.** Criticism can be constructive and valid. It may provide the feedback you need to grow in your relationships or your work. Actors, speakers, artists, and performers of all kinds seek constructive criticism from those they trust.

   The only way to assess criticism is to probe. Make sure that you know exactly what the critic means. People are so uncomfortable with criticism that they often avoid questioning the critic. They're afraid of the painful emotions that criticism stirs. But only when you probe to understand exactly what the critic means can you determine if it's useful to you. Before you fly into anger, retreat in defeat, or collapse in agreement, make sure you know exactly what the critic is conveying. Dave, a recent high school graduate, just started a new job in construction. His foreman approached him and said, "You need to improve your attitude if you're going to get along." Dave asked him what he meant. The foreman elaborated. "The contractors notice when you come and when you go. You were fifteen minutes late twice this week. It makes our whole team look bad and the other guys resent it." Dave learned that, on this job, coming to work late was interpreted as a "bad attitude."

   Jim's wife was sick with the flu. Her criticism was attacking and angry: "You're just never there for me. All you care about is yourself." Jim asked what she meant. "Here I am, sick, and you show no concern for me at all. When you had the flu last week, I called you twice from work, I fixed dinner, and I stayed home from my karate class just to be with you. You just go on with your life with hardly a 'How are you?'" Now Jim has more information. His wife would feel more cared for if he did those kinds of special things for her. Jim doesn't have to accept or agree with her attack. But now he knows more about his wife and more about how his behavior affects her sense of being cared for.

   Mat and Rich were old friends from grade school through college. Now that they are both working, they seem to be drifting apart. They have less time to do things together. Rich was surprised when Mat attacked him. He managed to control his hurt feelings long enough to determine what lay at the heart of some rather hostile criticism.

Mat:	You've turned into quite a social climber.
Rich:	What do you mean by "social climber"?
Mat:	You're always hanging out with friends at work now, you hardly have time anymore.
Rich:	What is it about my hanging out with work friends that bothers you?
Mat:	You all vacation and party together. You go to their yuppie sports club. How can I compete? You'd rather hang out with them than be with the real people.
Rich:	What do you mean by "real people"?
Mat:	People from the old neighborhood, like me.
Rich:	Since I've been working, do you feel like I've been going places and doing things with my new friends and we don't have as much time to do things together?
Mat:	Yeah, I miss the old days when we did everything together. It's kind of lonely without you.

What started out sounding angry was really Mat's feelings of loss and jealousy and a need to be closer. Once you've determined exactly what the complaint is, you can start to evaluate its accuracy. The new nurse really did need to work on time management skills. The two old friends were really drifting apart and their relationship was changing. Dave, the construction worker, was fifteen minutes late twice last week. Jim did not nurture his wife when she was ill.

Recognize also the part of the criticism that is not accurate. Dave's lateness does not necessarily indicate that he has an "attitude problem," but only that he didn't count on traffic delays. Rich was not snubbing his old friends and becoming a social climber. It isn't true that Jim is "never there" for his wife, only that it never occurred to him to nurture her when she was feeling ill. The new nurse's difficulty organizing her work doesn't mean that she was a bad nurse and a bad person, only that she is new and inexperienced.

One way to spot inaccurate, harmful criticism is to listen for generalizations. "You never _____ ." "I'm always the one who _____ ." "Everyone else knows about _____ but me." There are plenty of exceptions to such globalized statements. Look for them. Also be alert for global indictments that attack you as a person, not just complain about your behavior. When you hear yourself condemned as selfish or stupid or uncaring, refocus on the specifics of the situation. These attacks on your identity are wrong by definition. No one is totally anything. You are a complex person with many different (sometimes contradictory) motivations and needs.

3. **Deflect.** Here are four techniques you can use to disarm the critic and prevent escalation.

In *clouding,* you agree in part with the criticism, without accepting it completely. It requires that you listen carefully to the critic and agree with the part of the criticism that is accurate.

Critic: You are never around when I need you.

Response: I have been working a lot this month and I haven't been around as much in the evenings.

Critic: If you keep spending money at this rate, we'll be broke in no time.

Response: We have been spending more money since we moved into the new house.

Notice that you don't have to agree with everything. You don't have to buy that you're *never* around, or that you'll go broke. You acknowledge the grain of truth without accepting the entire exaggerated statement.

Another way to cloud is to *agree in probability.* "It may be . . ." or "You could be right . . ." are ways you can imply agreement without total capitulation. Using agreement in probability with the previous examples, you might reply:

"You may be right that I haven't been around much lately."

"It's probably true that we're spending quite a bit."

A third form of clouding is to *agree in principle.* The trick here is to accept the conclusion without accepting the premise.

Father to son: "If you don't work harder, you'll never get into law school." The young man can agree with the principle that hard work is necessary to get into law school. But he doesn't have to buy the *premise* that he isn't working hard. Here is how he might agree in principle: "You're right, you have to work hard to get into law school."

When you agree in part or in principle with the critic, the critic feels listened to and his opinion and concern is, in part, accepted. He'll be less likely to continue arguing to prove he is right and you are wrong.

Assertive preference is a way of shutting off the critic. Using this technique, you acknowledge the criticism but disagree with it. Don't feel you have to provide a long explanation. Just state that you prefer to do it your way. "I hear that you don't agree with how I'm handling this situation, but I prefer to do it this way." "I hear what you're saying. I guess we just don't agree on this point." "Thanks for your concern, but I'm willing to take the risk." This technique is used when you have the power to do things your way and you want the critic to back off and stop badgering you. It stops further discussion without attacking the other person and without getting angry.

Assertive delay is an important and powerful technique for responding to criticism without anger. If you take a time-out (even for a few minutes) you allow yourself to calm down, think, activate some coping strategies, consult with another, get support, gather information, and so on. When the critic is talking, you can just pretend that you are a tape recorder. Record, clarify, and understand the criticism. Don't feel you have to respond, apologize, fix the problem, or throw in the towel. You can delay responding until later when you can "play it back" in your mind, assess it, determine what is accurate and what is not. A few minutes alone can provide the perspective and awareness that you don't have when you feel under attack. "I hear what you're saying. Let me think about it and I'll call you in the morning." "What you're saying is important, but I frankly am feeling a little overwhelmed right now. Let's get together after work for coffee and we can talk some more."

Don't get pressured into responding if you're not ready. Don't try to get in the last word or get into an argument about whether or not you have the right to delay responding. Use your three-part statement for setting limits. "I understand that you are not happy with the job I've been doing (*acknowledgment*). I'm feeling like I need some time to think before I respond to you (*your position*). I'll call you tomorrow (*setting the limit*)."

A *content-to-process shift* is useful when the discussion is escalating into a battle, you feel that the critic is over- or underreacting to something, or you suspect the critic is not saying what's really bothering him. When you use the content-to-process shift, you stop talking about the issue (content) and talk about the angry feelings or your sense of being attacked (process). It is a way of putting on the brakes and exploring the quality of the interaction between you. "I don't know about you, but I'm kind of frustrated. We always get stuck in this sort of argument." "This is the third time today that you've criticized how I've handled the kids. What's happening?" "You say you're not upset about my canceling our date, but you sound like you're almost in tears." "We always end up arguing about how much money to spend on new equipment. I'm feeling accused and attacked. What's going on between us that we end up feeling angry like this?" A content-to-process shift allows you to get to the real issue or the more important issue that lies at the bottom of a conflict.

The Payoff

People who are not able to communicate assertively are usually angry. They're angry because they are not able to ask for what they want or to protect themselves by setting limits. They are angry because they can't motivate others to cooperate or negotiate successfully. They blame instead of listen, they defend instead of problem solve. Your efforts toward becoming assertive will eliminate many anger-generating situations. Now you can begin to acknowledge your needs, ask for changes, set limits, and cope with criticism. This work will have an immediate payoff in the quality of your relationships.

17

Anger as a Defense

Two boys square off in a schoolyard. One is larger and louder; he shoves the smaller boy. It was an error in judgment, because the smaller boy explodes like a grenade. He goes for the stomach, the groin, the chest. And when the bigger boy falls, he kicks him in the face and ribs. It's over in less than a minute. A teacher drags the smaller boy to a bench, where he sits waiting for the principal. The boy relives the scene again and again. He wonders what gave him the quickness, the strength, and most amazingly the courage to beat up the bully.

The answer of course is anger. The hormonal changes triggered by anger do five important things to protect you from attack. Anger provides:

- A feeling of empowerment. Suddenly you don't doubt yourself. You can do whatever needs to be done.

- Energy to cope. Not only do you have the confidence, but anger gives you the strength to mobilize yourself for action.

- A blocking mechanism for nonadaptive feelings such as fear and guilt. Anger drives out or obscures any feeling that might inhibit protective action. Anger's vector is always forward, to attack and push away the source of pain. There's no room for feelings that would slow you down at the moment of combat.

- Adaptive egocentricity. Anger allows you to forget the other person's needs. His or her pain doesn't matter. All that counts is your pain and your needs.

- The conviction of rightness. Anger strengthens the feeling that you are right and that whatever you do is justified. There is a temporary suspension of any sense of wrongness or badness in the self in order to maximize the commitment to self-protection.

Protection versus Psychological Defense

The same five properties of anger that help you respond to attack adaptively make it very useful as a psychological defense. A psychological defense is something you do that obscures or covers an important inner experience. Anger is often used as a defense because it can block painful feelings such as anxiety or fear, hurt, guilt, shame, embarrassment, the sense of being wrong or bad or unworthy, loss, emptiness, frustrated desire, helplessness, and many others. Anger can be a buffer against feelings that you would rather not experience. The properties of anger that block fear and guilt, which make you self-centered and fill you with a temporary sense of rightness, can help you push away literally any feeling or inner experience that threatens you.

Using Anger for Defense

The easiest way to understand how anger works as a defense is to see it in action. Consider the following examples.

Defending against guilt. A woman points out to her husband that he spends so much time at business and Rotary Club meetings that he is a stranger to his children. He defends himself from the guilt with the trigger thought that his wife has turned his children into self-indulgent brats. "The whole house is a playpen," he says. "You let them wreck it, you live with it." Then follows the explosion.

Defending against hurt. Marjorie has her first major job with an ad agency. When she brings home a direct mail piece that she wrote for an important client, her father makes several nitpicking suggestions. Marjorie defends against this hurt with a trigger thought: "He never changes. The same perfectionist shit." Abruptly she rises. "Thanks for the support," she says in a deadly voice.

Defending against loss. Sheila's best friend, Anne, is marrying and moving to Canada. Anne is preoccupied with finishing at work, packing, out-of-town guests, and last-minute details. Sheila defends against feelings of loss with a trigger thought that Anne is stupid and unliberated to sacrifice her career and friends for this one relationship. Sheila has to really fire up her anger to cover the enormity of the loss. Two days before the wedding she attacks Anne for "dumping everyone who ever cared about her." At the reception they barely speak, and Anne leaves town before the damage is repaired.

Defending against feeling helpless or trapped. Last year, Mateo had a heart attack. For twenty years he's worked as the only typesetter for a small weekly newspaper. He's expected to stay long, unpredictable hours to meet production deadlines. He has two girls in college and a feeling that his age and health history would make it hard to find new employment. The newspaper seems familiar and safe, but the deadlines create overwhelming stress. Mateo defends against the feeling of helplessness with the trigger thought that his girls wanted to go to "expensive party schools" even if it killed him to pay for it. Whenever his daughters come home to visit, he picks fights with them.

Defending against anxiety or fear. Tony screams and then spanks his two-year-old son for venturing off the curb. The anger blocks the jolt of fear he feels that a car might hit his child.

Rebecca is afraid that Jim is slipping away from her. He calls less often and their dates are spaced further apart. She defends herself with the trigger thought that Jim abuses women. She thinks that he keeps her waiting as part of a game of deliberate mental cruelty. And Rebecca grows more remote with each date.

Andy is secretary of a union local. Recent bargaining reversals make him expect that he'll be voted out. He cuts off his anxiety with the trigger thought, "They want everything, but they're too spineless to get it." He becomes increasingly abrasive with members.

Defending against the feeling of being bad, wrong, or unworthy. A driver waits at an intersection while a pedestrian saunters slowly in front of him. He feels rage. The pedestrian's message seems to be "You don't count, you're nothing." And that message ties directly into feelings he had as a child of being ignored and discounted. His anger defends him from all those feelings as he hits the horn and shouts through the window.

A woman's boyfriend declines a sexual advance. Immediately she is flooded with feelings of being unattractive. She defends herself with the trigger thought that "He's controlling, he's only interested in sex if he can be in charge." She rolls him over to tell him so.

A couple's daughter is caught stealing at school. On the way to a conference with the principal, they both feel inadequate as parents. They conspire to fight about who should take the car in for a tune-up as a cover for these feelings.

Defending against emptiness. Two graduate students are trying to have a relationship. As the semester progresses, Arthur finds himself more and more out of contact with Jean. Their evenings are spent reading and working on papers. An emptiness, very much like the ache for attention and nourishment he felt as a child, begins to grow in Arthur. He withdraws sexually. He begins to do crossword puzzles compulsively. He buys a telescope to look into people's windows. When these lesser measures fail to hold the emptiness in check, Arthur covers it with the trigger thought that Jean doesn't care about him and simply uses him for stability to get through grad school. He screams this charge one night, and they actually have sex. But within a week things are the same as ever.

Defending against frustrated desire (sour grapes). A divorced dad spends Saturdays with his son. He yearns for the child during the week and rents the boy's favorite *Tweety and Sylvester* cartoons for the coming visit. During the cartoon, he wants his son to sit next to him, to be close. But the boy keeps jumping up to play and make noise. To block the pain of his frustrated desire, the father thinks, "He's acting wild." So he shouts, "You can't control yourself. Sit down now or I'll never rent cartoons again."

Nearly everyone has at some time used anger to defend against painful feelings. The problem comes when you make a habit of it, when the frequency and intensity of your anger defense begins to affect your health or your relationships. Some people become addicted to anger as a way to spare themselves any experience that is threatening or painful. The person who deep down feels bad or worthless learns to blow up at the slightest criticism rather than experience even a moment of self-doubt. The person who is afraid to feel fear learns to attack and blame rather than endure a moment of anxiety.

The Addictive Nature of Defense

It's hard to let go of anger after you've learned to employ it as a defense. It always seems as if the anger is easier to feel than fear or hurt or guilt or emptiness. And of course it is. *At that moment.* All addictions feel good at the moment, all addictions serve to block pain, and all addictions offer a short-term feeling of control and well-being.

The problem with addiction is never in the moment, but in the aftermath. The long-term effects of chronic anger on health and relationships have been discussed in previous chapters. There is a third and equally damaging effect from addictive anger. *In everything except direct threat, anger tends to lead you away from appropriate action.* When you use anger to block painful feelings, you never get to deal with the feelings themselves. And you never get to address the problem that generated the feelings to begin with.

Anger keeps you from dealing with the source of fear. Fear derives from one of two things: misattributions (distorted and exaggerated perceptions of danger) or actual danger. Consider Irma's case as an example of misattribution. She was convinced that her sixteen-year-old son was a heavy drug user. She buried her fear underneath frequent outbursts about his clothes, choice of friends, sexual activities and, of course, his suspected drug use. Her son, whose drug use consisted of smoking marijuana once a week, dismissed her as a "person whose IQ approaches absolute zero." Anger prevented her from getting accurate information about her fears. She had no way of correcting her misattribution because her communications had a blaming rather than fact-finding function.

Anger not only prevents you from correcting fear-inducing distortions, it stops you from effectively coping with real threats. A man who had been mugged in a dangerous neighborhood railed against his company for relocating in the "knock-you-down-for-a-dollar part of town." For months he talked about the details of the mugging and the poor treatment he received from the police, made racial slurs, and began referring to every young man on the street as a "fucking thief." His anger prevented him from dealing effectively with the danger. There were choices he could make: he could buy a car, stop working late, arrange for a lift home, or even get a job in a safer part of town. He failed to explore a single one of these options because he wasn't motivated to. His anger was masking most of his fear; he simply wasn't scared enough to make an adaptive decision.

Anger keeps you from dealing with your pathological critic. This is the voice inside of you, spawned by hurt, neglect, and criticism from your parents, that attacks you for every flaw and imperfection. It's the pathological critic who makes you feel wrong and bad and worthless when you make a mistake or when you're criticized. It's the critic who internally abuses you when you fail to live up to your highest standards. Some people are in so much pain from their critic that they learn to turn it loose on the world rather than go on feeling worthless and bad. If they can just make the mistake someone else's fault, if they can just find some reason to attack and blame, they can shut off the chanting inner voice that keeps saying "bad, bad, wrong."

The trouble with using anger to calm your critic is that you never learn to talk back to its abuse. You never cope directly with the crippling things it says to you. Harold was a trombone player in a major symphony orchestra and a perfectionist about his playing. His pathological critic would denigrate an entire performance if his tone was unsatisfactory for a few notes. But he learned to shut these feelings off by focusing on the performance of other musicians in his section. He raged about sloppiness, lack of preparation, and "musical incompetence that should have been obvious at their audition." Expecting the worst from others became a psychological trademark. The real problem was never addressed: low self-esteem and a killer critic.

Anger keeps you from examining the values that generate your guilt. Guilt results from a collision between needs and values. Sometimes the values are healthy and appropriate; sometimes they are not. Arlene worked for an attorney who frequently was poorly prepared for hearings. She helped him by preparing one- or two- page summaries of the salient issues in each case before he appeared in court. Whenever he was embarrassed or lost a case, she blamed herself and then defended against the guilt by criticizing her daughter's schoolwork when she got home. Anger kept Arlene from questioning her values. Was she really responsible for the incompetence of her employer? Was it her job to anticipate every pitfall of a case?

The other side of the coin is also true. Many people run from guilt generated by appropriate and healthy values. A man who had custody of his fifteen-year-old daughter was rarely home to supervise her. He dealt with his guilt by denouncing her as "undisciplined and irresponsible, a nightmare on 12th Street." Here, the anger prevented a reexamination of his behavior and a square look at how his night life was incompatible with good parenting.

Anger keeps you from facing loss. Chronic anger prevents you from grieving, from letting go. You just keep replaying the sins and violations of the person who abandoned you. The short-term effect is that you don't have to feel sad. The long-term consequences are symptoms of unresolved grief and the inability to trust or bond with others. Serena was a topflight model who suffered minor facial scarring in an auto accident. She railed at the plastic surgeon's incompetence, filed a lawsuit, and dumped the boyfriend whose driving led to the accident. Anger helped to keep the grief away. She thought very little about a new career, about decisions that lay ahead. But her bitterness was palpable when she interviewed for jobs as a receptionist or salesperson.

Anger keeps you from saying what hurts. Angry people don't talk about their pain. They talk about the faults of others. No one knows how much they hurt, how wounded they are by a remark or gesture. While the short-term effect of anger is to block feelings of hurt, the long-term consequences are that no one ever learns to recognize or accommodate vulnerabilities.

Arnie feels hurt whenever his wife mentions his recent six-month period of unemployment. He sees himself as an incompetent breadwinner, so he counters with a discussion of her spending habits or picks a fight about their inability to save. Arnie's wife never hears about his hurt, and the core problem is never communicated. The truth is that she would gladly change her behavior if she only knew.

Anger keeps you helpless by stopping problem solving. When you're angry it's hard to fix things. You feel like a victim; life seems out of your control. Although the deep frustration of feeling stuck can be somewhat masked by anger, the impulse to blame or attack prevents you from real problem solving. As in the case of the man who was mugged or the model who was disfigured, anger works in the short term to keep feelings of helplessness at bay. The long-term consequence is that important decisions never get made. And your self-defeating behavior remains unexamined.

Anger keeps you empty. Anger damages the very relationships that are the source of nourishment. Laurie's husband is a sports addict; she hates the sound of football because she associates it with loneliness and isolation. But the more she complains, the more her husband withdraws into the games. Anger keeps Laurie from taking more effective steps to increase the level of intimacy in her relationship.

Coping with the Underlying Feeling

It's a hard thing to face, but your anger defense is more harmful than the pain that it's designed to obscure. To understand the role your anger plays in defense, go back to your anger diary. Review every anger incident for the past three-week period. Analyze these events; ask yourself which feeling the anger covered. Write the feeling down in red ink next to each anger entry.

Now you have some hard data. You may notice that one or two feelings predominate. Or that you experience different underlying feelings with different people. One man found that he frequently felt guilt about his daughter but helplessness with his wife. Another reported feeling an underlying experience of fear in nearly every anger episode.

If you have trouble contacting the underlying feeling, ask yourself this question for each anger incident: "What would I have to feel if I *didn't* get angry in this scene?" Imagine yourself continuing the scene and the dialogue or action unfolding without the protection of your anger. Use your visualization skills to fully experience the sights, sounds, and sensations of the event. Without anger, what are you left to feel inside?

The work that lies ahead now may be difficult, and it will require a real commitment. It's time to begin to face and feel the emotions your anger has blocked. What follows are specific steps you may wish to take in working with these underlying feelings.

Facing fear. Step 1 is to identify your catastrophic thoughts. Examine the anger scenes where the underlying feeling is fear or anxiety. Fear is always generated by a catastrophic image or belief. What dangerous or painful thing are you expecting to happen? What vision of the future does your fear paint for you? What's the nightmare, the worst-case scenario? As you review situations where you've covered fear with anger, make a list of your catastrophic expectations. For some it will be the same fear over and over—for example, the fear of being rejected or humiliated. Others will have great variety in their catastrophic projections.

Now for each catastrophic fear that you uncover, try to restate your concern using three guidelines:

- Strive for accuracy rather than exaggeration.

- Be specific rather than general.

- Include your tools to cope if the worst should happen.

Raymond's catastrophic fear was that his supervisor was displeased with his work and planning to fire him and that he would end up losing his newly purchased home. He realized that a more accurate statement about his job was that he had no idea how his supervisor felt about him. His supervisor had asked him to be more prompt with sales reports, but there had been no other feedback. Raymond decided that he needed to do two things to cope. First, he needed to ask his supervisor for some informal feedback on his performance. Second, he needed a fallback plan to handle his worst-case scenario of losing his job.

Here's how Raymond restated his catastrophic fear: "I have no idea how my supervisor feels. The only feedback I have is that he wants the sales reports on time. I'm going to arrange a worst-case contingency plan with my parents for getting a loan if I can't meet house payments. Then I'll ask my supervisor how I'm doing."

In Maria's log, she found again and again the fear of being exposed as incompetent. She was enraged if her boyfriend said anything about her cooking, her driving, her use of makeup, or her parenting of her six-year-old daughter. The catastrophic fear was "Everyone will see how incompetent I am." Striving for accuracy, Maria reminded herself that her boyfriend generally liked her cooking, she had a good driving record, men obviously thought her attractive, and her daughter seemed basically loving and happy. In none of these areas had she been exposed as incompetent to the world. The only evidence against her were private observations made by her boyfriend. She decided to cope by forcing herself to hear out his criticism, acknowledge it, and point out to him any balancing realities. Maria restated her catastrophic fear like this: "I'm an adequate cook, I'm attractive, I'm a good driver, and my daughter is clearly happy. My boyfriend's criticisms are just between us, and no one needs to know about it. I can hear what he says, but I'll also tell him the balancing realities."

When it's clear to you that your perception of danger is very real and very accurate, put your energy into brainstorming new ways to cope. Here's a condensation of the problem-solving strategies presented in chapter 11.

- List as many alternative solutions as you can think of. Quantity is better than quality. Don't evaluate your ideas, just keep them coming. The more fresh, unusual, or bizarre the better.

- When you have a list of between ten and twenty alternative solutions, begin ruling out the obviously unworkable ones. With the solutions that remain, list the positive and negative consequences for each one. Make sure that the consequences include both short- and long-term outcomes.

- Now select one or more alternative solutions that you would like to try. Decide on the first step you need to take toward implementation.

The key to dealing with real danger is effective action. You need to make a decision and carry it out.

Facing the fear of unworthiness. This is perhaps the greatest psychological pain a human being can endure: the feeling of not being good enough, not being adequate. Although its roots lie in your relationship with your parents, the feeling of unworthiness is promoted every day of your life by the constant attacks of your pathological inner critic. The first step to coping with feelings of unworthiness is to really hear what the critic is saying to you. Go back to anger situations where the underlying feeling was being wrong or bad. What were you saying to yourself? How is your critic putting you down?

It's time to restate what the critic is saying. Use these four rules:

1. Make the statement accurate rather than exaggerated.

2. Make it specific rather than general.

3. Use nonpejorative language.

4. Include balancing realities.

The critic always exaggerates, always generalizes, and frequently uses language that has demeaning connotations. On the other side of the ledger, the critic never points out your strengths, abilities, or good points. Jane's critic was always on her for being "ugly." Jane's sister and girlfriends frequently brought up the issue of her weight and endless dieting. Sometimes they joked, sometimes they asked serious questions about her eating habits. On each occasion, Jane seethed inside. Her angry trigger thoughts helped drown for a while the critic who was shouting, "You're fat, you're fat." Jane decided to state the critic's attack using accurate, specific, nonpejorative language: "I weigh 150. I'd like to lose 30 pounds." For a balancing reality, Jane pointed out to herself that she had not gained weight in two years, that she had bought an attractive wardrobe rather than waiting to lose the pounds, and that she liked certain parts of her body (her legs, eyes, and breasts). Jane resolved to use her new statement as a way of talking back each time her critic harangued her. It felt particularly important to her to make the balancing statements that acknowledge things that she valued in herself.

Special note. A deeply held belief in your badness may be a result of early trauma. People who were abandoned, neglected, or seriously abused often feel that the trauma happened because they were bad or because they invited it. If this feels true for you, it could be extremely helpful to see a trained psychotherapist.

Facing guilt. As you review the scenes in your anger diary where anger covers an underlying experience of guilt, ask yourself this question: "What is the rule for how I am supposed to be or act that I violated in this situation?" You may have one rule that emerges again and again, or there may be a variety of rules that strongly influence your behavior. Whether there are one or many, these rules have a rigid, absolute quality. To break them is to be bad. These rules also stand in opposition to some important need you have. Otherwise, you wouldn't be acting to violate them.

Once you've identified a rule that generates guilt, you can begin to examine it. Is this your rule? Does it come from your own experience? Or is it the rule of a parent or some authority figure that you've accepted without question? Is the rule flexible? Does it allow for unusual or mitigating circumstances? Or is it written in stone without possible exceptions? Is the rule realistic? Is it based on real and likely consequences for your acts? Or is it based on strict, unbending concepts of what's right and wrong? Is your rule life-affirming? Does it support taking care of yourself in a way that's healthy for you and those you love? Or is it life-constricting, denying you access to important sources of nourishment and satisfaction?

You are feeling guilt because your needs are in conflict with a rule or value. Now ask yourself this question: Is your need more important in this situation than the rule? Should the rule be made more flexible, more supportive? You may wish to rewrite the rule so that you are allowed to pursue certain needs in specific situations.

If you feel good about your rule, if your value makes sense to you, then your guilt is a healthy response to behavior you want to stop. Your greatest enemy now is denial, the response of running away from a feeling that signals a need to change. The guilt is your ally, a necessary source of pain that can push you to make the tough choice between your rule and the behavior that conflicts with it.

If guilt alone is insufficient to motivate change, this can only mean that you don't have enough support to stop the harmful or inappropriate behavior. You may need to join an appropriate twelve-step program or a support group to stop violence or improve your communication or deal with sexual acting out. Perhaps you need a training group such as those offered by parent-effectiveness programs. Many people get support by telling their friends about a problem and making a contract for specific changes. Regular check-in times are built into the contract and the friend agrees to monitor your progress.

Cheryl was guilty about blowing up at her children. She covered the guilt with more anger about the condition of their room, their slowness getting dressed, their dawdling over meals, and so on. She asked herself what rule she was violating to generate such guilt. She recognized that she felt a very strong prohibition against shouting at her kids. The rule seemed to be her own, rather than an old idea borrowed from her parents. The rule seemed flexible (it was okay for her to shout sometimes). The rule seemed realistic in that she felt that very negative consequences could develop for her children's self-esteem if she barraged them with angry criticism. The rule was also life affirming in that it supported her children's growth while allowing her to express needs and criticism in a nonpejorative way.

Cheryl decided that her rule was okay, and the guilt was appropriate. It was her behavior that had to change. She enrolled in a parent-training group and found more effective ways to set limits than her old strategy of shouting.

Facing grief. When you become aware that anger is covering loss, you can arm yourself with this mantra: "He (or She or It) is gone. I am angry so that I won't feel the loss." If you say this each time that the anger emerges, you will gradually develop greater contact with your basic feelings of grief. Whatever the nature of the loss, your work now is to begin letting go. Set at least half an hour aside each day to mourn (or more if your loss is a recent or grave one). Mourning means reminiscing, appreciating, regretting, but most of all feeling the sadness of surrendering and giving up the lost person or object.

It is important to trust the grief process. People run from grief because they (1) resist pain and (2) are afraid of being overwhelmed and engulfed by the powerful feelings. The truth is that the human psyche is set up to experience grief (or any pain) in a sequence of waves. The awareness of a loss hits with crushing intensity. The pain goes on until you reach a natural shutting down process. There's a respite, a quietness, perhaps even a numbness in the middle of the pain. After the rest and numbness comes another wave, and so on.

Grief can be enormous. But when it reaches overwhelming proportions, the natural shutting down process gives you time to get your breath. You can "work through" grief by letting the waves happen and remembering they will pass before their intensity overwhelms your abilities to cope.

Two years ago, Harold's girlfriend moved out. He is still angry and still talks about her to friends. He focuses on her withdrawal and her failure to communicate and on a conviction he has that she secretly planned to leave for many months. He counts her sins and transgressions like beads on a rosary of blame. But the real function of Harold's anger is to effectively block feelings of grief. While he holds on to her with his anger, he never has to face the loss.

Harold began his recovery process by using the mantra "She's gone, I get angry to stop feeling sad." He repeated this sentence internally each time he noticed himself slipping into his familiar obsession. He decided to set aside a half hour each day from 6:30 to 7:00 to mourn their time together. He assembled a group of pictures and mementos. Harold focused on the good that was lost and let the grief well up in him. Over time, he began to recognize that he could rarely sustain feelings of grief for more than five to ten minutes. He saw this as the natural limits of the wave and reduced his sessions of mourning to a shorter interval.

Facing hurt. Hurt ranges from feeling slightly neglected or discounted all the way to an overwhelming sense of abandonment. If you find a propensity to cover hurt with anger in your diary, then anger should be a signal for you to ask yourself, "What hurts me?"

Hurt is either realistic or unrealistic. Unrealistic hurt occurs when a small slight or criticism triggers deep feelings of unworthiness based on your early relationship with your parents. If you feel that this describes your case, return to the section earlier in this chapter on facing the fear of unworthiness. Hurt can also be a realistic response to a current slight, criticism, or rejection. Realistic hurt is usually far less painful. You still feel basically good about yourself, even though something is wrong with your current interaction. Sometimes hurt has both realistic and unrealistic components. The hurt that you feel when a friend arrives late may also trigger echoes of earlier experiences of neglect.

The active work in facing your hurt is to acknowledge it— openly and directly. Anger is always blaming and accusatory. It's focused on the other person. To communicate hurt, you must find a way to convey what hurts without implying that the other person is bad or wrong to have caused it.

Ariel was a short-order cook who felt close to most of the waitresses in the diner. Susan had an acerbic, biting humor that Ariel usually liked, but also found grating at times. Whenever a customer sent food back, Susan would joke about Ariel's incompetence. "Eggs a little slimy, babe?" These remarks hurt. Ariel found herself reacting with trigger thoughts such as "You want to cook, bitch?" As a result, she grew more distant from Susan.

After Ariel began to recognize her use of anger to cover hurt, she would ask herself "What hurts?" whenever Susan's behavior triggered anger. She decided to express her feelings to Susan and settled on this response: "When you joke like that, it makes me feel bad about my cooking." It was important not to convey in the message that Susan was doing something wrong. Only that Ariel was feeling hurt and hoped that Susan would cool the cooking jokes.

Facing helplessness. Anger obscures the feeling of helplessness in two ways. First, it keeps you from experiencing how stuck you are by putting all your attention on the failings of others. You're so concerned with their selfishness, their mistakes, and their stupidity that your own sense of impotence is never fully faced. Second, by shifting the blame to other people, you don't have to take responsibility for your own decisions or failures to act that led you to feeling so stuck.

Facing helplessness requires that you give up the crutch of blame. Anger won't change anything. People will keep doing what *they* need to do, not what *you* need them to do. The first step in facing helplessness is to take full responsibility for being stuck right now. Look back at the specific choices you made, both to act and not to act, that led you to your current circumstances. Right now you need to accept that the ways you chose to cope, your game plan, your strategy for getting your needs met, fell short of the mark.

Step 2 in dealing with helplessness is to generate a new set of coping options. If you've begun to face your own responsibility for being stuck, then you are ready to face the fact that *you are the only one who can solve your problem*. You are the one in pain, you are the one whose needs are unmet. You are also the one who knows best what you require to feel better.

To generate new options for coping, you should develop a clearly stated goal. What must you achieve to feel unstuck, to lift the burden of helplessness? Make sure that the goal is concrete and specific. Write it down. If you're having trouble formulating a goal, ask yourself what specific thing you want that you don't have or what source of pain you want remedied. Now brainstorm some alternative solutions and proceed with the problem-solving strategies described in the beginning of this section on facing fear. If none of your solutions seem to offer much improvement over the current situation, it's time to go back to brainstorming. But this time involve your friends, your family, and any trusted adviser in the process of developing new ideas. Tell them that you don't expect them to give you the right answer, but that you just want to hear all the new ideas or perspectives that they can think of. Don't forget to remind them that wild and crazy ideas are acceptable too. The third step in coping with helplessness is to take action. You have decided on a new coping strategy. You need to take the initial step toward implementing it. Decide now on what that step is and when exactly you will begin.

Joe had worked for the past three years as a gofer at a major newspaper. He was stuck on the lowest rung of the ladder and he blamed his boss for it. "He won't give me any responsibility. He trusts me with nothing. He's a condescending, rat-faced little man." Joe's first task was to begin taking responsibility for his own experience of helplessness. He looked back at the things he had done and not done over the past years. He had decided to take a high-paying warehouse job when he was eighteen, rather than go to college. He lost this job when he picked a fight with his boss. He had enjoyed a vacation paid for by unemployment insurance for the next six months and then taken his current job in desperation when his money ran out. He had wanted to go back to school, but felt intimidated by the effort that he'd need to make to hold down a nine-to-five job plus evening classes. He had also thought of applying for other jobs inside the newspaper, but had never really mobilized himself. He knew that he should do a resume, but had never written one.

Having taken responsibility for his current dilemma, Joe identified a specific goal. "I want to be a reporter. I want to see my byline." He generated over two dozen alternative solutions. Joe settled on starting night classes in journalism at a local community college. He planned to assemble a portfolio of writing that he could use later in job applications. The first step toward action would be calling the college to request an application packet.

Facing feelings of emptiness. Feelings of loneliness and emptiness are so painful that some people will do anything to block them from awareness. The key here, as with all the other difficult feelings, is to separate blame from pain. You need to experience your loneliness directly without linking it to a fault or failing in others. To accomplish this, you will need to literally encourage the feeling.

Since loneliness is extremely painful, you will have to arrange for it to come up in brief, manageable chunks. Set a time limit so that the feeling doesn't overwhelm you:

- Take a ten-minute walk on an isolated part of the beach.

- Sit alone for ten minutes, concentrating only on counting your breaths.

- Spend fifteen minutes in a place where you once felt happy and close to someone.

- Concentrate on exploring feelings of boredom and loneliness for ten minutes just before turning to some distracting activity.

- Turn off the radio and TV and just sit in silence for twenty minutes in your living room.

- Resist your impulse to call someone. Notice what it's like to postpone the contact for ten minutes or so.

- Place a chair in the middle of the backyard and sit in it for fifteen minutes.

Some of these exercises will make you more aware of your loneliness. Paradoxically, some of them may generate a strange sense of calm. The important thing is to notice what you feel like when you're not running away from your experience by getting angry. When you can just feel your loneliness without blaming anyone, you're taking a big step toward improving relationships with others. At this point, you have two ways to go. One is to learn more about yourself by expanding the periods during which you contact your aloneness. You may learn that aloneness brings up other uncomfortable feelings: guilt, grief, or a sense of unworthiness. These underlying feelings may require special attention and working through (as described in earlier sections of this chapter). Or you may learn that your emptiness includes painful memories from the past. (You may find it helpful to seek professional help if these memories are disturbing or hard to shake.)

Your loneliness may just be an ache, a yearning for attachment. It may be a long-held dream of a certain kind of closeness and partnership. Here the second part for dealing with loneliness presents itself. If your loneliness does seem focused on a need for intimacy, then direct action may really help. It may be time to make a clear decision (frightening as it may seem) to join a hiking group or go to a single's dance or begin participating in a political action group. If you already have close relationships, yet are haunted by feelings of dissatisfaction, you may take action by initiating activities that promote closeness and intimacy. Create a candlelight evening of massage, a weekend in the country, an interesting sexual variation, a great dinner out, and so on. Just turning the television off so that you can talk may be an important decision. Whatever you decide to do, make sure that you take full responsibility for generating the experience that you want. You are going to have to lead; hopefully your friend or partner will follow. Years of blaming the other person can make initiating the hardest task in the world. Why should you suggest anything new when it's always their turn to do something, their responsibility to fix what's wrong. In truth, the only one who can make a difference is you. You need the closeness, and you will have to find a way to ask for it or create experiences of sharing that meet this fundamental need.

Maria's boyfriend is a tennis nut who plays two evenings a week and both mornings on the weekend. For Maria, the loneliness and anger were always interwoven. She considered his tennis playing to be selfish and compulsive.

In the initial stages of facing the emptiness, Maria began taking brief walks on the beach while her boyfriend played on the weekend. She practiced just feeling the loneliness without making him responsible for the pain. Somehow, by removing the anger, several solutions became clear to her. She decided to continue her walks on Sunday and sign up for a painting class on Saturday. She asked her boyfriend to spend one weekend afternoon taking a country hike with her. In this new shared activity, she found it possible to have a closeness that she looked forward to all week. The emptiness was still there sometimes, but Maria felt more confident in her ability to cope.

Making Your Own Plan

As you begin to let go of anger as a defense, you can experiment with the suggestions offered in this chapter. Some will help, and some won't work for you at all. In time you may develop strategies of your own to deal with underlying feelings. What's important is to stick with your commitment to see through your anger to the feelings underneath and to find new ways of responding to parts of yourself that once lay buried under layers of blame and upset.

18

Road Rage

Anger displays behind the wheel have become the norm rather than the exception. It has been established that, in the United States alone, road rage contributes to 1,673 accidents per year, 2,102 injuries, and 40 fatalities. (AAA Foundation for Traffic Safety 1997). The plain truth is that angry people are impulsive and they often do very unwise things. When they are behind the wheel controlling several thousand pounds of machinery, the itch for payback and revenge can too easily end in catastrophe. There are hidden consequences of road rage that no one's writing about in the newspapers. First among them is the helpless suffering of passengers whose driver has gone berserk—yelling, honking, gesturing, weaving, chasing. Road rage is responsible for literally millions of hours of fear and stress on the part of auto passengers each year. It's no fun wondering if you'll be killed because someone you ordinarily trust has gone crazy in the driver's seat. And it's no fun listening to the venom, the curses. It's a safe bet that road rage affects relationships—long after everyone gets out of the car.

The second hidden consequence of road rage is its impact on your body. Chapter 3, "The Physiological Costs of Anger," documents how hostility negatively affects your cardiovascular system and increases mortality from all causes. It's no accident that commuters have shorter life spans than folks who do less driving. One probable contributor to their increased mortality is that they are exposed for hours each day to high levels of frustration, with large and small spikes of anger throughout.

Enough said—road rage is no good for you. The big question now is what can you do about it? As it turns out, there's a lot you can do to change and cope with your anger behind the wheel. The first step is learn to relax in the car.

How to Relax While Driving

Relaxing your body. A physical change you can make involves learning to relax your diaphragm, the locus of much physical stress. In chapter 10, "Controlling Stress Step by Step," you learned about a technique called cue-controlled relaxation. This involves using cue words, such as "let go" or "relax," or "release," while exhaling a deep, diaphragmatic breath. The idea is to relax away the tension in every muscle of your body—while you simultaneously let go of the breath and mentally say your cue words.

If you haven't learned cue-controlled relaxation, do it now. Read the instructions and practice the technique over the next week. As you'll see in chapter 10, there are two foundation skills you have to learn before you can do cue-controlled relaxation. These are (1) progressive muscle relaxation, and (2) relaxation without tension. Cue-controlled relaxation will not be nearly as effective without first mastering these two prerequisite skills.

Cue-controlled relaxation is such a powerful technique that you can use it to fully relax your body in thirty to sixty seconds—any time, anywhere. It's great behind the wheel because it's so quick and easy. We recommend taking three cue-controlled breaths before starting your engine—every time you get in the car. That way you will begin your trip in a relaxed state.

As your trip progresses, keep taking cue-controlled breaths. Take one every time a new song comes on the radio, every time you have to slow down, every time someone pulls in front of you. Take three when traffic congestion gets bad, when someone drives foolishly, when someone honks at you and looks angry. Keep doing cue-controlled breathing until it becomes second nature. And use it *particularly* when there's provocation—when people slow you down, cut you off, or drive disrespectfully or dangerously.

Changing your attitude. People who get angry behind the wheel share a number of common attitudes. Here are some of them:

1. Everyone in a car should be skilled and courteous, and if they aren't (here's the important part) they are bad or stupid people who deserve to be punished. The problem is that a percentage of people who drive *aren't* skilled or courteous, and most people who drive have occasional lapses. This is reality. It won't change. There's nothing you can do about it. Getting angry just damages your health and the relationships with your passengers.

Now let's look at a key assumption—people who drive badly should be punished. Why? Because it will make them better drivers? You already know that doesn't work. Because justice requires they be paid back for driving misdeeds? Imagine if everyone on the road saw him- or herself as a vigilante, punishing driving mistakes as they saw fit. The road would be a far more scary, more dangerous place. Ask yourself, "Who appointed me judge and jury of Highway 5?"

2. No one on the road should impede your progress toward your destination. But there are dozens of ways other drivers slow you down—cutting in front, doing the snail crawl, being too timid during a left turn, looking for an address or street sign, double parking, and so on. What can you really do about it? Folks in front of you will keep driving like that as long as there are cars and roads. The only choice you have is how you react to it. While in the car, say to yourself, "I choose not to react."

3. You have to arrive on time or when you're expected. But the world isn't arranged to help you be punctual. People gawk at accidents. They travel at a slow crawl. They speed by on the inside lane, then cut in front of you. It never fails. The only answer is to plan to be delayed. Assume that people are going to slow you down. Expect the inevitable delays.

4. People only care about themselves, they don't think about anyone else on the road. That's right. A lot of drivers are like that. And no amount of road rage will change human nature. What matters is not how things should be, but how things are. Fighting reality will just result in high blood pressure or an early stroke.

5. If you're in pain, it's someone else's fault. When you feel frustrated, stressed, or scared of the testosterone-driven nitwits, it feels good, for a moment, to blame someone else. But this is just the way it is—the road, the people on it. Life is often painful, and driving makes it worse. But the crazy, incompetent drivers are not responsible for your suffering. Anymore than the car is. Or the road. They are just part of the driving experience. Like potholes— or a sign that says, "No gas next 47 miles."

6. Bad or selfish drivers are being personally disrespectful to you. They can certainly seem that way, but how *personal* is it? They don't know you. If they notice you at all, you're just another car on the road. A hunk of moving metal—not a person. They're just trying to get where they're going—no doubt thoughtlessly, perhaps unsafely. Remind yourself: "This (the other person's driving) has nothing to do with me."

Now we know the attitudes that don't work. Are there attitudes that can keep you more relaxed behind the wheel? The answer is a resounding yes. There are four key attitude shifts that greatly reduce anger on the road.

1. *I'll get there when I get there.* Let go of control; you can't change any of the conditions on the road. From the moment you get in the car, you have to surrender both to the traffic and every decision made by other drivers. Your key coping thought: "Let go, I can't make this any different."

2. *People are people.* Some are foolish, rushed, inconsiderate, or aggressive. They are what they are, not what you want them to be. Can you change them? No. Can you teach them? Not on your life. Will you feel any better if you rage at them? Not in the long run. So what can you do? Before you get in the car, make a decision to accept everything you see and experience on the road. You won't fight it—you're going to let people be themselves.

3. *People do what they want to do, not what they should do.* No one really cares about your rules of driving behavior and etiquette. They stop to let people out, blocking traffic whenever they want to. Your rule that they should pull into a driveway means diddly-squat to them. Your rule that they should think about the folks behind them ranks exactly *nada* among their concerns. What can you do? Accept the "People do what they want to do" rule of human nature; repeat it to yourself when you see some lunatic at the wheel.

4. *It's just a bad moment—that's all.* How long is this road bummer going to last? Thirty seconds? Two minutes? Five minutes, tops? Most driving affronts don't last long, so put them in perspective. It's not cancer, you're not getting fired, your son didn't flunk out of college. It's just an irritating moment in time—and it will soon be over. Focus on how minor and time-limited this is. Remind yourself in the car: "This is a small problem in the scheme of things."

Choose Three Coping Thoughts

Review the four key attitudes listed above, and extract three coping thoughts that would help you behind the wheel. Write them down on a file card or small piece of paper. Tape it to your dashboard. Read your coping thoughts *every* time you start the engine. Memorize them. Take a deep breath and say them to yourself each time some idiot does something he (or she) shouldn't.

Ten Key Road Rage Strategies

1. **Keep taking cue-controlled breaths and reminding yourself of your coping thoughts.** If you wait till you're upset to initiate relaxation strategies, you simply won't remember to do them.

2. **Take a mental time-out when another driver provokes you.** At the first sign of annoyance, shift your attention to something interesting. For a mental time-out to be effective, you have to decide what you're going to think about *before* you start driving. Maybe you'd like to begin planning your next vacation, or a wonderful night out, or focus on sexual or romantic fantasies. The point is to identify something you'll enjoy thinking about, and hold it in reserve to distract yourself with when you start to feel irritated.

3. **Make sure you have relaxing music tapes or CDs in your car.** Be sure to *play* them when you begin to feel stressed.

4. **Make use of distracting activities.** Radio talk shows, books on tape, or news stations usually offer something to distract your attention from the problems of driving. If there's someone in the car, try to start up a conversation that gets your mind off all the fools on the road. Whatever you do, however, don't talk about the drivers who annoy you—that's only going to inflame your anger.

5. **Occupy yourself with problem solving.** Plan out a work project, mentally rearrange the living room, develop a strategy to keep track of your kid's homework. Some people plan whole books (like this one) in the car.

6. **Ignore provocations.** When you witness poor driving, look elsewhere and say to yourself, "It's just the road," or "That's par for the course," or "It's the usual."

7. **Avoid epithets.** Never describe another driver with pejorative labels—either out loud or in your own mind. That just inflames you; it pushes the anger meter way up. Instead, say to yourself, "There goes another pothole," or "He's doing the Social Security crawl," or "There's a guy in a big hurry—must be rushing for the toilet." If you must describe bad driving, make it light. Humor helps to distance you from the provocation; it's a great antidote for irritation.

8. **Accept reality.** Tell yourself: "This guy is doing the best he can. It's not very good, but that's how he drives."

9. **Control yourself, not the other driver.** At the root of road rage is a sense of profound helplessness. People drive the way they drive—sometimes quite badly—and you have no control over

them. No matter how much you yell or fume, they just go on with their unfortunate driving behavior. What *can* you do to end the helplessness? Commit yourself to controlling your own reactions (i.e., cue-controlled breathing, distracting yourself, avoiding epithets, taking a mental time-out, etc.).

10. **Plan ahead.** When you know you're going to be faced with a stressful or provocative driving experience, decide in advance how you will cope. If you're heading into traffic, or an area of town where people double park, or a place where parking is tight and competitive, assume that you're going to be frustrated and annoyed. Then make sure you're prepared by relaxing and distracting yourself. And by reviewing the coping thoughts taped to your dashboard.

Dealing with Another Driver's Anger—The Five Don'ts

1. **Don't look.** Absolutely, the number one response is not to look at the other driver. No glaring. No eye contact whatsoever.

2. **Don't gesture.** Never make a gesture of any kind. Don't point, don't throw up your hands. Do nothing but continue to drive. Nothing.

3. **Don't touch the window.** Never roll down your window. And never make a noise the other person can hear.

4. **Don't lean on your horn**. Don't honk—ever. It will only inflame a bad situation.

5. **Don't pull over.** Never pull over to engage the offending driver. And *never* get out of your car.

The road's never going to get any better, nor are other drivers going to get nicer. Or smarter. The only thing that can change on the road is you. A commitment to relaxation and using key coping thoughts can make a huge difference in your driving experience—and for those who drive with you.

19

Anger and Children

Vicki, seven months pregnant, sat in a café drinking cappuccino and talking to her friend, Bonnie. With them was Bonnie's eighteen-month-old, whining, squirming daughter. The two adults tried in vain to talk. Bonnie was so distracted trying to keep her baby restrained in the high chair that Vicki soon gave up any attempt at conversation. Vicki could feel her unborn baby moving within her, and she imagined how wonderful it would be when the baby finally arrived. Her baby would be calm—not fussy and crying all the time like Bonnie's. In this moment of perfect symbiosis, Vicki felt that her baby was close and quiet and perfect.

Before you had children, you might have had fantasies about how you would feel and act as a parent. You would strive to be loving and patient. You would provide explanations, not give orders. You would discuss, not overpower. You may have been critical of other parents who were impatient, inconsistent, too lenient, or too strict. You certainly would never feel anger.

You now know how difficult it is to achieve those ideals. It is not necessarily true that if you love your children, if you are conscientious and aware, you will be immune to anger. You cannot automatically assume that you will always rise above the little upsets in parenting and handle conflict with intelligence and good humor. Being a parent tests your patience, your flexibility, wisdom, and endurance like no other career and no other relationship.

When you look at the working conditions of your job as a parent, you can see why many parents feel exhausted and stressed.

1. **Long hours.** You are "in charge" every hour of every day (including weekends and holidays). If you work outside the home, your parenting job starts well before you leave the house in the

morning and resumes the moment you come home. And it doesn't end at bedtime. Infants and babies may wake frequently during the night, and your sleep might be broken by a child who is ill or has a nightmare.

2. **Children are incredibly messy.** A lot of your time and energy is spent picking up, cleaning up, or wiping up. Food, toys, clothing, and dirt spread throughout the house. Even parents of children who are responsible about cleaning up their own toys find themselves involved with encouraging, supervising, training, organizing, and supporting the cleanup effort.

3. **Children are noisy.** A household with children is a house filled with laughter, screaming, and crying. Children are constantly asking questions. Any activity that requires quiet, such as reading, phone calls, or conversation, is always a struggle.

4. **Caring for children requires that you do many repetitive and time-consuming tasks.** The laundry, shopping, and cooking never end. Children need you to transport them everywhere—to sporting events and dance classes and to the dentist.

5. **Children are self-centered.** They aren't usually aware that you are worn out, losing patience, or under a great deal of stress. Social skills, such as empathy or sensitivity to others, are learned over a long period of time.

6. **Children push the limits.** Normal children are constantly seeking autonomy. They want and need to do more for themselves, and they question your judgment and authority. From the two-year-old who has learned to say no to the rebellious teen, children push and challenge the rules in order to grow up.

7. **Children need tremendous amounts of attention and approval.** They compete with anything and anyone that takes you away from them. Their attention-getting strategies may be overt and obvious (look at me, see me, watch me), or covert and indirect (sibling rivalry, destructive behavior, low achievement at school).

8. **Children require vigilance.** They must be protected from immediate and potential dangers. Parents of young children must constantly watch the child, remaining alert for anything breakable, hot, sharp, or small enough to be swallowed. Parents of older children who play and travel away from home are always worried about bike or car accidents, the dangers of the playground, the dangers posed by strangers, and so on. No matter how vigilant you are, you never feel that your children are completely safe.

The Functions of Anger

As discussed earlier, anger helps you to block or discharge painful levels of stress. It enables you to defend against painful feelings of anxiety, hurt, guilt, worry, or loss.

Meg's fourteen-year-old daughter Kim was supposed to be home by 10:00 P.M. When Meg heard Kim's key in the lock at midnight, her anger discharged the pain of two solid hours of worry.

Eight-year-old Bobby was showing his dad a new trick he had learned on his skateboard. A car turned the corner and just narrowly missed hitting him. His father's anger at Bobby helped discharge the pain of anxiety.

Matt's mom was doing well in the hospital. But at 7:00 A.M. a nurse called to inform him that his mother had been moved to the intensive care unit. The pain of anxiety triggered an impatient outburst at his four-year-old as she dressed and prepared for school in her usual "slow as molasses" way.

Anger also helps block the stress of painful physical sensations.

After an hour of noisy and rough play, Martin's nerves were shot. When one of his children accidentally kicked him in the shin, he blew up and sent them all to bed.

Peggy was helping her daughter study for an important French test. At 10:00 at night Peggy was exhausted and found that she was being irritable and sarcastic to her daughter.

Anger also blocks the stress that develops when you are frustrated in your attempt to do something that you need or want to do.

Nancy complains that she can't even go to the bathroom alone. Her toddlers follow after her. If she closed the door, they shout and bang and cry. By midafternoon, when both children are supposed to be napping, she finally sat down with her favorite magazine and a cup of tea. When her three-year-old woke the ten-month-old, she was in a rage. She slapped the boy and tossed him back into bed. Now, with the sound of both children crying, she feels even angrier.

Children suffer from fear of abandonment, but parents are also threatened by fear of being abandoned by their children. This often leads to anger.

Sue and her parents were in perpetual conflict during her senior year in high school. She wanted to work and share an apartment with her boyfriend after graduation instead of going to junior college and living at home. The threat of losing her fueled constant fights and bickering with her parents.

Justin looked forward to seeing his dad on weekends. As he excitedly packed his bags, his mother felt rejected. She suppressed this with a stream of irritable remarks.

Effects of Anger on Children

Anger is a concern for a large percentage of parents. Over half the parents in one study said they had lost their temper and hit their child "really hard" (Frude and Goss 1979). Another 40 percent feared they might lose their temper and really hurt their child in the future. A study by McKay et al. (1996) found that two-thirds of the parents reported feeling anger to the point of shouting or screaming at their children an average of five times a week. These were normal parents with normal kids, but these parents had an intense anger episode *almost every day.*

Because anger is so common and frequent in parent-child relationships, some people have the illusion that it's harmless. But anger has a devastating effect on the emotional lives of children. It distorts their sense of self ("I must be very bad to make Mommy so mad."). It makes them feel scared and unsafe and that their lives are out of control ("Who will take care of me? Who will protect me?"). Anger makes them feel alone.

Frequent and intense parental anger helps shape a child's future behavior, academic success, social functioning, ability to be empathetic, and ability to establish and maintain healthy adult relationships. The research proves it. Korbanka and McKay (1995) found that, overall, emotional support diminishes as parental yelling, threatening, and hitting increases. In other words, as parents get more angry, their kids get less of every kind of nurturing and encouragement.

Parental Anger, Aggression, and Empathy

A study by Susan Crockenberg (1987) revealed that the children of angry and punitive mothers were themselves angry, more resistant, and noncompliant compared to children of less angry mothers. She also observed that frequent maternal anger was associated with more frequent nonempathetic reactions by toddlers when they were bystanders to someone else's distress.

For children to learn kindness, they must be treated kindly. For children to discover alternatives to anger and aggression, they have to see those alternatives demonstrated. For children to be considerate of others, their feelings and needs must be treated with consideration.

Use of Physical Punishment

The research also shows that frequency and intensity of parental anger is strongly related to the use of physical punishment.

Parents who yell often are the ones most likely to hit often (Hemenway, Solnick, and Carter 1994). Korbanka and McKay (1995) found that parents who frequently engage in verbal attacks are more likely to cross over into physical attacks such as hitting, spanking, and slapping.

If the purpose of physical punishment is to correct a child's behavior, and to "teach the child a lesson," spanking actually creates the opposite effect. Sociologist Murray Straus (1994) concluded that corporal punishment does not help a child develop an internalized conscience. It leads, instead, to more physically aggressive behavior by the child. Furthermore, the more that parents rely on hitting, the more they will have to hit to physically punish the child over time.

Hoffman (1970) studied the moral development of children and found that children who fear physical punishment tend to feel less guilt, are less willing to accept responsibility, are less resistant to temptation, and have fewer internal behavioral controls than children who are not physically punished. The child may feel that it is okay to misbehave if he is willing to take being hit, as the appropriate punishment.

Herman (1985) cites studies that show a correlation between corporal punishment and stealing, truancy, aggression, hostility, lying, depression, and low self-esteem.

Parental Anger and Overall Adjustment and Success.

A study by Abraham Tesser, et al. (1989) looked at the relationship between angry parent-child disagreements and adolescent adjustment. The researchers kept track of disagreements about forty-four specific issues, such as TV use and homework. The mothers, fathers, and adolescents rated the degree of anger on each occasion. The researchers then measured the children's adjustment, including assessments of academic competence, social competence, acting-out, depression, and grade-point average. The level of adjustment in every one of these areas was negatively related to the number of angry parent-child discussions. Moreover, adjustment in each area was *positively* related to the number of calm discussions about the same issues.

Trigger Thoughts and Escalation

As you have learned, there is nothing automatic about anger. Neither stress nor pain make you angry. A child's misbehavior, defiance, carelessness, brattiness, or acting-out is not the cause of anger. What makes you lose your temper are the beliefs and assumptions you have about that behavior. Those are trigger thoughts.

Trigger thoughts can distort a situation, making it seem bigger and the child's behavior worse than it really is. Trigger thoughts contribute to the illusion that children are "bad" on purpose, to make you mad, to frustrate or defeat you. Problem behavior is seen as intentional acts of defiance, disrespect, selfishness, or cruelty. Trigger thoughts cause you to forget to consider *other reasons* for your child's behavior. They get in the way of problem solving and addressing the underlying causes of the problem behavior. They leave you feeling helpless and out of control.

Changing the outcome of a potentially anger provoking situation requires that you be aware of the *trigger thoughts* that are fueling your anger, and replace them with *coping thoughts* that will help you calm down. Coping thoughts keep matters in perspective, acknowledge your child's level of development, his or her temperament, and possible underlying needs. They do not magnify and dramatize the situation. They keep you in control so you can communicate clearly, set limits, and solve problems.

Parental Anger Study

In a study by McKay et al. (1996), parents were interviewed about the situations that made them angry, how they dealt with those situations, and what they were thinking during the angry episode. Parents who felt more anger at their children tended to use provoking trigger thoughts significantly more often than parents who were less angry. Eighteen trigger thoughts were used much more frequently by the parents with higher anger levels. The trigger thoughts associated with the highest levels of anger were grouped into three major themes.

1. **Assumed intent.** These trigger thoughts assume that the child is misbehaving deliberately to upset you.

2. **Magnification.** These kinds of trigger thoughts make you feel the situation is worse than it actually may be.

3. **Labeling.** These trigger thoughts use negative or pejorative words or terms to describe your child.

Here is the list of the eighteen trigger thoughts associated with the highest levels of anger.

Put a checkmark in the box of any trigger thought that you recognize influences your anger at your child.

Assumed Intent

☐ 1. You're doing it to annoy me.

☐ 2. You're defying me.

☐ 3. You're trying to drive me crazy.

☐ 4. You're trying to test me (to see how far you can go).

☐ 5. You're tuning me out intentionally.

☐ 6. You're taking advantage of me.

☐ 7. You're doing this deliberately (to get back at me, hurt me, spite me).

Magnification

☐ 8. I can't stand it.

☐ 9. This behavior is intolerable.

☐ 10. You've gone too far this time.

☐ 11. You never listen.

☐ 12. How dare you (look at me like that, talk to me like that, do that, etc.).

☐ 13. You turn everything into a (power struggle, fight, lousy time together, nightmare, etc.).

Labeling

☐ 14. You're getting out of control.

☐ 15. This is manipulation.

☐ 16. You're so (lazy, malicious, stubborn, disrespectful, ungrateful, willful, selfish, cruel, stupid, bratty, spoiled, contrary, etc.).

☐ 17. You're deliberately being mean, a jerk, etc.

☐ 18. You don't care (what happens, how I feel, who you hurt, etc.).

You can see how trigger thoughts can inflame any anger-provoking situation, but they are especially dangerous to kids. An adult will probably be able to correct your mistaken *assumed intent*. Adults have the awareness and vocabulary to tell you they were late due to car trouble, not disrespect. A small child will whine, cry, or throw a tantrum, but won't be able to articulate that he or she is tired, hungry, overstimulated, or suffering from separation anxiety.

When you use *magnification* in an already volatile situation, you end up feeling totally out of control. We depend on our friends and partners to help us calm down and regain control when we're feeling distraught. "I think that vase can be fixed, let me work on it." "Calm down kiddo, It's not the end of the world. We can work it out." Children look to you to define reality: how serious something is, whether it's safe or dangerous. They are more likely to join you in feeling out of control, making the situation even more volatile.

Because children are learning to define themselves by the reactions of adults *labeling* them in a derogatory way, will eventually damage their self-esteem, (I really must be selfish, stupid, careless, irresponsible, etc). When the child believes the labels, there is little motivation to change. Why bother?

In the McKay, et al., study cited above, the researchers found that parents who were *less angry* tended to use specific coping thoughts more frequently than their angrier counterparts. Here is a list of the seven most frequently used coping thoughts used by low anger parents in this study.

1. It's just a stage. Kids have to go through these stages.

2. This is natural for his or her age.

3. Don't take it seriously. Keep a sense of humor.

4. This is just natural impulsiveness.

5. He or she isn't really trying to infuriate me. It's just how he or she is coping right now.

6. He or she can't help (crying, being angry, interrupting, needing attention, etc.).

7. Just get through it. You can cope. You don't have to get angry.

Looking at the list of calming thoughts, you can see that some of them (1, 2, and 4) reframe the behavior as normal for the child's level of development, or temperament. Some help you to stop magnifying (3, 7). Coping thoughts 5 and 6 steer you away from assumed intent by reframing the problem as something the child can't deal with any other way. When you are extremely upset, the first most important coping thoughts are those that will calm you (coping thought No.7). Take a deep breath, turn away, don't do or say anything. You cannot deal effectively with any situation when you are "seeing red".

Exercise. Identify your triggers and coping thoughts.

Read back over the list of trigger thoughts while you think of a situation with your child that was particularly infuriating, a situation that caused a lot of anger and upset at the time. On a fresh page in your anger diary, list any of the trigger thoughts that you used in the heat of the moment. Were there *labeling* thoughts? Is there a child whom you tend to see as careless, or stubborn, defiant, or bratty? Was there *assumed intent*? (You're doing this to annoy me, test me, defy me). Did you magnify the problem situation (I'm going crazy. I can't stand it.)?

Now review the list of coping thoughts while you think of the same provoking situation. Which ones might help you to control anger stirred up by these triggers? Write them down, as well as anything that might better explain your child's behavior. What need was your child trying to satisfy in that situation? Think of how your child's age and temperament contributed to his behavior. This selection of coping thoughts is a good start toward better managing your anger during a particular event. Now repeat the exercise for four more high-frequency anger situations. Use separate pages for each. When you complete this exercise, you'll have, in essence, five coping plans for some of the most provocative situations you face as a parent.

Example: Wanda's Trigger Thoughts

Wanda was walking home from the park with her eight month-old baby girl and her two-and-a-half year-old son, Richie. The usual group of kids Richie played with had not been at the park today, so he had been very demanding. He wanted her to play with him in the sandbox, push his swing, and catch him as he jumped off the slide. The baby was fussy, as well, eating the sand, and wanting to be held. When it was time to leave, Richie ran away from Wanda, and refused to collect his toys as he usually did. By the time they started walking home, her nerves were shot.

Richie knew he could walk ahead but had to stop at the corner and wait until Wanda caught up. But this time, he was following a neighborhood puppy he liked. When he got to the corner, Richie took a right turn and ran down the block after the dog. Wanda was furious. "Stop!" she yelled, and had to leave the stroller to run after him. Richie didn't even look back. Eventually, Wanda grabbed the boy roughly and carried him screaming back to the corner. The baby woke and started crying as well.

"Now look what you've done. You're driving me crazy. What makes you think you can run off like that? Are you getting back at me for making you leave the park early?

"You are so demanding and selfish. I took you to the park and played with you all morning. But are you grateful? Do you listen when I call you? No, you run away and ignore me." Any parent of young children has had moments like this. You're stressed, tired, then your child does something that is heedless and unpredictable. You're full of adrenaline, and find yourself feeling completely out of control. You can see in Wanda's situation how trigger thoughts add to the upset.

Assuming intention: You ignore me. You're getting back at me.

Magnifying: You're driving me crazy.

Labeling: You are demanding, ungrateful, selfish.

Of course, no amount of coping thoughts would have made this a wonderful day in the park. But, after the fact, Wanda was able to write down several coping thoughts that might help her the next time.

"Just get through it. You can cope." (Tomorrow his buddies will be back, and it will be more fun for all of us.)

"He couldn't help being demanding today. There was no one else to play with!"

"It's not unusual for a two-year-old to forget the rules when in hot pursuit of something as fascinating as a dog."

"He isn't doing it to me, he's just being a kid."

"I'm not crazy, I'm just stressed."

Sample Trigger and Coping Thoughts

Trigger: "They've destroyed the house."

Coping: "The kids left clothes, books, and dishes in several rooms. It's natural, you can cope."

Trigger: "She is lazy, selfish, stupid."

Coping: "Lucy got a C in chemistry because she didn't consistently turn in her homework."

Trigger: "If he keeps that up he's going to flunk out.

Coping: "With his grade-point average, he will probably not be able to get into a four-year university, and will have to attend community college."

Trigger: "All you think about is yourself."

Coping: "I can see that she really wants her way. Being self-focused is natural at this age."

Trigger: "This is manipulation."

Coping: "I can set limits without getting mad."

Trigger: "He looks like a bum in those sloppy pants."

Coping: "It's a stage. Kids wear crazy stuff."

Trigger: "She looks like a prostitute in that skimpy skirt."

Coping: "Kids have great needs to fit in. They want to look and act like their friends."

"Don't take it seriously. Keep a sense of humor."

Tune in and Talk Back

Because trigger thoughts can be so automatic and habitual, some parents aren't t even aware of them. They resolve to be calmer, but when a provocative situation occurs they are right back in the same old fights.

In order to become aware of your automatic trigger thoughts try to imagine that there is a video camera in your home for a twenty-four-hour period. It shows you in the morning, getting the kids off to school or child care. It shows you in the evening coming home after work, preparing dinner, helping the kids with homework, the bedtime routines. The video shows your kids playing, fighting, laughing, and eating. The video camera records your conversations, body language, and tone of voice.

Do something to remind yourself that you are being "taped" all day. You might wear a bright ribbon on your wrist, or put bright stickers or ribbons on the refrigerator, bathroom mirror, the toy chest, or the dashboard of your car to remind you that the "cameras are rolling" all day.

Next, on a piece of paper, divide the day into time zones: morning activities, midday, after work, dinner time, after dinner activities, and bedtime routines.

At the end of the day "play back" the imaginary tape and analyze every stressful, frustrating, anger-provoking interaction you had with your kids. Write down in each time zone the behavior or events that upset you. What made you angry? What made you impatient? *What were you saying to yourself at the time?* Tune in to your *trigger thoughts* that make a difficult situation worse. Record the anger-provoking events.

Here is an example of what may have happened through the day.

You think your daughter is getting dressed in the morning , but she went back to sleep.

Your son needs a permission slip signed for school, but he can't find it.

Your toddler screams and whines while you are on the phone.

You have a headache, and the electronic sounds of the video game are making it worse.

You prepare his favorite dinner, but your five-year-old won't eat anything but bread and jam again.

The kids are bickering and fighting in the backseat of the car.

You come home and find that your daughter and her friends have made cookies, used every utensil in the kitchen, and covered the floor with flour.

You trip over your daughter's skates and twist your ankle.

Next to each event, record the trigger thoughts that made a difficult situation worse.

"How can she do that to me? She is so careless, thoughtless, selfish . . ."

"I just can't stand it, I'm going nuts with that noise."

"If I told her once, I've told her a million times. . . ."

"She is manipulating me, defying me, testing me, . . ."

Once you can tune into the trigger thought, you can begin to talk back with coping thoughts.

"Take a deep breath, calm down, I can get through it"

"It's not the end of the world if . . . she is late . . . it's lost . . . he doesn't eat tonight."

"This is the age for separation anxiety, . . . autonomy issues, . . . being negative. . . ."

"Kids are so focused on the game, they are not aware of the noise . . . the danger . . . the time . . . etc."

"The kids are tired and hungry. They're falling apart, but I don't have to fall apart too."

"He's a kid who needs a lot of attention, and he is having a hard time sharing me."

"No labels, she's just doing what kids do . . . that's what teens do . . . that's what babies do."

Now you have a worksheet with the specific situations in your family that are upsetting, as well as an awareness of the kind of thoughts that pop into your mind that trigger your anger. You also have some practice using coping thoughts to defuse the situation and keep your cool.

Your Expectations

What you expect of your children has enormous impact on your anger. Not the expectation of who and what they'll be when they grow up, but your values and needs as they affect the daily activities of family life. What you expect at family meals, at bedtime, regarding schoolwork, hygiene, and dress. What you expect around cleanup, friends, chores, and private time.

Why do certain expectations cause so much stress and anger? Sometimes you may expect things of your kids that are just not reasonable. You may have two expectations that are mutually exclusive or contradictory. Your child may not be capable of meeting your expectations or you may have expectations that are no longer appropriate for the age of your child. To begin to understand how your expectations affect every aspect of family life, complete the following exercise.

> **Exercise. Make a list of your childrens' activities and behaviors.**

The list might include such items as mealtime, bedtime, cleanup, playtime, time alone, noise, following directions, allowance, chores, fighting, homework, school performance, watching TV, sports activities, and so on. For younger children, you might also include potty training, sleeping in your bed, sleeping through the night, nursing, sharing, interrupting adults, and so on. The list for older children should include visiting other children, other children visiting you, sleepovers, parties, being alone in the house, dating, driving, working, makeup, music, and sexuality.

Next to each activity write a belief, value, or need that you associate with that activity. Your beliefs and needs together form your expectations of your child in each of these situations. List as many as you can.

Here are a few items from Rochelle's list to give you an idea of how your list might be constructed.

Mealtime: The family should eat together. One person at a time should talk. No playing with food.

Bedtime: I need the kids to go to sleep at a consistent, reasonable hour so that I can relax and have time with my husband.

Homework: Kids should take responsibility to do their own work. I try to be available if they need help, but I won't stand over them until it's done.

Television: Kids should not be allowed to space out watching TV without limits. I allow my kids to watch one hour of TV each evening, and they can watch anything they want during that hour.

If you have a partner, have him or her do this exercise also. Are you surprised by your partner's responses? How are they different than yours? Do those differences contribute to stress in your relationship?

Now that you have a list of all the issues that are relevant to you and your expectations about them, put a check next to the items that cause stress and conflict in your family. Which expectations are a source of fights? These are the items that you will want to work on later. But now you need more information.

Looking at Your Child

Sometimes it's hard to see your children as they really are. They remind you of yourself, or they remind you of someone else. Often they pick up labels that describe one aspect of their personality or developmental state. This kind of generalization can stay with them for a lifetime. Meg is the "princess." Bill is the "rebel." Cheryl is "sixteen going on fifty." Even positive labels describe only one aspect of the child. Mike is the "smart one." Gary is an "angel."

These descriptions are a kind of shorthand that limit how you see your child. But of greater concern, they can trigger anger. You start with a generalization. "He's lazy." "She can't be trusted." "She's a bully." Then you become hyperalert to the behavior that exemplifies that generalization. You say to yourself, "Here she goes again", "I don't have to put up with that," and so on. You fail to see even a single exception to the expected behavior. If your children accept the negative labels, they may live up to your expectations by persisting in that behavior, thus making you angrier.

Perhaps the most damaging part of labeling and generalizing is that you miss seeing your children as they really are. You miss seeing your son's potential, his talents. You miss knowing the things that motivate your daughter, that challenge her, interest her. Steve felt that his twelve-year-old son was ignoring him. "He never hears me when I talk to him" (*generalization*). "He deliberately tunes me out" (*trigger thought*). What Steve failed to appreciate was that Joe had an incredible ability to concentrate. He loved learning math, especially algebra. He enjoyed working on his model planes and actually built a remote control plane by himself. He liked to read. He just didn't hear Steve (or anything else) when he was concentrating on these things. Labels were keeping Steve from seeing how focused and competent his son really was.

Exercise. Take a fresh look.

One way to get a fresh look at your children is to describe them to someone who doesn't know them at all. The best way to do this is in the form of a letter. Think of someone you haven't seen since becoming a parent (like an old college friend or a relative who lives far away). In your "letter," describe your child as completely as you can. What is your daughter good at? What is hard for her? How does she relate to you, to her other friends? What does your son like to do? What is his best subject in school? What are his needs for privacy or social contact? How is he creative? How does your daughter deal with frustration? How does she express her feelings of affection or anger? How does she get support? What are your son's needs for order, for limits, for autonomy? How is he different from you when you were his age?

Make this exercise a real treasure hunt. Get more information and fill out your description by watching and listening carefully. Ask others who know your children—their teachers, parents of their friends, their siblings. You might find yourself looking at your children more carefully than you ever have before.

The goal of this exercise is to see who your children really are and become more aware of their specialness, their talents, their limits, and their potential. If you started with some overgeneralizations, look for the exceptions to the "rules." Is your daughter careless? Or is she just easily distracted? Is she careless about everything? What things is she careful about? Take several days to complete the letter, adding to it over time, watching, observing, and gathering more information. When both you and your partner have done this exercise, share the letters with each other. Does your partner's letter differ much from your own?

Rachel's father saw her as being totally self-involved and unconcerned about the needs of other family members. She complained about her few chores. She'd stay on the phone most of the evening.

Rachel's door was often closed, and the closed door seemed symbolic to her father of how he felt shut out of her life. Every time he passed her door, he felt angry. He'd say to himself and to his wife, "She doesn't participate in this family at all, yet she wants us to give her an allowance, lend her the car, and pay for a college education. Well, who does she think she is?"

To research his letter, Rachel's dad started talking to her about things that were happening in her life. And he started to notice things. He noticed that although Rachel didn't want to accompany her parents to large family gatherings, she did enjoy going to the movies with them. Although she complained about her chores, she would occasionally take on a project without being asked. She decided to plant flowers in the front yard. She also helped hang wallpaper in the bathroom.

He noticed that her friends often confided in her, and she seemed to have great insight about them and their relationships. In fact, it seemed that she was very mature when helping others deal with crises and make decisions. When Rachel's dad was able to see beyond the limited view he had of her, he was less hurt when she did withdraw. He also had some information about how to create and preserve a connection to her during her teen years.

Seeing Clearly

Once you have completed the "letter," use the information and new awarenesses that you have discovered to make two lists. The first list is for the child's positive characteristics and the potential that he or she shows. These are the areas that you need to recognize, support, and encourage. When you see your children's best selves, their talents and emerging abilities, you will be less likely to carry with you negative generalizations that create and intensify anger.

Make a second list of all the negative characteristics that annoy you, disappoint you, and tend to make you angry. Put a check mark next to the ones on the list that are especially irritating. Start with these "hot" items and ask yourself what makes them so irritating. Do they violate one of your important values? Is it behavior that reminds you of someone else? Does it remind you of yourself now or how you used to be? Does this behavior end up being embarrassing to you, or do you feel that others would disapprove of it? It is important to recognize how you bring your own history, values, and needs to a conflict situation. You can then replace your trigger thoughts ("This behavior is intolerable") with ones that are less anger-provoking and more accurate ("This behavior is embarrassing to me, or disappointing, or makes me feel that he is out of control").

Look again at the items on the negative list. Make note of the items that you probably won't be able to change. Here are some common reasons that certain behaviors might persist despite all your efforts to change them.

1. **The child's basic nature.** Children have their own personalities, tastes, preferences, sensitivities, and strengths. There is little you can do to make a shy child into a social butterfly by reminding, nagging, or pushing. The pressure that children feel to go against their basic nature might make them more withdrawn or inauthentic.

2. **Fads and fashion.** It is certainly useless to argue fashion, fads, hairstyles, and music with your children when these tastes are so strongly influenced by peer groups. You may limit how and when they listen to their music, but you won't talk them into liking yours or disliking their own.

3. **States of development.** Some behavior is almost inevitable at certain stages of development. Typical two-year-olds can be very negative. Being able to use the word *no* enables them to assert their autonomy and separate themselves from the world around them. Children go through stages of imaginary friends, fear of being alone, identifying with superheroes, fascination with movie and rock idols. Older children will predictably reject their parents' values and seek their own. It helps to read about child development, talk to other parents, and talk to your child's teachers. Check out what is typical behavior at certain ages so that you can see your child's behavior in the context of developmental norms.

Accepting that you won't change certain behaviors, that they are basic to the child or the developmental stage, may help you let go of blaming trigger thoughts.

Ask Why

You need to do one more thing with your list of negative behaviors: ask *why* this behavior persists. Any attempt to eradicate a behavior by punishments, restrictions, distractions, or indulgence is useless unless you look at what function that behavior has in the child's life. All behavior has a purpose. Ask yourself, "What need is being expressed by this behavior?" Look for basic needs like safety, attention, belonging, and approval. Then ask, "How can I help my child express that need in a more successful and acceptable way?" Do this for every remaining item on your negative list.

These questions move you beyond anger to real problem solving. Instead of saying, "How dare he do this to me?" (trigger thought), you say "What need does this behavior try to satisfy?" which establishes that your son acted as he did in a legitimate attempt to take care of himself. Your job is to help him find healthier or more effective ways to meet those needs.

High-Risk Situations

Review your relationship with your children. See if you can find some pattern. Is there a particular time of day or day of the week that the conflict occurs? Is there a particular activity or issue that sets you off? Is there some predisposing event or feeling that sets the scene for later anger-generating interactions with your child?

A common predisposing factor is *fatigue.* Parents who come home tired after working and commuting have no time to revive. Their children may also be tired, hungry, and needy for attention. The after-work hours may therefore be a danger zone.

Another predisposing factor is feeling *rushed.* The early morning challenge of getting everyone out the door is a common source of chronic conflict.

Feeling *disappointed* in your child or feeling that your child compares poorly with other children can be a source of chronic anger.

Conflict can also become a habit around *control* issues. Are rules about food, bedtime, friends, dress, language, or curfew a source of conflict for you?

A common source of anger is *interruption.* It is very frustrating to be interrupted when you're struggling to complete a task, concentrate, talk on the phone, or have a conversation with another adult.

Other contributing factors might include worry, symptoms of illness, interpersonal conflict, and literally any significant source of stress.

When you've identified that you are in a high-risk situation, one that traditionally leads to anger at your child, you are forearmed. You can plan ahead for the coping strategies that may be required. You can anticipate the impulse to blame or attack and prepare a less destructive response.

Reinforcement

All behavior persists because it is reinforced. You can only change your child's behavior by changing the reinforcers.

Positive Reinforcements

Positive reinforcement is a powerful tool to get children to change their behavior. The most powerful reinforcement of all is your approval and attention. This truth cannot be overemphasized. The child's goal is to be accepted and to belong. You are the one, through praise and support, who can provide the motivation for nearly any positive behavior.

You can shape behavior by positively reinforcing each step in the right direction. Let's say that you want your son to clean his room. As he goes toward his room, you could say, "Great, Jack, I see you're getting right on it. I appreciate not having to remind you." He picks up his dirty clothes and puts them in the hamper and you say,

"It looks better already. You are doing a great job." And so on. If he slows down or stops, you can be encouraging with more praise and approval by saying, "You've done so well. Just a few more things and you'll be through." When the job is completed, you can make it even more reinforcing by praising him to others. "Jack did a beautiful job on his room, and he did it all by himself except for the puzzles. I'm really proud of him." Other reinforcers could be as simple as a gold star for a job completed or a special treat such as staying up later, reading a story, or some favorite food.

Older children respond to positive reinforcement as well. Teens, who may be in conflict with parents about many ideas, often complain that their cooperation is never noticed. Praise encourages cooperation. Just saying, "Thanks for getting home on time; I'm glad you're here," makes a teen want to please you again.

When you praise and reward behavior, you build a child's self-esteem. He can feel like a good, cooperative, capable, smart, important person and is more likely to continue behaving in ways that gain your approval.

Discipline and Consequences

Discipline is an important tool for helping children learn. It needn't come from anger and needn't involve revenge, threat, or aggression. Discipline that is reasonable, supportive, and consistent allows your children to learn and grow with their self-esteem intact.

But many parents only think about discipline when they are already angry. It is often imposed without thought or planning. "How many times have I told you not to do that? Now you'll be sorry." The next step is some shouted punishment that may alienate your child and actually make him *more* likely to misbehave in the future.

Remember that there is an imbalance of power in your relationship with your child. You are much stronger, and you are more articulate. You make the rules, you control the resources, you are in charge. You have the power to impose any punishment or restriction you want, and the child has no direct recourse. This imbalance of power makes it all the more important that punishments be implemented without a lot of anger. When you're angry, you are more likely to make rash, extreme, and inappropriate decisions. You're more likely to make threats and use violence. You're more likely to hit, squeeze, push, or shake a child. Your body is surging with adrenaline, your judgment is impaired, and your response is likely to be dangerous—physically and psychologically. "If you as much as lay a finger on that baby, I'll break your hands." "If you're not home on time, you'll never see that boy again."

Imposing negative consequences without anger is possible. Here are some suggestions.

1. **Natural consequences.** Every action has its consequence. It is a fact of life. If you don't put gas in the car, it won't run. If you miss eating breakfast, you feel hungry. If you don't take your jacket, you'll be cold. Natural consequences aren't imposed by any authority, but arise inevitably from the situation. Allowing the natural consequence to occur to children may be the easiest and least anger-provoking form of discipline. If you don't get involved with trying to save them from natural consequences, they will learn the lesson without feeling criticized or manipulated by you. You can even be sympathetic to their problem and encourage them to do better next time. "It's hard when you have to leave the house in your pajamas and dress in the car because you didn't dress in time at home." "You must be terribly disappointed that the school won't let you play on the team because of your report card." "I was sorry to see you forgot your lunch. You must have been hungry all afternoon."

There is no need to threaten or rub it in. Children are capable of figuring out how to change their behavior so that the consequences won't recur. Even though it might make you uncomfortable to think of your daughter going hungry or going to school unprepared, even though you are tempted to "save" her, remember that when you prevent natural consequences from occurring, you are *reinforcing* the problematic behavior. If you deliver her forgotten lunch to school, she is less motivated to remember it next time. If you take responsibility for completing her homework, it becomes your homework. When you allow natural consequences to occur, you teach your children the real facts of life—and they learn to own and solve many of their own problems.

2. **Reasonable consequences.** Sometimes, of course, allowing natural consequences to occur is neither reasonable nor safe. You can't let a small child play in the road to learn how dangerous cars are. You may not be able to allow a child to miss school because he has overslept. In such cases, you have to create negative consequences for the behavior. The negative consequences should be reasonable, appropriate, timely, and consistently applied. Here are some guidelines for creating reasonable consequences.

(a) Consequences should take into account the age and ability of the child. If you take television away from a five-year-old for one day because he hit another child, he might learn something about impulse control. Bigger punishments create unnecessary deprivation for a child that young.

(b) Whenever possible, consequences should relate to the offense. If your child has lost or broken something, the consequence should involve saving or earning the money to replace that item. If your children are roughhousing in the car, the consequence might be to stop driving and wait until they have settled down. If the children are fighting over a toy, the consequence might be the loss of the toy while they work out how they are going to share it. If your child doesn't complete a chore in the time allotted, the consequence might involve losing a part of her allowance or delaying some other activity until the chore is done.

3. **Time-out.** This can be an effective strategy in handling younger children who are being noncompliant, having a temper tantrum, or are acting in other antisocial ways. A short period of time (five minutes, for instance) in a boring but safe environment (a room with no TV or toys) enables children to reassess their behavior and choose to act differently so that they can reenter the social environment. It also enables you to regain control of the situation without getting upset. Explain to the child that the consequences of certain behaviors result in five minutes of time-out and that he can choose to change his behavior or not. Place a portable egg timer outside of the door to keep track of the minutes so that it is the sound of the timer and not you who determines when he gets out. He can come out after the set period of time if he is willing to follow the rules (no hitting, help cleaning up, willingness to share, quiet play, and so on).

4. **Avoid long-lasting or delayed punishments.** Long-term restrictions mean that you are tied to enforcing the consequence long after children have forgotten what they are being punished for.

5. **Make sure that your children know exactly what is expected of them.** Define what you mean by "behave in the restaurant." Also make sure that your children are capable of what you want. Is your five-year-old daughter really able to "sit still" for a half hour? If you expect your son to clean the kitchen, does he know how to fill the dishwasher and turn it on? Does he know that you also want him to sweep the floor?

6. **Tell your children in advance what the consequences of misbehavior will be.** This way they can make a reasonable decision about how they will act. Then, when it's time to impose the consequences, children are less likely to protest or try to convince you to change your mind. You don't have to get angry or prove that they are wrong. Reasonable consequences, clearly communicated, lower the stress level in your family.

7. **Once you have established a reasonable consequence, don't continue to harp or nag about it.** Avoid teasing, reminding, or rubbing it in. Nora knew that the consequence for any driving violation was that she would lose her use of the family car for a month. John knew that if he hit his sister with the robot arm, it would be taken away for an hour. Sue and Millie knew that if they didn't finish their homework by 8:00 P.M., they would not get to watch their favorite TV show. The beauty of reasonable consequences is that *it's your child's choice:* appropriate behavior or face an unpleasant outcome.

8. **Consequences should be consistently applied.** Do what you said you would do every time. If you aren't consistent, then your children will be constantly testing you. And they'll have little motivation to change their behavior. One time they are punished for something that is ignored the next time. When you are inconsistent, you are forced to "really get angry" in order to be taken seriously.

   Don't threaten a consequence that you are not prepared to carry out. If you say "No more fighting in the car or I'll turn around and take you home," then be prepared to do it—even if you are disappointed as well. If you say "Get dressed so we can leave by 8:15, or you'll need to finishing dressing in the car," be prepared to enforce the consequences—even if it's raining. You'll probably not have to impose the consequence more than once or twice before your child will get the point that you mean it. It's the consistency, not the strictness or severity of consequences, that make them effective.

Assertive Communication with Your Child

Parental anger is often fueled by feeling ignored. "They just don't listen." "How many times do I have to say it?" "She just tunes me out." Learning to be clear and assertive in your communication will go a long way to lowering your frustration and anger. Assertive communication makes it more likely for your child to meet your expectations, and it promotes cooperation.

Before you begin, be sure that you are calm. If you're already angry, take a moment to cool down (use your relaxation and coping skills). Most kids will tune out everything you say if it has an angry edge. Also be sure you have your child's attention. This will save you from repeating and nagging. Have the child turn off the television, music, or computer so he is able to hear you. Talk to your child privately, away from the other kids.

Assertive communication is a four-step process. It's simple, but it works. Here's how it's done.

- State your feelings (or reactions) to the child's behavior.

- State the problem.

- State what you want the child to do.

- Describe the reinforcement.

Step 1. State your feelings. Be open about how you feel when your child is misbehaving. Sometimes our expectations or limits might seem random or unfair to a child.

Do you feel *embarrassed* when your four-year-old throws a screaming fit in the supermarket?

Do you feeling *disappointed* when your son leaves his bike out in the rain?

Do you feel *anxious* when your daughter wanders away from you on a crowded beach?

Do you feel *frustrated* when you are picking up your son from a play date and he refuses to get in the car?

Step 2. State the problem. Keep it simple; without insult, without blame, or assumed intent. Note the generic format: "I was (the feeling) because (the problem)."

"I was anxious because I thought you might get hurt."

"I was frustrated because I couldn't hear my sister on the phone."

"I was concerned because you didn't call me when you were late."

"I was resentful because I got stuck cleaning up the mess you made."

Step 3. State what you want the child to do now, or your expectation of what you want him to do in the future. Be as specific as you can about the behavior that's expected. Instead of "I want you to behave in the movies," tell him what he should do (stay in your chair) or not do (no loud voices, don't put your feet up on the seat in front of you). Be specific about the expected time frame. "I want your room cleaned up (right now . . . by the time I get home . . . by tomorrow at suppertime)."

Step 4. State the consequences for noncompliance. (See the previous section on *natural* or *reasonable* consequences.) Once you've chosen an appropriate consequence, explain it in simple terms. "If you haven't cleaned up your room when I get home, there won't be any afternoon TV." Or, "If the fighting in the backseat continues, the CD player goes off until further notice." Or, "If you aren't dressed by the time we're ready to go out the door, you'll have to walk out to the car in your pajamas."

Exercise. Assertive communications

Refer back to the problem situations you wrote about in the "Tune In, Talk Back" section, above. Assertive communication could be useful for many of those situations. Choose the top five and write an assertive statement that expresses your feeling, the problem, your expectations, and the reinforcement. Here are some examples:

"I get anxious when you kids are running and hiding in the supermarket."

"It makes it hard for me to concentrate on shopping."

"I want you both to stay with me."

"If you run off again, I'm going to put the cookies back on the shelf."

"I have a headache, and the noise of that video game is making it worse."

"I need you to turn it off, or play the game with the sound on mute."

"If I keep hearing the game, I'll have to put it away."

"When you go back to sleep instead of getting dressed, I worry that you'll miss your bus and be late for school."

"I also feel resentful that I can't trust you to get dressed without reminders."

"If you run late again this morning, I won't have time to braid your hair."

Next time any of these situations occur, follow the four assertive steps. Notice whether you feel differently when you acknowledge your emotions. Notice if your child responds differently when given clear information about your emotional state, and specific expected behaviors. Were you less frustrated because you felt heard?

Putting It All Together— Solving Problems

Exercise. Working toward solutions

Now return to the recurrent problems that tend to cause stress and fighting in your family. By following the six steps listed below, you can begin to work toward a solution that will change old patterns of conflict. Do this exercise when you are not feeling angry or frustrated, so that you can be creative and optimistic about solving the problems.

1. *The problem.* State the problem in behavioral terms. Be very specific about the exact behavior that causes the conflict.

2. *State what need you think the child is expressing by behaving this way.* Is the child trying to satisfy her need for attention, safety, approval, or autonomy? Is she frustrated, bored, or overwhelmed? You may not know for sure what need is being expressed, but try to figure it out using your knowledge of your child's personality, needs, interests, and motivating drives. You may have to get more information from your son, his teachers, or others who know him. You can also get information from reading about other children who are at your child's level of development.

3. *What value or expectation of yours is being violated?* Earlier you wrote down some of your beliefs, values, and expectations relating to your child's behavior. Apply what you learned to this particular situation.

4. *How can you help your children express their needs in a more acceptable way?* Try to be creative and open-minded. There doesn't have to be a winner or a loser. You may be able to find an alternative way to take care of everyone's needs. It might mean that you compromise. It might require changing your priorities or doing things differently. It might require that you let go of some expectation that causes or intensifies stress.

5. *Positive reinforcements.* How can you motivate your children to want to change their behavior? What would make them want to cooperate?

6. *Negative consequences.* What consequences would your children want to avoid by changing their behavior? Would allowing a natural consequence to occur work? Can you create a reasonable consequence that would motivate your child to change?

Here are two examples of how these six steps can be used to solve problems.

Dinnertime was a disaster for Caroline, Fred, and their two small sons, ages four and six. Both parents preferred that the whole family eat together, but this preference was not a high priority. Fred didn't get home until 6:30 most nights. By the time they all sat down to eat it was 7:00 and both boys were irritable from being hungry and tired. Caroline and Fred were tired as well, and had little patience for the mess and noise and fighting that ensued. Neither child was very skilled at using utensils, and they usually spilled food on the table and floor. Caroline and Fred found themselves correcting, warning, threatening, and finally sending one or both boys from the table. This is how they used the six steps to assess the problem and work toward a solution.

1. *The problem:* The children are messy and noisy and they fight at the table.

2. *The need being expressed by this behavior:* The children are hungry and tired. Neither child knows how to use utensils properly. Both children fight because they are competing for attention from their parents.

3. *Values and expectations violated:* The whole family should eat together without fighting. Children should be able to use utensils and not make a mess.

4. *How can the children express their needs in a more appropriate way:*
   - Feed the children earlier on weekdays and let them join the adults for dessert. The family would eat together on weekends.
   - Have the children take turns talking at the table and don't allow interruption.

5. *Positive reinforcements:*
   - Have children practice using utensils in a way that is enjoyable. For instance, they could practice using a soup spoon by eating ice cream "soup." They could practice using a knife and fork to eat brownies.
   - Make the conversation interesting and enjoyable for them at the dinner table and let each child take a turn talking without being interrupted.
   - Acknowledge and praise improvement in table manners.

6. *Negative consequences:*
   - Require that the children clean up and sweep up any spilled food after a meal.
   - If there is any fighting, they will have to leave the table.

Ten-year-old Zack had always been shy and small for his age, but he was agile and very coordinated. The previous summer he had learned how to ride a skateboard. He devoted a lot of time to practicing until he was the best skateboard rider in his class. Along with his competence in skateboarding came confidence and new friendships with other boys who enjoyed this sport. His father, Jerry, was concerned that Zack would be seriously injured if he fell and bought his son a helmet and protective pads. Zack promised his father that he would not ride in the street and would always wear the protective gear on the skateboard.

One rainy day Jerry saw his son riding in the middle of traffic without his helmet or pads. His first inclination was to burn the board. But skateboarding provided a lot for Zack—challenge, confidence, and the respect of other boys. This is how Jerry used the six steps to assess the problem and work toward a solution.

1. *The problem:* Zack riding his skateboard in the street without protective gear and deceiving his father about it.

2. *The need being expressed by his behavior:* Zack's need to be accepted by his peer group (by riding unprotected) is greater than his need to be honest with his father or his need for safety.

3. *Values and expectations violated:*

   - Children should be honest with their parents.

   - Children should not ride without protective gear and should not ride in the street. (Both expectations had a high priority for Jerry.)

4. *How could he express his need in a more appropriate way?*

   - Jerry would try to get others in Zack's peer group to wear helmets and pads. He could call the parents of the other children and encourage them to buy pads and helmets for their kids.

   - Encourage Zack to participate in other sports where he would probably excel (wrestling, gymnastics) and gain more confidence and prestige.

5. *Positive reinforcement:*

   - If Zack will wear his helmet and pads when riding his skateboard, Jerry will take him and a friend to a skate park where he can practice on the ramps and tracks. (Protective gear is required in these parks.)

- If Zack will wear his helmet and pads, Jerry will buy him a subscription to a skateboard magazine so that he can learn more about professional skateboarders.

6. *Negative reinforcement:*

- If Zack is caught riding in the street or without his protective gear, he will lose his skateboard for a week.

The Antianger Prescription

1. **Your relationship.** The first and most important step in avoiding anger at your children is to establish and preserve a good feeling between you. If children feel safe and accepted at home, they are less likely to act out and misbehave. They prefer to maintain the feelings of warmth and respect between you.

   You communicate your acceptance by listening, spending time together, and sharing activities that are fun. Share yourself as well. Children of all ages enjoy hearing stories from their parents' childhood and stories about themselves at an earlier age. Spending time alone with your child helps establish good feelings. Each child needs time when he or she doesn't have to compete with other children or activities for your attention. When you make time for your daughter, you are saying to her, "You are important. I want to know what you think and feel." When you listen, you learn about your child's perceptions, fears, motivations, and limits. You can more accurately predict problem situations and avoid them. You can more frequently recognize the pressures your son is under in his efforts to manage his own life. When he does misbehave, you're more likely to understand why and indulge in fewer trigger thoughts.

2. **Be aware of your stress.** Watch out for the danger times when you are under stress and are more likely to be annoyed by the common frustrations of parenting. After work or when you're tired are two typical times when you should be on the alert. Other times to be careful are when you are in pain or don't feel well, when you are rushed, or when you are angry at someone else. Children, unfortunately, are easy targets for your anger at these times.

   Some parents come home from work in a physically aroused state, looking for a fight in order to discharge their stress. If this happens to you, absolutely avoid difficult or conflict situations with your children during these danger periods. If bath time is a battle, skip the bath. Don't add to your stress by taking on more obligations or starting new projects, even if you think you ought to. Delay, avoid, or cancel whatever is not absolutely necessary.

3. **Communicate to your children that you are feeling stress (upset, frustrated, worried, unhappy).** Even very young children can understand that you are upset and they need to be careful around you. You may also communicate what they can do to help or at least not add to the problem.

> "I need a half an hour of quiet now."

> "I'm worried about Grandma because she's sick. I need you to be quiet and not interrupt me while I call the hospital."

> "That man at the garage really made me mad. I'm very grumpy right now, but I'll be better in a few minutes."

Communicating clearly about your own emotional state helps the kids learn about you, your limits, and your needs. It also teaches them how to express their own needs and limits in appropriate ways. If they are frustrated or stressed, they'll learn to ask for what they need without being angry or aggressive.

4. **Take care of yourself—right away if possible.** Do something that will lower your stress level. A hot bath, a phone conversation with someone who is supportive, or just taking off your work clothes and sitting down with a cool soft drink and listening to some music can take the edge off and help you feel more able to cope.

5. **Be prepared for a disaster and avoid it when possible.** If you give a three-year-old a glass of milk, there is some chance that she will spill it. If she is sitting on the old couch, you will feel annoyed. If she spills it while sitting on the new couch, how would you feel? If you know that you'd "go nuts," then *don't let her drink milk on the new couch.* How would you feel if your son lost your jacket at the school dance? Would you be somewhat disappointed? How would you feel if he lost your old, favorite, irreplaceable, cherished denim jacket that you've had since college? If you think you would be "out of your mind," then *don't lend him the jacket.* Know you own limits and avoid feeling pushed beyond what is tolerable. By doing that you avoid setting yourself up for the pain and the stress that cause anger.

6. **Plan ahead.** You can probably predict and prevent some problems if you plan ahead. Plan ahead by letting the children know exactly what is expected of them. What exactly do you mean by "Don't bother me now" or "Don't give the sitter any trouble"? Plan ahead by helping children cope. Long car rides are stressful for everyone. Snack food, quiet activity toys, story or music tapes that they enjoy, frequent stops—all help to make a trip more pleasant.

You are aware of your child's particular strengths and limits. Avoid putting your son in a situation where you can predict that he will feel pushed beyond his limits or capabilities and be likely to misbehave. Let him feel prepared by explaining and rehearsing what will happen in a new situation (first day of school, first visit to the dentist). Some children need more physical activity. Some need less stimulation. Some children need very clear limits and are always testing you. Some kids get extremely irritable when they are hungry or tired. It is up to you to discover what makes each child tick, what situations will be most difficult, and how you can help your son or daughter cope and be successful. Not only is each child different, but his or her needs will change as he or she gets older. Planning ahead means staying attuned to a child's unique and changing needs.

Seeing Red

The above suggestions in the antianger prescription will help you control and limit feelings of anger at your children. But when you do get angry, you need some guidelines to help you cope, avoid the danger of escalation, and recover.

1. **Don't touch your child when you are angry.** The adrenaline charge in your body makes it difficult to gauge the amount of force you are using and your physiological arousal could easily turn to aggression. This is no time for a spanking! When you are angry, it is safest to have your son go to his room or otherwise separate himself from you on his own power. If this is not possible, you should leave. If your children are old enough to leave alone, take a walk around the block. If you cannot leave them alone, sit outside the house, or sit in your car (do not drive!) where you can easily hear or see them. If you must handle a child to put him in his crib or restrict him to a safe environment, do so in a calm and controlled way. Move in slow motion and be aware of any overreaction. Do not shout or slam the door. These actions increase the adrenaline charge and the risk of losing control.

2. **Combat your trigger thoughts.** Replace them with self-talk that is calming and comforting to you. "I can control myself." "I am really worn out, and I need a break." "I don't need to make a decision now, I'll think of a solution when I'm calm." "I can get help figuring this out later." See chapter 13 on coping through healthy self-talk for more suggestions about keeping control when you're angry.

3. **Get support.** It may help to talk to another person, but avoid complaining about your child to someone who will fan the flames of anger. It doesn't help to hear "You're right, what a little beast. I

would never put up with that kind of behavior." You might make an agreement with a friend or relative whom you can call when you feel really stressed. Choose a person who will allow you to ventilate and just listen or will help you calm down *without* agreeing with you, arguing, or giving advice.

4. **Use time-out when necessary.** (See chapter 12.) When you are angry, you may be fearful that what you do or say may be damaging to your child. You need time to calm down, regroup your resources, and look at things with a new and calmer point of view. If your child is old enough, explain the concept and rules of time-out when you are *not* in conflict. Establish what signal you will use to call time-out, how long you will be away, when you will return, and what you expect of him or her. When you are gone, use the time to calm down or expend the physical energy generated by the anger. Brisk walking, hitting a pillow, aerobic exercise, or crying are all good ways of releasing the pent-up energy that goes along with anger. Some household tasks are very conducive to discharging anger, such as vacuuming the rugs, polishing, hammering, or mowing. A cup of tea, listening to a favorite album, or spending a few minutes reading can help you recover. Do not try to solve the problem. Your aim is to recover from anger, not find the solution.

5. **Stick with assertive messages and avoid blaming, sarcasm, insults, or generalizations.** Attacking statements intensify your angry feelings. Angry attacks on children are devastating to their self-esteem and do not inspire regret or cooperation. Long after the fight is over, the insults that children have heard will linger in their memory and affect their image of themselves. Stick to the point. If you are confronting your son about teasing his brother, don't bring up difficulties he is having at school or his failure to feed the dog that morning.

6. **Listen.** Repeat what you heard your child say to make sure you heard it. Ask if you got it right. If not, ask your child to explain again the part you missed. Listening to your daughter's position doesn't mean that you agree with it. When people feel heard, they are less resistant and provocative.

7. **If you feel overwhelmed, call a parent stress hotline.** The counselors who answer phones are supportive, not critical—they know the stress you are under. They can handle the immediate problem as well as refer you to other community resources. Sometimes just talking to someone on the phone or reaching out for help will lower your arousal level and enable you to better cope. Parents having difficulty coping with a child's demands can call CHILD

HELP (1-800-422-4453), a twenty-four-hour national hotline that provides phone counseling.

Making It Happen

Your relationship with your child is different from any other relationship in your life. As a parent, you are responsible to teach your children, socialize them, and prepare them to be able to live in the world successfully without you. In no other relationship are you 100 percent responsible to set the limits and provide both discipline and love. In no other relationship is the other person so dependent and vulnerable. In no other relationship are the effects of anger so devastating and the importance of finding ways to solve problems without anger so important. The fact that you are reading this book indicates that you are aware of the importance of finding a way to live with your children without feeling so angry so much of the time.

Making changes in any relationship takes patience and perseverance. Children expect their parents to act a certain way. When you change your style of communication and respond to conflict or stress without lashing out, they may be surprised—even confused.

The changes you make may seem strange or unnatural to you at first. It may take a while to get used to allowing natural consequences to occur instead of stepping in to rescue the child. It may take time to get used to planning reasonable consequences instead of blowing up and feeling guilty later.

Parent support and education groups (Parent Effectiveness Training, Tough Love, Positive Discipline) can put you in contact with a network of supportive teachers and other parents who are going through similar experiences with their children. You are not alone. When you hear how other parents cope with similar problems, you can gain a better perspective on your own.

Family therapy may be helpful to identify problems and patterns that trigger anger. It can be a place where everyone in the family can participate in exploring solutions and finding alternatives.

There will be times when you are successful in changing your usual responses to stress and you don't get angry. There may be times when you fall into the old anger-generating habits—magnifying, labeling, and assumed intent. At these times you may wonder if it's too late to change old patterns. But even long-established negative patterns can change. Sometimes even the smallest changes in the language that you use or the things you tell yourself when you get upset can make a tremendous difference in how you feel and how you cope. The effort you expend will help protect the most important thing in your life—your kids.

20

Spouse Abuse

by Kim Paleg, Ph.D.*

Jim couldn't find his blue striped shirt. "Damn! Not again!" He stormed into the kitchen where his wife, Alison, was cooking his breakfast. "I didn't have time to iron yesterday," she began. Jim grabbed the omelet pan from her hand and hurled it across the kitchen. "Pay attention when I tell you something!" he screamed. Her meekness infuriated him even more as she shrank against the refrigerator and edged toward the kitchen door. He became enraged. He punched at her wildly, then grabbed her and threw her out of his way before marching back into the bedroom to finish dressing and slam out of the house.

Vicki told her husband of her mother's intended visit. Joe hated his mother-in-law's visits; he always felt excluded by the two of them talking and laughing—about him, he often thought. And Vicki knew how he felt, so why was she doing this to him again? He was livid. The argument escalated rapidly until Joe screamed, "If she steps one foot in my house, I don't know what I'll do." He slammed out of the room, returning a few minutes later carrying his shotgun. Vicki watched with terror as Joe sat and cleaned the gun, staring white-faced and threatening.

* Kim Paleg is in private practice. She specializes in couple and family psychotherapy. Dr. Paleg is coauthor of *Focal Group Psychotherapy* (New Harbinger Publications), *When Anger Hurts Your Kids* (New Harbinger Publications), and *When Anger Hurts Your Relationship* (New Harbinger Publications).

Julie was tired after a long week of working hard. Her boy-friend, David, was due to arrive any minute; Julie was hoping he'd like the idea of ordering a pizza and cuddling in front of the TV. He didn't. "You never want to do anything anymore," he complained. "Don't be silly," Julie retorted, "I'm usually the one who makes the suggestions for going out." David knew that was true, and he knew he was being silly, but he hated hearing it from Julie. He already felt inferior in comparison with her; she was more articulate and had a better memory, and when they argued he always lost. Suddenly he was furious. "Why do you always have to argue?" he yelled. "Why can't you just do what I want for a change?" David stood, clenching and unclenching his fists. Suddenly he swung around and punched the wall about two feet from her head, skinning his knuckles and making a hole in the wall. Then he turned and left.

When anger escalates out of control, violence and abuse can easily result. The line between what's abusive and what's not is often difficult to determine. Sometimes the line is crossed without either person being totally aware of the transition. It seems clear that Alison was being abused when her husband punched and threw her against the wall. But what about Vicki? Was her husband being abusive when he sat, white-faced and menacing, cleaning his shotgun? Or what about Julie's boyfriend, who broke her wall instead of her jaw? In truth, these are all examples of abuse. Abuse occurs any time someone is induced to act in ways that they would not otherwise have chosen to act, by violence, threats, or intimidation. Abuse includes not only habitual beatings, but the occasional slap or shove and even the threat of such behavior.

It has been estimated that one out of every two American fami-lies experiences some form of domestic violence each year. One fam-ily in five experiences violence on an ongoing basis. More often than not, the abusing partner is the man, and the victim, the woman.

Sometimes an abusive incident will occur once and never be repeated. Jan described one argument with her husband where she accused him of not caring about her feelings. She'd had a fight with her boss that day and wanted Tony's comfort and support. Tired from his own day, Tony at first retreated behind his newspaper. After a while he became defensive and counterattacked. As Jan's frustration mounted, she not only lashed out at Tony verbally, but physically as well. Tony caught her fist in mid-punch and threw her backwards, where she fell heavily, hitting her head on the coffee table. Both were horrified and shaken. Now, eight years later, Jan reports that the shock of that incident left an indelible mark on their relationship and provided the necessary restraints to ensure that no further violence would occur.

At the other end of the scale, Sarah described from her hospital bed a nightmare of five years of almost daily beatings. She and Peter had heated arguments in the year following their marriage. There had been some violence—a few slaps, a shove or two—but she'd never thought of it as abuse. The first major beating occurred when they'd returned home from a party where, according to Peter, Sarah had flirted with "anything in pants." After this, escalation was rapid. Every argument and every disagreement led to a beating, and soon Sarah began to dread the sound of Peter's car in the driveway. The last episode left Sarah in the hospital with a ruptured spleen and the realization that if something didn't change she might soon be dead. Sarah's case demonstrates an important fact about abuse: left unchecked, abuse tends to escalate into increasingly violent episodes.

The first time violence occurs, it's usually a shock to both partners. The victim feels stunned: how can someone who supposedly loves her treat her this way? She rationalizes that it must have been an exceptional, isolated incident in which he overreacted. The abuser validates this perception, promising that it will never happen again. Wanting to believe him, the victim searches for what she might have done wrong to cause her partner's reaction so that she can avoid triggering him again. In this way they convince themselves that it's not a problem and minimize the seriousness of the episode.

Patterns of Abuse

Various theories describe the cycle of violence. Walker's (1984) three-step model includes (1) the phase of tension building, (2) the explosion or acute violent episode, and (3) the remorse phase. During the tension-building phase frustrations gradually mount. Spouses often report being aware that things are leading to a blowup. Sometimes the tension becomes so intolerable that the eventual violence is a relief. When the explosion or acute violent episode occurs, the victim might be pushed, grabbed, held, slapped, shoved, kicked, bitten, choked, punched, hit with an object, or threatened or attacked with a knife or a gun. The remorse phase occurs in the period after the violence, when the abuser often feels embarrassed or humiliated about his loss of control. He swears it will never happen again and finds ways to reassure his partner of his devotion. This period has also been called the "honeymoon phase." Jim would bring Alison flowers and gifts; Joe would take Vicki out for a romantic dinner at a fancy restaurant. Over time, less and less remorse is shown, and the couple experiences more frequently repeated periods of tension building and violence.

Deschner's (1984) model is more complex and consists of seven phases. The first phase is that of mutual dependency. In abusive relationships, partners often rely on each other for the satisfaction of all their needs, emotional and otherwise. When there are no outside sources of reward, having a need frustrated by a spouse becomes much more serious. Any irritating event (the second phase) such as dinner not being ready on time or a shirt not being ironed can lead rapidly to the third phase, where each partner attempts to force the other to meet his or her needs through coercion. The "last straw" decision (phase four) occurs at the point at which the abuser feels that the stressful situation is no longer tolerable. He feels as if he's exhausted his alternatives and has to resort to expressing his anger and frustration in violence. At this point, he gives way to the primitive rage that is the hallmark of phase five. Phase six provides the abuser with reinforcement for his battering. Since the abuse results in an immediate cessation of whatever was causing the stress, violence is reinforced as an effective way to deal with frustration and pain. For the victim, the end of the battering provides negative reinforcement. Phase seven is the repentance phase. Both partners are initially shocked at the outbreak of violence. The batterer swears earnestly that it will never happen again and attempts to prove his love and devotion. The victim is only too willing to believe him. For the victim, this honeymoon phase can reinforce the cycle of violence. This phase may be the only time that she ever feels close in the relationship and experiences her partner as warm and loving. It's also a time when the power in the relationship shifts temporarily to the victim, and this reversal of roles is also very reinforcing. After repeated battering episodes, the seven steps are often truncated to more rapidly completed cycles of buildup (phase three) and attack (phase five).

Why Does Abuse Occur?

Complex answers to the question of violence include factors outside the family as well as within it. In this society, violence is a part of daily life. As a child, you watched cartoons that showed brutal violence between the cartoon characters that seems to do no lasting harm. Wiley E. Coyote is killed and reborn an average of five times in each *Road Runner* episode. As an adult, you see violence in the media and read newspapers that describe countless incidents of violence here and around the world.

Societal Factors

In all but nine states across the U.S., paddling is allowed in schools. This paddling can be hard and is inflicted on both teens and small children. Once again the message from society is that violence solves problems.

The socialization process also increases a propensity for violence in men. Males are taught that to be considered "real men" they must be strong and tough and ready to defend their manhood at any time. They're discouraged from talking about feelings that could be perceived as "weak," such as fear, sadness, neediness, or hurt. To deal with vulnerability and pain, some men turn to alcohol and drugs; others simply bury the feelings under episodes of explosive rage (see chapter 17 on anger as a defense).

Women are given a different set of instructions. It's okay for women to express vulnerable feelings, but they are encouraged to be passive and "ladylike" in their interactions with men. Direct expressions of anger are discouraged. Thus in any violent exchange, women are more likely to be victims and men to be abusers.

Society also reinforces the forceful domination of women by men in many subtle ways. Religious doctrine emphasizes the superiority of men and assigns women an adjunct role. Family law until recently gave men rights over their wives as though they were possessions (including the right to beat them when necessary). Only a few states today have laws prohibiting rape in marriage. Many people in law enforcement still don't acknowledge spouse abuse or marital rape as crimes. An economic system in which women are paid less than 73 cents for every dollar paid to men keeps women financially dependent on their husbands. These often unquestioned social characteristics contribute to the inequality of a relationship that gives one sex power over the other and makes spouse abuse possible.

Family Factors

An important piece in the puzzle of domestic violence is the abuse that each partner may have experienced in his or her own family of origin. As a child, your earliest role models were, of course, your parents. If you saw your parents engaged in an abusive relationship, you may have acquired a template for future relationships. As a boy, you may have learned that anger is most effectively expressed in violence and that violence is useful as a means of influencing or controlling others. As a girl, you may have learned that your lot in life is to be subjected to such violence. Research (Strauss, Gelles, and Steinmetz 1981) indicates that men who grew up with violent parents are ten times more likely to batter their wives than men who weren't exposed to violence in their family of origin. Additionally, men who received heavy physical punishment as teenagers become batterers at a rate four times that of men who weren't punished physically.

If you were abused as a child, it's likely that the violence affected how you view yourself. Most children believe that they deserve what happens to them, and so you may have developed the deep belief that you were not a very worthwhile person. Feelings of unworthiness can contribute to low self-esteem and a dependency on others for validation. Both of these factors can produce a heightened vulnerability to frustration and criticism.

Characteristics of Batterers

Men who batter represent a wide spectrum of age, race, religion, socioeconomic status, education, and career. However, some characteristics are present across the board. For the most part, the abuser is a man who doesn't feel very good about himself, believes that he's not very worthwhile, and looks to others for reassurance. He holds traditional views about sex roles and looks to his partner for nearly all of his emotional support and nurturance. If he doesn't feel good about himself, he's likely to suspect that others may feel the same. So he anticipates rejection and he can perceive almost anything as a rejection. Since he finds it difficult to express feelings of hurt and disappointment, he's more likely to respond with anger. Responding to perceived insults with violence increases his negative feelings about himself and makes the cycle all the more likely to recur. His limited ability to empathize makes it difficult for him to understand his wife's feelings. He has little or no insight into her pain and fear, so his violent acting-out goes unrestrained.

Pathological Jealousy

Another related characteristic of a man who abuses his partner is pathological jealousy. If he's dependent on his spouse for all of his emotional support, then he may be constantly terrified that she'll leave him for another man. After all, if she can see that he's as worthless as he often feels, then she would naturally want to be with someone else. The fear of abandonment underlying jealousy typically provokes irrational suspiciousness and frequent questioning and accusations. Mary's husband monitored her activities in and out of the house. He insisted on driving her to work every day and picking her up in the evening. He grilled her about her social contacts at the office. On weekends he refused to allow her to visit friends and strictly limited her use of the phone.

Pathological jealousy can also lead to sexual violence. Rape frequently occurs in battering relationships. Some men force their partners to have sex with them as a way of feeling reassured about their own sexual identity. Some equate physical and psychological abuse with sexual arousal and desire sex in the aftermath of a beating.

Isolation

One of the most important characteristics of battering relationships is their isolation. The more anxious and in need of reassurance the man becomes, the more likely he is to bond tightly with his partner. Outsiders are seen as threats to his control and to his relationship. He may forbid her to go out without him, to exercise, to meet with friends, or to do the weekly grocery shopping. He may restrict her money and her phone contacts with friends and family. Eventually he may even monitor her mail. Gradually the partners become more and more isolated, which in turn increases their dependency on each other for most emotional and practical needs. Increasing dependency usually leads to decreasing flexibility in meeting the demands of everyday life. That means more stress. And the more stress, the greater the chances of conflict and eventual violence.

The abuser tends to lack the skills both to ask for what he wants and to say no to his partner. He holds society's stereotype of what it means to be a man, which includes the ability to control his wife and not to be "henpecked." Thus his self-esteem is bruised again and again when he's unable to live up to all of his standards. The result is a building resentment and a growing willingness to use violence to get his needs met. Violence becomes a way of controlling and incapacitating the partner. He's less threatened by her independence and the possibility of her leaving him. He feels more powerful and more in control. In this way, violence is positively reinforced, increasing the likelihood that it will be used again.

Instrumental Aggression

One of the most frightening and dangerous types of abuse, which is usually seen in long-term battering relationships, is called "instrumental aggression." In most cases of abuse, each violent episode is accompanied by a rush of primitive rage, during which the batterer feels out of control. Afterward he may feel embarrassed and remorseful, temporarily upset about his behavior and determined to prevent its recurrence. But sometimes the violence is so rewarded that it becomes ingrained as an habitual way of getting what's wanted. It's no longer simply an out-of-control rage response, but a calculated way of gaining a desired reward. The violence becomes "instrumental" in gaining the reward.

This batterer seems to show no emotion during the violence and no remorse afterwards. This is a man who can beat his wife daily for no apparent reason and no longer seems to be responding to any internal feeling of anger or rage. He is unlikely to give up the habit, even in treatment, since he sees it as a justified and useful tactic for getting his needs met.

Drugs and Alcohol

Drugs and alcohol are involved in more than 80 percent of violent episodes (Sonkin, Martin, and Walker 1985). Alcohol lowers inhibitions against violence, while heavy use of drugs like cocaine increases paranoia, which increases the likelihood of violence. Some men attribute their violence to the drugs or alcohol, claiming to feel out of control when under their influence. In most cases, however, the man has been abusive before the substance became a problem. And since he often aims for places that don't show—breasts, stomach, base of the spine, parts of the head hidden by hair—he apparently knows what he's doing. Considerable control is required to wound only where it won't be seen.

Military Men

Men in the military have added factors that contribute to problems with anger and violence. These men are given specific training in the use of violence and combat skills that become part of their day-to-day lives. When the conflict occurs at home instead of on the battlefield, it's not surprising that violence can result. In addition to the indoctrination process, military men and their families also experience a number of other stresses. Most military personnel tend to hold traditional sex roles, where the man must be strong, competent, and in charge. But the work is hard, long, and poorly paid and frequently involves experiences that lead to feelings of humiliation or powerlessness. These factors may all increase the need to feel in control at home. Families may be separated for extended periods of time while the men are on tours of duty. Absence of regular contact makes it harder to maintain marital and parental relationships. Moreover, the pattern of moving from place to place makes it difficult to establish and maintain friendships for everyone in the family. This in turn leads to increased isolation, one of the most important factors in battering relationships.

Estimates of the percentage of batterers that have had prior military experience range from 58 percent (Walker 1983) to 90 percent (Eisenberg and Micklow 1979).

The Battered Woman

There are many myths about the woman who remains in a battering relationship. Some people suggest that she is less a victim than a masochist who enjoys being abused. Or that she causes her partner to become violent. The battered woman has been described as passive, manipulative, and compliant. These notions are confirmed for some by the fact that women often return home to the abusive situation after a brief respite in a battered women's shelter.

The truth is that the woman who remains in a battering relationship does so because she sees no way out. Often she's financially dependent on her husband, untrained for any profession, and unable to support herself and her children. Frequently the man will threaten to kill her or her children, family, or friends if she leaves. And if the beatings have been severe enough, she may have good reason to believe him.

The potential for violence forces the woman to accept her husband's rigid view of her role, since this course is plainly safer for her than that of provoking his rage by acting any other way. So it's not hard to see why she is often seen as more traditional in her attitudes and more willing to accept a passive, compliant, "feminine" role. One recent study (Walker 1984) found that many battered women are actually more liberal in their sex-role attitudes than the norm. But when faced with an angry, potentially violent man, the woman will try to appease him and calm his anger. Over time, this behavior becomes the automatic response to anger—anyone's anger.

Since any direct expression of her own anger is likely to result in violence, the battered woman must resort to a more indirect way of voicing her feelings. She may say yes to her husband's requests, but find ways of sabotaging his plans without any indication of deliberate intention. Although this behavior could be labeled manipulative or passive-aggressive, it clearly helps her meet important needs while protecting her from abuse.

Abuse and Self-Esteem

By far the most devastating effect of physical or psychological abuse is the impact it has on the victim's self-esteem. The woman's realization that she has lost her ability to protect herself can result in constantly feeling afraid and off balance. She becomes hypervigilent, watching for any sign from her husband that might lead to anger and a beating.

After the first violent episode, a woman may convince herself that it was a mistake and that it will never happen again. Then it happens again ... and again. She can no longer escape from the sense that her love and trust has been violated, nor the terror of being unable to trust her own perceptions. After all, if this man was abusive before she met him, why couldn't she see it? And if he wasn't, what does that say about her? Is there some part of her that provokes violence, or worse, that deserves violence?

Feeling unable to prevent the abuse, the victim often develops a "learned helplessness." Time and time again the woman's attempts to stop the cycle of violence are ineffective. She comes to believe that she is unable to change anything, and so she simply stops trying. Instead, she learns to behave in ways that help her avoid the violence. She hides her feelings—sometimes even from herself—and assumes a passive, compliant role.

The feeling of helplessness can also lead to a tendency to deny and minimize the seriousness of the abuse. If the abuse isn't so severe or frequent, then it's not so terrible to be stuck in the relationship. This rationalization helps reduce the fear to a tolerable level. Sometimes the woman tells of her abuse to a friend or acquaintance, pastor or doctor, whose response is to minimize her complaints or not take them seriously. No one likes to acknowledge violence in an outwardly "lovely couple." But this response invalidates the woman's experience while reinforcing her denial. Doreen was told by her pastor that her husband was a "good man" and that she should be more understanding of the pressures he was under. Her doctor offered her a prescription for Valium.

In addition to all of these assaults on her self-esteem, the woman may be constantly belittled by her husband. During the buildup and abuse phases, she may be subjected to endless accounts of her faults and failings. Her husband may even blame her for the violent episodes, telling her that if she were a better wife (cook, mother, housekeeper, lover) the abuse wouldn't occur. After a while, it's not surprising that many women get profoundly depressed, even while maintaining a cheerful exterior facade. Often the depression is manifested in physical symptoms: back pain, headaches, menstrual problems, and low energy.

Who's Responsible?

So what keeps the abusive cycle going? Contrary to the myths described above, women do NOT cause or provoke spousal abuse. It's never the woman's fault that she's the victim of violence. No matter what she does, she never "deserves" to be beaten—no one does. There is absolutely no justification for violence. No matter how angry a man is, there are always alternatives to violence, and his choice of violence is quite simply that: his choice. Even if the man feels that he has no other resources in dealing with his anger, he is never justified in using violence. He alone is responsible for the abuse, and unless he acknowledges his problem with anger and wants to stop his violent behavior, the outlook for the relationship is grim.

Nevertheless, both partners *are* responsible for the stress and conflict in a relationship, and the woman can and often does behave in ways that provoke frustration and anxiety in her partner. Every relationship can be thought of as a unique dance, with each partner engaging in complementary steps that maintain the nature and direction of the dance. The battered woman can't stop the abuse, and attempting to do so only reinforces the erroneous belief that somehow she's to blame for the violence. Her partner must address his abusive behavior and learn new skills in anger management. But if she wants to stay in the relationship, she must also learn new skills in dealing with conflict.

Can Things Change?

The first question that must be addressed is whether there is any hope of the relationship changing, or whether the only logical option for the woman is to leave. If the history of violence in the relationship is short and the frequency and severity of the beatings are low, then the chances of success are increased. As the abuse becomes more entrenched and habitual, it becomes more resistant to change.

There must also be motivation to change. Does the batterer acknowledge his problems with anger and violence? Does he feel sorry after each abusive episode and wish to change sincerely enough to work on developing new behaviors? Is he willing to admit his problem to helping professionals and work with them long enough to stop the cycle?

The presence of remorse is an important indication of motivation. If the batterer shows no remorse after an episode of violence, then you may be dealing with a case of instrumental aggression. If so, the only reasonable option may be to work toward leaving. Finally, ongoing substance abuse weighs heavily against the possibility of stopping the violence.

Leaving

If your partner refuses to acknowledge his problem with anger and violence or refuses to work with others toward ending it, there may be very little that you can do to change your situation other than leave. Making the decision to leave can be extremely difficult. If you've found yourself going around and around in a struggle to decide, do an exercise suggested by Ginny NiCarthy in her book *Getting Free* (1982). Make a list of your fears of the worst that can happen if you leave. Be specific. Will you get so lonely and depressed that you'll take an overdose of sleeping pills? Will you be unable to provide for or discipline your children alone? Under each fear, write the reasons that it's *likely* to happen and the reasons that it's *unlikely* to happen. Then make a list of the worst that can happen if you stay with the abuser. Consider the most likely bad things to happen if you stay. Include the physical and psychological damage to you and your children. Remember the last time you were battered and list the things that you were afraid would happen then. Maybe you were afraid of being killed or of killing your partner. Maybe you feared being permanently injured. Do you get enough from the relationship to risk these things? Comparing the lists and weighing the different items on each can sometimes make the decision a little easier.

Without a job or any means of support, leaving can be a terrifying prospect, especially if you have children. There's probably a battered women's shelter in your community or nearby (listed in your local yellow pages under "Crisis Services") whose staff would be willing to talk to you. Call them and find out what resources are available for you and your children with respect to financial and legal aid, housing, and job training. If there are no shelters listed, call the National Coalition Against Domestic Violence crisis line: 1-800-799-7233 (twenty-four hours a day, seven days a week) for referrals. Seek an assertive lawyer who specializes in spouse abuse cases. Some lawyers will offer low-cost services, and some will work on a contingency basis. Look under "Legal Aid" in the phone book, or ask your local shelter for a referral. Try to solicit help and support from friends and family. Although you may feel reluctant to ask others for help, most friends would rather help you leave before you're injured than see the nightmare continue. But be careful of those people who, with the best of intentions, might attempt to "save your marriage" by informing your partner of your plans or whereabouts.

Protecting Yourself Now

One of the first and foremost considerations for you if you're a victim of domestic violence is safety for you and your children. Whether or not you ultimately decide to leave the relationship, you may still be at risk right now. Your husband might agree that he has a problem with anger and be committed to changing his behavior. But he isn't going to change overnight. It's crucial that you have a place where you and your children can go when you feel you're at risk. Friends or relatives are good options, but if your partner decides to look for you, these places may be at the top of his list. Battered women's shelters are another alternative. They provide crisis counseling and safety from an abusive situation.

Make a plan to exercise this option. Set aside some money, an extra set of car keys, and any personal business documents you might need for the few days or longer that you might be away. It might help to have a small overnight bag packed and ready for the occasion—preferably stored at a friend's or neighbor's house. If children are involved, include some toys for them. When you feel in danger, get out fast. Don't hang around wondering if there's something you've forgotten. Although unconfirmed, statistics suggest that the highest risk period for homicides against women is while leaving. You can always return at a later date with police support to collect anything you need.

If possible, call the police when violence has occurred. In some places, the police are required to respond to calls and make an arrest if a felony has been committed. Beating someone, even one's wife, is usually a felony. Arrest has a sobering effect on offenders and tends to reduce the recidivism rate, even when the offender is released within twenty-four hours. Prosecution further lowers recidivism, even if no conviction occurs. The court may require that the batterer attend counseling to address the problems. It may also issue a temporary restraining order (TRO) or stay-away order that forces the batterer to keep away from you and the children. These orders can be issued by the court without an arrest or prosecution proceedings and don't even require the involvement of a lawyer.

Find out what kind of police support exists in your area. Unfortunately, in some places the police are reluctant to respond to domestic violence calls and often wait for several days before coming to the house. The staff at your local women's shelter should be able to tell you whether this is true in your community.

When Children Are Involved

Sometimes the decision to stay or leave involves considerations about children. You may be concerned about disrupting your children's lives or depriving them of a father. You might fear being unable to provide for them in the way you'd like. Some women try to postpone leaving till their children are all in school, are toilet trained, have all left home, or have reached some other milestone. And sometimes it works out for the best. But staying in a frightening, violent situation can often be more harmful for children than any temporary disruption or material deprivation.

You might be afraid that your partner will gain custody of the children if you leave or try to punish you by hurting them. Unfortunately, these fears are sometimes justified, and custody and visitation rulings are often unfair. Think through your plan of action with a lawyer who specializes in domestic violence cases.

If the children are being abused, the decision to stay or leave becomes even more crucial. Child abuse can be just as subtle and difficult to identify as spouse abuse. It can include constant belittling and threats of violence as well as physical beatings. Usually, all the battering in a family is done by the one violent person. And you may feel just as helpless to protect your children as to ensure your own safety. If so, leaving the relationship may be the only option that offers the safe environment that children need. Call the children's protective service agency in your area or the National Child Abuse Hotline, operated by Childhelp USA: 1-800-4-A-CHILD (twenty-four hours a day, seven days a week). These agencies can help you clarify your options and provide counseling and referrals.

If you are abusing your children, recognizing that you have a problem with your own anger is the first step. You may be angry at their father for his abuse of you and unable to express it to him. Or you may be jealous of the fact that the abuse is only directed at you and not at them. Or your tolerance for conflict may be very low as a result of having to live in a constant state of stress and vigilance. In any case, your abuse, although understandable, is unacceptable. Once you're out of the violent situation, this abuse might automatically stop. Meanwhile, call Parents Anonymous: 1-909-621-6184 (open seven days a week) or the hotlines listed above for crisis counseling and referrals. Although it will be difficult to make the calls, you will probably feel relieved to finally get help in dealing with your children more effectively. Reading the following sections on resources for batterers can give you some tools for dealing with your own frustration and anger. Counseling and support groups can increase your parenting skills and improve your ability to set limits.

If You Stay: Seeing the Cycle

If you decide to stay and work on the relationship, there are several factors to explore. The following suggestions assume that the batterer has acknowledged his problem with anger and violence and is actively working on changing his behavior with the help of a professional. If not, the chances of the violence stopping and the relationship improving are minimal.

Although the ultimate decision to use violence is solely the batterer's responsibility, the conflict that precedes the violence often involves both partners.

Think about the cycle that usually occurs in your relationship. When do you become aware that violence is inevitable? Can you detect early warning signs? Does the man drink heavily before a violent interaction? Does he get upset about innocuous events? Maybe he gets silent and withdrawn. What goes on immediately before that "point of inevitability"? Review chapter 12 on stopping escalation to see how aversive chains develop. These may begin with a relatively trivial exchange and rapidly and predictably escalate to the expression of anger and violence. The more links (or interchanges) on a chain, the more likely violence will result. The last link that often precedes a violent outburst is called the trigger behavior, it is a link that usually stirs up feelings of abandonment or rejection in the abuser.

There are many possible links that can build aversive chains, including a variety of verbal behaviors (blaming, threatening, complaining), nonverbal sounds (groaning or sighing), tone and quality of voice (mocking, cold, loud), facial expressions (scowling or frowning), gestures (shaking a fist), and body movements (turning or moving away, throwing something). Think back over the past several incidents that have occurred in your relationship. Try to identify the different links in the chain and see if you can detect patterns. Does your partner always get furious when you try to defend yourself against his accusations? Does he seem to respond negatively to your visible signs of fear? Do things get worse when you attempt to end the interaction by walking away from him? There are usually (but not always) a series of progressive stages that precede a violent outburst.

Changing the Cycle

Once you've begun to identify the early warning signs that indicate potential violence, you can begin to use the time-out model described in chapter 12. (If your partner is in treatment, he may already have been introduced to the concept.) At the instant you recognize a warning sign that an aversive chain is beginning, call "Time-out" and make the T sign with your hands. It helps to discuss the procedure ahead of time, at a moment when tension is low, and reach an agreement about who's going to leave first, where each of you are going to go, and for how long. Because anger is often triggered by feelings of rejection and abandonment, your partner may prefer to be the first to leave in order to avoid the experience of being "left." Since there is a risk that when the next episode occurs your partner might forget or simply not care that he made an agreement with you, you should be sure to make plans for your own safety. Come back and check in with each other at a specified interval after the time-out. Be careful that you're not putting yourself in danger again by coming back. You might arrange to initiate the check-in with a phone call in order to assess the level of anger still present.

Rechanneling

Another technique described in chapter 12 is that of rechanneling. More subtle than time-out, this technique redirects the sequence at a critical junction or "weak link" in the aversive chain. A weak link is a point in the chain where a new behavior could be most easily substituted for the old.

Examine the patterns you were able to detect in your relationship. At what points might you be able to say or do something different? Vicki knew that her husband, Joe, felt left out whenever her mother came to visit. She felt guilty about enjoying time with her mother away from Joe, yet knew she didn't want to give up those special times. Vicki identified a weak link at the point when Joe said, "Oh great! Just what I need! That old bag visiting again." Instead of her usual defensive, blaming response, Vicki realized that she could have acknowledged how left out Joe felt at those times and offered to try to include him in some of their activities. For Julie, a weak link existed at the point at which she said to her husband, "Don't be silly!" in a patronizing voice. The scene might have been rechanneled with acknowledgment and compromise: "I guess you were really looking forward to going out tonight. Maybe we could compromise and go to an early show?"

Rechanneling can be effective only if your partner is also involved in substituting new behaviors for his old violent patterns. While identifying the weak links and attempting alternative behaviors can often alter the pattern of conflict, the responsibility for changing the violent response still remains strictly with the man. Unless your partner is actively working on finding his own weak links in the chain, your efforts may be futile. If your partner is uncommitted to making the necessary changes in his behavior, you might wish to reconsider whether staying in the relationship is the best decision after all.

One very important part of changing your old pattern of isolation and mutual dependency is for you to join a group for women who've been victims of domestic violence. The battered women's shelter in your area can probably give you referrals to such groups. In the group, you can establish relationships with other women and get support for the decisions you make about your relationship. You can practice assertive behaviors and explore the potential impact that taking such different steps will have on your relationship.

Psychological Fallout

The psychological aftermath of being in an abusive relationship often resembles the post-traumatic stress syndrome that many war veterans experience. You may feel that you're constantly under siege because the memory of past violence and the uncertainty of when it might occur again lead to a state of constant fear and anticipation. Common symptoms include anxiety, fear, depression, shock, anger, inappropriate compassion, guilt, humiliation, confused thinking, intrusive memories, uncontrolled reexperiencing of traumatic events, rigidity, lack of trust, suspiciousness, hypervigilance, and increased startle response to cues of possible violence. A professional counselor who's been trained to assist victims of abuse can help you slowly heal the hidden wounds that remain after the physical scars have disappeared.

Discovering Your Needs

You need to explore and discover what *your* needs are, so that you can learn how to be more assertive in attempting to meet them. Abusive relationships are characterized by mutual dependency, where the batterer expects that all his needs will be met by his partner. As a consequence, the victim begins to stifle her own needs and desires and to focus on those of her partner. Eventually, even her awareness of her needs dims. Rediscovering your own needs and desires and learning how you can meet them can lead to increased feelings of competence and independence. It won't stop the abuse, but knowing what you want to change can push you to get help or get out.

Challenging Beliefs

It's important to evaluate the abusive patterns you may have learned in your own family of origin and relearn healthier, more self-affirming patterns. If you were abused as a child or witnessed abuse between your parents, you may have learned that violence was an unavoidable part of life. You will need to challenge your beliefs and assumptions about how you deserve to be treated in a relationship. Do you deserve to be abused? Do you deserve to be "punished" for doing something for yourself that your partner doesn't like? Does any adult have the right to punish, physically or otherwise, another adult?

Strengthening Self-Esteem

Most importantly, you need to restore your feelings of worth. Your abusive partner has probably attacked your basic value as a person as well as your behavior. It's difficult to hear frequent attacks without, on some level, starting to agree. Perhaps you already had secret doubts about your worth; perhaps you already criticize yourself for certain failures. Everyone has a critical inner voice. But when that voice constantly attacks and berates you, it can do tremendous damage to your self-esteem. To assess the strength of your inner critic, make a list of the things that you did right today. Add everything that you feel good about. If you can't think of very many things, chances are that your critic is working overtime.

The first step in strengthening your self-esteem is to identify the critic and determine exactly what it says to you. Because the attacks are so frequent and familiar, they may be hardly noticeable. Try to hear what your critic is saying when you've made a mistake, when your partner is criticizing you, or when you're feeling depressed or down on yourself. Keep a notebook and write down exactly what's said, from single words ("Idiot!") to whole sentences ("If I hadn't been such a stubborn fool, I might not have made such a stupid mistake").

Notice whether the criticisms are general or specific. General criticisms are those that make a global judgment about you or your behavior ("What a slob!" "Boy, are you stupid!" "You never do anything right!"). Criticisms like these are destructive because they don't allow any room for improvement, but simply hack away at any feelings of worth. Specific criticisms are limited to a particular incident or behavior. They don't condemn you totally as a person for each minor mistake or failure ("I didn't express myself very assertively with Dennis today;" "the promo piece wasn't catchy enough").

Go back over your list of things the critic has been saying to you. Analyze each attack. Is it general or specific? Is it a global indictment or does it refer to a specific situation without condemning you as a person? Try substituting a simple statement of fact for each criticism. Use language that's specific (avoid words like *never, always, everything*) and nonpejorative (avoid adjectives that have negative connotations like *lazy, illogical, stupid, stubborn, crazy*). Sally was able to substitute, "I forgot Fred's birthday and sent him a card that was a few days late," for, "What an idiot! You never remember anything on time!" Pat changed, "You're such a manipulative bitch!" to "Sometimes I don't express my needs directly to Larry because I'm afraid he might respond with anger and violence."

Now try and find exceptions or strengths that correspond to the critic's statements. Pat could see that although she didn't express herself directly with Larry, she had no difficulty with her mother or sister. Sally acknowledged that although she forgot Fred's birthday she had remembered everything else on her list of things to do for the week. Doing this last step is particularly important in the pursuit of higher self-esteem.

Some of the strengths you identify can be turned into positive affirmations. Make a list of qualities and abilities that you like about yourself. Remind yourself of your strengths when the critic goes on the attack.

Once you've begun to hear the critic and practiced writing down the criticisms, analyzing them, and substituting more realistic and self-affirming statements, you can begin to practice the process without writing. The more you practice, the sooner you'll begin to feel less depressed and more positive about yourself.

Seeing a Professional

Although there are many things that you can do to take care of yourself, a professional counselor can make an important contribution to your recovery. A variety of counselors have been trained in helping victims of spouse abuse. You can find marriage and family counselors, psychiatrists, psychologists, social workers, and religious counselors in your local yellow pages. More specifically, domestic violence programs can be found under the headings of "Crisis Intervention Services" or "Social Service Agencies." Suicide prevention or child abuse hotlines can also be helpful. Keep in mind the fact that some professionals, like many others in society, believe that a man's wife and children are his possessions and that he has the right to treat them as he chooses. Check with the local battered women's shelter or with the local chapter of NOW (National Organization of Women) to discover which counselors hold attitudes that will benefit your progress.

If You Use Violence

If you're a man and want to change your pattern of anger and violence, the most important step is to GET HELP. Changing the cycle of violent behavior is difficult at best, and virtually impossible without outside help. A treatment group for offenders is probably the most helpful, and can be found in the yellow pages under "Crisis Intervention Services" or "Social Service Agencies." You could also call the National Coalition Against Domestic Violence (1-800-799-7233) for referrals. A group setting is especially helpful for breaking the isolation and mutual dependency that exist in most abusive relationships. It can also provide a forum for developing and rehearsing anger-management skills.

Individual counseling can also be useful. If you're in the military, there are usually counseling services on the base which are set up to address problems that active duty personnel and their families experience. Or check out your regional military hospital or branch clinic. Sometimes the chaplain can be a useful source of referrals

Remember that your willingness to enter some sort of treatment program is the best sign of your commitment to changing your violent behavior. Without this commitment, the chances of change occurring are remote.

Substance Abuse

If you use alcohol or other drugs, it's essential that you evaluate how these substances contribute to the abusive pattern in which you're involved. If you're in doubt about the impact that alcohol or drugs have, then go to a treatment center where you can get the assessment and help you need. Look in your local yellow pages under "Alcoholism Information and Treatment" or "Drug Abuse Information and Treatment." If you need more intensive treatment, hospital-based programs offer short-term in-patient care, while residential programs provide longer term assistance. Attempts to change violent behavior are unlikely to succeed if you continue to abuse drugs or alcohol.

Anger Control

There's little hope of managing your anger within the context of your relationship unless you are committed to the belief that there are no justifications for violence against your partner under any circumstances. No matter what the provocation, she does not deserve to be hit. Because violence is a behavior that you learned, it follows that you can also learn nonviolent alternatives.

Anger-control skills involve five major components: (1) taking responsibility for your pain and stress, (2) giving up blame and challenging the thoughts that trigger anger, (3) identifying the physical early warning cues and patterns of escalation, (4) learning stress-reduction behaviors, and (5) learning assertive, problem-solving communication.

Taking Responsibility

The first step in managing your anger and violence is to understand the two-step model of anger (chapter 6) and the principle of personal responsibility (chapter 7). This principle suggests that you are responsible for the outcome of all your interactions. It's stressful not to get what you want or need, and it's easy to mask the resulting feelings of frustration and helplessness by blaming the other person for your pain. But you are the only one who knows your exact desires and needs. The other person is aware of his or her needs, and is doing the best that he or she can at the time to get those needs met. Trying to force the other person to change with anger or violence is destructive to each of you and to the relationship. Only by changing your own behavior can you produce a more satisfying outcome.

It doesn't make sense to ask who's responsible for your pain. When needs conflict, as they often do, it's inevitable that one or both partners will be frustrated or disappointed. What does make sense is to use your anger or frustration as a cue to ask yourself, "What hurts?" and, "Since I'm responsible for my pain, what can I do to fix it?" Try different strategies to discover the ones that work best for you. If a strategy fails, don't fall into the "helpless victim" role—try another. Each time his mother-in-law visited, Joe felt angry and abandoned. He blamed Vicki for his frustration and believed that she should change things. That only led to resistance from Vicki and escalation of anger on both sides. When Joe asked himself the two questions above, he realized that what hurt was feeling excluded. He decided to explore ways *he* could change the situation. He might suggest activities that included the three of them. Or he could spend some time really getting to know his mother-in-law so that he understood more of her jokes and idiosyncratic humor. Or he could plan fun activities for himself so that he wasn't sitting at home waiting when they were out together.

Owen found himself furious every time Betsy smiled at another man. His jealousy was reaching pathological levels. When he asked himself "What hurts?" Owen identified feelings of fear and insecurity. He was interpreting Betsy's smiles as interest in having an affair and was terrified at the potential of losing her—her time, attention, and love. If he were to take full responsibility for changing the situation, Owen would realize that he had several choices. He could express his concerns directly to Betsy and ask for reassurance. He experienced less jealousy when his level of stress was low, so he could practice his stress-reduction techniques. Finally, he could avoid situations that he could predict might trigger his jealousy.

Giving Up Blame

There are many ways of coping with the stress and frustration of not getting your needs met. Blaming is one of them. You decide that your pain was caused by someone else. Underlying blame is the

belief that other people *should* be feeling, thinking, or behaving differently. The fact that they're not makes them bad, wrong, and
deserving of punishment. Chapter 9 describes how these "blamers"
and "shoulds," added to the stress itself, trigger anger.

The problem with this process is that the people you're judging
rarely agree with your rules about what's right and wrong and what
they should and shouldn't be doing, feeling, and thinking. Although
any kind of "should" can trigger anger, chapter 9 describes several
that are extremely damaging in intimate relationships. Review in
particular the entitlement fallacy ("I want it very much, therefore I
should have it"), the fallacy of fairness ("If my needs aren't met, it's
not fair"), the fallacy of change ("If I just apply enough pressure, I
can make you change and meet my needs"), conditional assumptions
("If you really loved me, you'd meet my needs"), and the letting it
out fallacy ("If you don't meet my needs, you deserve to be punished
with my anger").

The important blamers to understand are good-bad dichotomizing ("What you do to me is either good or bad, right or
wrong"), assumed intent ("You're deliberately not meeting my needs
in order to hurt me"), magnifying ("Things are really terrible,
awful!"), and global labeling ("You're such a dimwit!").

In order to change your pattern of anger and violence, you
need to combat these trigger thoughts. First, think back over the past
few incidents that provoked an anger response. What stress were
you experiencing before the particular incident occurred? What
needs weren't being met and what method did you use in your
attempt to meet those needs? Notice the pattern of escalation from
frustration to anger to violence. If you haven't already started an
anger journal, begin one now. Whenever you feel angry, write down
what you're saying to yourself. Identify the trigger thoughts that you
are using. It may help to review the general examples for the
"should" fallacies described above. And finally, rewrite your original
statement so that it is more realistic and no longer contains the
distorted trigger thought.

Adrian's first entry in his anger journal was, "This house is a
bloody pigsty! And she knows it drives me crazy coming home to
such a mess after a long day at work!" He identified his trigger
thoughts as assumed intent, magnifying, and the fallacy of fairness. After some consideration, Adrian rewrote his original statement. "I don't like it when the kids' toys are scattered around the
living room when I come home. I assume Melanie is doing the best
she can because other than the kids' stuff the house is pretty neat.
And it's quite a handful trying to pick up after three children.
Maybe we need to talk about hiring someone to help with the
cleaning."

Stopping Escalation

You may have attempted to control your violence by trying not to get angry. What usually happens under these circumstances is that the anger you feel builds up and eventually explodes into more violence. You need to become aware of your anger at the stages *before* it builds to an explosion. Most men are only aware of very high levels of anger, those that would score above 5 on a scale of 1 to 10. Lower levels of anger, which you probably call annoyance or irritation, are the ones most likely to be ignored until they build to an explosion. Read through chapter 10 again and learn the physiological cues that go along with early anger. Think back to recent times when you were frustrated or irritated. How did your body feel? Did you begin to feel tension in your jaw or neck? Did your hands ball into fists? Did your stomach feel tight or twisted? Go back to your anger journal. Each time you're angry or frustrated, write down the physiological cues you notice, the intensity of your anger on a scale of 1 to 10 (10 being high anger), and the situation that made you angry. Once you've identified your particular early warning signs, you can begin to make changes in the pattern of escalation that usually follows.

The most effective way to stop escalation is to employ the time-out model. Using chapter 12 as a guide, discuss with your partner how each of you will initiate a time-out, who's going to leave first, where each of you will go, and the length of the interval you'll be gone. It's essential that you call a time-out at the first sign of escalation. It's also crucial that if your partner calls a time-out before you're aware of feeling angry or even irritated, you respect her need to disengage from the discussion. Because your anger is the biggest threat in these situations, you should be the one to leave the house. You probably learned years ago that only cowards walk away from a fight. But the really courageous person is the one who can recognize a no-win, potentially disastrous situation and walk away without resorting to violence.

Stress Reduction

In chapter 10, you read how anger and relaxation are physiologically incompatible. Anger involves an increase in physiological tension, while relaxation leads to a decrease in tension. It's impossible to be relaxed and angry at the same time. If you can use your early warning signs of tension as a cue to relax, you can reduce the possibility of escalation even further. Chapter 10 describes several techniques for effectively reducing stress. Read the chapter again, and practice each technique several times before going on to the next one. In this way, you can determine which ones work best for you.

Then practice. Relaxing, like any other skill, requires a certain discipline and commitment.

The next step is to identify the situations that produce tension. If you've been keeping your anger journal, you're probably already able to see patterns. Perhaps your job is the most stressful component of your life right now, or perhaps your family or social demands. Perhaps a series of apparently minor setbacks has produced enough irritation and frustration to result in a state of chronic stress. Knowing your particular patterns will enable you to prepare yourself ahead of time and approach the situation as calmly as possible. Relaxation is most effective when used as a preventative measure. It's far easier to relax tight jaw muscles or a knotted stomach than it is to combat the tension accompanying overwhelming rage.

Adrian noticed that as soon as he walked into his living room and saw his children's toys scattered around, his neck and shoulder muscles began to tighten. Rather than making his habitual response of "This house is a bloody pigsty!" Adrian sat down on the couch and took several deep breaths. Even before he started examining the trigger thoughts that elicited the old reaction, he noticed a sharp reduction in his level of tension.

Simon found that a fast, five-mile run to the beach and back during a time-out cleared his head and worked the tension from his muscles. To his surprise, he found that lying down and meditating for fifteen minutes was equally effective. Eventually, Simon discovered that he could reduce the need for time-outs at home by setting aside a couple of brief periods during the day for meditation. Combating his stress at work led to far less escalation at home.

Communication

Because anger and violence are often fueled by the stress of unmet needs, it's important to learn more appropriate ways of meeting those needs. You were probably never taught how to express your needs clearly and assertively. You might hope that others will know or guess your needs by the subtle cues you give and then get frustrated and angry when they guess wrong. The less you're able to verbally express yourself, the more likely you are to resort to violence when frustrated. Problem-solving communication recognizes the validity of both partners' needs and the importance of compromise. Before continuing, make sure you've read and understood the concepts described in chapter 16 on problem-solving communication.

1. **Making requests.** To express your needs assertively, you must first be able to define those needs. When you're feeling angry or frustrated, ask yourself that old question, "What hurts?" Then

ask, "What do I want in order to fix it?" Formulate a statement that begins, "I feel . . ." and continues, ". . . and I want . . ." Take responsibility for your needs without blaming; "I feel lonely and want a hug," is more assertive than, "You're always so cold and distant." Say, "I'm feeling bored and I'd like to go to a movie tonight," rather than, "You're so boring! You never want to go out anymore."

Sometimes you'll need to describe the problem before getting into your feelings and needs. State the problem simply, exactly, and nonpejoratively. Just the facts, without blaming or making a case. "The TV usually goes on after dinner (*fact*). I feel a bit overwhelmed by the noise and I'd like to keep it off until nine."

Restate questions as statements. Questions are often perceived as criticisms or attacks and can lead to defensiveness and escalation. Say, "I feel anxious about running late for work when breakfast isn't ready on time," rather than, "Why can't you ever have breakfast ready on time?" "When you question my judgment in front of the kids, I feel embarrassed and humiliated . . . I'd rather you talked to me in private," will probably lead to less defensiveness than, "What the hell do you think you're doing, making a fool of me in front of the kids?"

2. **Setting limits.** Saying no clearly and directly is probably very difficult for you. You may fear that your partner will reject you if you refuse a request. Or you may have been told as a child that it's selfish and thoughtless to refuse a request. Some people say yes verbally, while saying no with their actions by completing the request slowly, ineffectively, and resentfully. These people are often chronically angry and feel exploited and unappreciated. Eventually a simple request might trigger an explosion of anger or violence. This is the kind of no that does damage to relationships. You might feel so afraid of not being able to say no that you say it all the time with an intensity that borders on violence. Setting limits *assertively* reduces the likelihood of anger and violence. It also ensures that when you do say yes you'll feel better about offering help willingly rather than grudgingly.

Think about the last time you said yes when you wanted to say no or said no in a way that felt excessive. Imagine yourself in the same situation using the three-part statement described in chapter 16—acknowledgment, your position, and saying no. George responded to Michelle's request with, "I know you'd like me to take the kids to school tomorrow morning (*acknowledgment*), but I have to be at work for an eight o'clock meeting with the board (*your position*). I can't take them (*saying no*)." Practice saying no, first in easy situations, then in increasingly difficult ones.

3. **Negotiation.** In any relationship there's bound to be conflict. No two people have identical needs. There will always be times when one partner's wants conflict with the other's. Giving up your needs or trying to force the other person to give up his or hers isn't very effective in the long run. It leads to anger, resentment, and often violence. Negotiation involves reaching a compromise that feels relatively satisfying to you both. It can be seen as a logical extension of the process you've already begun. You became aware of feeling angry, so you ask yourself, "What hurts?" and, "What do I want to do to fix it?" You may also ask yourself, "What are my limits?" Once you have a clear idea of what you want, present it to your partner. At this point, you must listen carefully to her needs and objections. It's often difficult to hear someone present needs that differ from your own without feeling criticized and getting defensive. Remind yourself that you're entitled to your needs and that your partner is entitled to hers.

When each of you has presented your needs, look for a compromise. Propose something that addresses both your concerns. If the first suggestion doesn't work, come up with another. Encourage your partner to come up with her own proposal. When negotiating, never say a flat no. Always offer a counterproposal so that you can continue to search for compromise. In the previous example, George was very clear and assertive in his response to Michelle's desire that he take the kids to school. Had he given his usual type of response, the interaction would have looked like this:

George: Jesus! You can't take them again? Well I can't either! So you'd better find some way to get them there.

Michelle: But my sister's arriving tomorrow ...

George: Whoopee for your sister. Isn't she capable of even getting herself on a bus? Is she as dumb as she looks?

Michelle: That's a crummy thing to say about Joan! All I'm asking is ...

George: Forget it! I said no and that's it!

Instead, the interaction continued:

Michelle: Well, my sister's flying in from Florida tomorrow morning. Her plane arrives at 8:25 and I'd like to meet her at the airport. (*Statement of needs*)

George: What if I pay for her to take a taxi from the airport? (*Suggested compromise*)

Michelle: No. I'd rather meet her in person.

George: What do you suggest?

Michelle: Perhaps I could call Andrea and see if she would take them to school with Kevin. If you could drop them at her house, you'd still have time to get to work before your meeting.

George: Well, if you can get them ready before you leave, I'm willing to take them to Andrea's.

If you practice these negotiation techniques, you won't have to get angry or violent to get your needs met. You'll be able to develop solutions that are satisfying to you both.

4. **Dealing with criticism.** Being criticized always hurts, and usually results in the desire to react defensively or counterattack. In your relationship, you probably find yourself criticizing and attacking. Your reaction may be partly the result of feeling attacked yourself or feeling unable to get your needs acknowledged. Chapter 16 describes how being criticized can make you feel inferior, imperfect, guilty, and worthless. It also describes how you can respond to criticism more effectively. You can limit the damage to your self-esteem by blocking the attack, reminding yourself that the criticism is just one person's opinion, and accepting that perfection is impossible. Evaluate the criticism for anything accurate in it that you can use or learn from. At the same time, recognize the part of the criticism that isn't accurate. Respond by agreeing with what's true and ignore the rest. Initially this may be difficult, and you may want to use a time-out to prevent escalation.

In battering relationships, the woman is often too frightened of incurring further violence to express her anger at the abuse she's already experienced. As you begin to work on taking responsibility for the abuse and making changes in your behavior, your partner may feel safer to express her feelings. You may find yourself being subjected to all the rage and anger that your partner has been stuffing for years. It's essential that you don't get pulled back into the pattern of defensiveness and counterattack that led so rapidly to violence. Call time-out as soon as you feel yourself getting tense or angry. Allow yourself to calm down, then approach the situation again using the skills described above and in chapter 16.

Self-Esteem

Most batterers feel ashamed of their violence and the fact that they can't control their behavior. In addition, they often suffer more global feelings of unworthiness. If you were abused as a child, you're even more likely to think that you're somehow bad or worthless. It's important that you learn to separate your behavior (which might be inappropriate and need changing) from you as a person. Go back and reread the section in this chapter on strengthening self-esteem. Begin to identify the internal critical voice that attacks you for your mistakes and imperfections. Keep a notebook in which you record all the things your critic says, from single words to entire monologues. Are the criticisms general indictments of you as a person ("You're a lying son-of-a-bitch")? Or are they specific references to specific behaviors ("What you just said was an exaggeration and a put-down")? Examine each of the critic's statements and substitute something more factual, less judgmental. Now identify your strengths and the exceptions to the criticisms. Use these to develop some positive affirmations and repeat these to yourself as often as you can. Incorporate them into the anger-control techniques described above. When you first become aware of feeling angry or stressed, you'll ask yourself, "What hurts?" and, "What do I want to do to fix it?" You might decide to take a time-out, do some relaxation, or assertively verbalize your feelings and needs. Using your positive affirmations at these times will give you added confidence to carry out your choice. Remind yourself that you're a worthwhile person, that you're doing the best you can, and that you can cope with stressful situations without resorting to violence.

When Violence Stops

When violence stops in a relationship, other problems don't disappear. Problems with dependency, isolation, and communication are common in abusive relationships, but can't be dealt with effectively until the violence has ended. Once the batterer has taken the responsibility for changing his violent behavior, you can work toward developing a healthier relationship based on mutual respect and affection.

This book offers some resources toward that end, but the process of change will most likely be slow and painful. After years of violence, you'll need to slowly reestablish trust in the relationship. The victim may need to see the batterer consistently choose nonviolent behaviors for some time before she can begin to relax her vigilance and trust the reality of the changes. It will take a lot of practice before you are both able to clearly express your feelings, both positive and negative. It takes practice to approach inevitable conflict with equanimity and assertively negotiate for satisfaction of your needs.

However, with a commitment on both sides to a healthy relationship, and with help of the resources listed in this book, you can develop a different kind of relationship than the scared and hurtful one you now experience.

Appendix

Response Choice Rehearsal (RCR) Group Protocol

Selection of Group Members

Success for an RCR group depends on appropriate selection. Pregroup interviews should be conducted. Ask questions about the duration and quality of relationships. Try to rule out personality disorders, particularly borderline conditions. Since RCR groups are less effective for clients struggling with generalized anger, try to determine if the anger is generalized (free-floating hostility that can attach itself to any situation) or limited to specific situations or settings. Ask questions to determine if the client enjoys his or her anger, nurtures it, relies on it, or is otherwise invested in maintaining an angry stance. Clients who find their anger to be highly rewarding tend to be less successful RCR group members.

Group Structure

Groups should consist of five to ten clients. Groups with more than ten members offer each client too few opportunities for role playing, questions, and shared experiences. Groups should meet for one and a half to two hours over a six- to eight-week period.

The Anger Diary

During the pregroup interview, ask clients to keep a daily anger diary. Each anger incident should be listed and rated on a 1 to 10 point scale (1 is minimal anger, 10 is the angriest the client has ever felt). Emphasize that the anger diary is an indispensable part of treatment and must be conscientiously maintained.

If you wish to do pre- and post-group testing, it is recommended that you use Charles Spielberger's excellent State-Trait Anger Inventory (Spielberger, et al. 1983)

Session 1

Overview of RCR

1. Six pre-learned strategies for adaptively coping with angry encounters.

2. Strategies are divided into active and passive responses.

3. RCR will help you to cope even when extremely angry.

4. RCR will enable you to learn adaptive reactions that help solve problems rather than escalate tension.

5. RCR will keep you from getting stuck with a response that isn't working, and make it more likely for you to find a response that will get you what you want.

6. RCR will help you experience anger as a signal to cope and try a new response rather than as a signal to intensify attack.

Describe each of the RCR responses. Emphasize that not all of the six responses will be appropriate for a particular anger situation. Emphasize the concept of switching from one response to another to cope with growing anger or escalation. Although a single anger-control strategy often fails during provocations, the ability to use a variety of strategies or responses in succession increases the likelihood of resolution.

Key Attitude

The key attitude is problem solving rather than avenging. An avenger wants to punish and injure the offending party to the same degree that he or she has been hurt. Pain must be paid back. A problem-solving attitude assumes that the conflict is a matter of conflicting needs; there is no right or wrong about it. Each person's needs are legitimate and important. The goal is to work toward agreement through discussion and compromise.

Hand out RCR Response Sheet.

1st RCR Response: Ask for What You Want

1. Pre-learn opening line:

"I'm feeling (What's bothering me is) _____ .
And what I think I need (or want or would like) in this situation
is _____ ."

2. Rules:

a. What is bothering you (your feeling) is optional. Include this if you think it is important information to help the other person to be more responsive, or if the other person is an intimate who deserves to know your reactions.

b. Ask for something behavioral, not attitudinal.

c. Ask for something specific, limited to one or two things.

d. Develop a fallback position, i.e., the minimum change that would be acceptable to you. This gives you room to negotiate.

3. Role-play by therapists to model RCR. (Include this section if the group has co-leaders.) Emphasize concept of voice control: keep voice low in volume without much inflection. So often voice tone and volume communicate anger, blame, contempt, sarcasm, and so on. Voice control guards against escalations that are triggered by meta-messages in your tone of voice.

4. Client visualization. Some groups find visualization difficult or unproductive. If this is the case, drop the visualization component and emphasize role plays. Homework should then focus on practicing the RCR response in vivo in low impact situations.

a. Brief lesson in visualization. Practice a beach scene, bringing in visual, auditory, and kinesthetic aspects of scene.

b. Clients visualize a scene from their anger diaries that grew out of some unmet or frustrated need. Clients visualize using RCR response and having success. Visualize second scene: initial RCR response is rebuffed but they are successful when offering fallback position.

5. Discussion of visualization:

a. Discuss visualized scenes and any problems clients encountered generating need statements.

b. Therapist helps clients who had trouble generating need statements and fallback positions to do so.

6. **Client role-play.** Using a scene from his or her anger diary, client takes role of provocateur. Second client practices RCR response after learning what presenting client wanted. Therapist coaches the provocateur and the client practicing RCR.

7. **Therapist discusses importance of expressing wants and needs.** Asks clients if there are concerns about what it's okay to ask for.

Homework

1. Pick three scenes from anger diary (low, medium, and high). Generate need statements and fallback positions for each one.

2. Practice visualizing each scene, using RCR response 1, successfully each day. Start with low impact scene and progress to high impact scene.

3. Learn RCR response 2.

Session 2

Review response 1. Discuss any problems experienced with homework.

2nd RCR Response: Negotiate

1. Review opening line:

"What would you propose to solve this problem?"

(*Note:* If clients don't feel comfortable with phrasing of opening line, let them modify it so that it feels right for them.)

2. Rules:

a. If you get resistance or a worthless proposal, offer your fallback position.

b. If you hear a proposal that has possibilities, begin negotiation. Look for compromise. Examples:

- "Let's do this part of what you want, this part of what I want."

- "My way this time, your way next time."

- "If you do _____ for me, I'll do _____ for you."

- "Let's split the difference."

- "Try it my way for a week. If you don't like it, we'll go back to the old way."

c. Compromise can be reached only when the solution takes into account BOTH people's needs.

Repeat sections 3, 4, 5, and 6 as described in first session.

3rd RCR Response: Self-Care

1. Pre-learn opening line:

"If (the problem) goes on, I'll have to (self-care solution) in order to take care of myself."

2. Rules:

a. The self-care solution should have as its main goal *meeting your needs*, not hurting the other person. This isn't something you do to the other person, it's something you do for yourself.

b. Emphasize that this is your way of solving the problem yourself, not a pushy ultimatum, nor a punishment.

Repeat sections 3, 4, 5, and 6 as described in the first session.

Homework

1. Using three scenes from anger diary (low, medium, and high), visualize using RCR response 2 successfully.

2. Using same three scenes, generate self-care statements and visualize using them.

3. Practice visualizations each day.

4. Learn RCR response 4.

Session 3

Review RCR responses 2 and 3. Discuss any problems with homework. Emphasize that responses 1 through 3 are "active" responses, while 4 through 6 are "passive" responses.

4th RCR Response: Get Information

1. Review opening line:

"What do you need in this situation?"

"What concerns (worries) you in this situation?"

"What's bothering (hurting) you in this situation?"

2. **Rules:**

   a. Use this response when someone is angry at you and there's something behind their anger you don't understand.

   b. If you don't already know what their need or worry is— GET INFORMATION.

Repeat sections 3, 4, 5, and 6 as described in the first session.

5th RCR Response: Acknowledge

1. **Pre-learn opening line:**

   "So what you want is _____ ."

   "So what concerns (worries) you is _____ ."

   "So what bothers (hurts) you is _____ ."

2. **Rules:**

   a. Use when someone has given you a clear message about his or her feelings.

   b. Expect the other person to correct or modify what you said if you didn't get it right. Then re-acknowledge the new information.

   c. Acknowledgment is not just to let people know you hear them, it is a way to clarify and correct your misconceptions.

Repeat sections 3, 4, 5, and 6 as described in the first session.

6th RCR Response: Withdrawal

1. **Pre-learn opening line:**

   "It feels like we're starting to get upset. I want to stop and cool off for a while."

2. **Rules:**

   a. Keep repeating, like a broken record, if you get resistance. Acknowledge the other person's desire to keep the discussion going or acknowledge his or her general distress, but keep repeating your withdrawal statement.

   b. Physically leave the situation. Don't just leave the vicinity.

   c. With intimates, give a specific time at which you'll return to resume the discussion.

Repeat sections 3, 4, 5, and 6 as described in the first session.

Homework

1. Pick three scenes from anger diary (low, medium, and high) and visualize using RCR responses 4 and 5.

2. Visualize same three scenes, but add needing to use RCR response 6 (withdrawal).

3. Do visualizations every day.

4. Review opening statements of responses 1 through 6 each day.

Session 4

Review homework and discuss any problems.

Switching

1. **Rules:**

   a. Memorize all opening lines. Test yourself daily.

   b. Whenever possible, rehearse in advance active response numbers 1 and 3. Decide if you wish to include your feelings about the situation. Then formulate your request and your fallback position. Make sure it's behavioral and specific. Also try to generate a self-care response. Ask yourself how you can take care of the problem *without* the other person's cooperation.

   c. Continued anger or escalation are your signals to SWITCH responses. Don't get stuck if a response isn't working. Move on to what you feel, intuitively, is the next best option.

   d. Don't be afraid to repeat responses. You may wish to return, several times, to questions that get more information. You may wish to acknowledge what you're learning about the other person's experience. And as the discussion progresses, you may wish to invite another round of negotiation.

   e. If you don't know what to do next, try shifting from active to passive responses (or vice versa). If you've been focusing on getting information, try expressing your own needs now. If you're stuck in fruitless negotiation, consider asking for information.

   f. As a rule, start with active response 1 (asking for what you want) when you're angry or want something changed. Start with passive response 4 (getting information) when the other person is angry and on the attack.

g. Keep shifting among responses until the problem feels resolved or further communication appears pointless. If you're still angry and stuck, go to one of the exit responses (either self-care or withdrawal).

2. **Coping thoughts: to be used whenever you feel your anger increasing:**

   a. "Take a deep breath and relax."

   b. "I have a plan to cope with this. What's the next step?"

Role-Play Switching

Divide the group into pairs.

1. **Using Anger Diaries:**

   a. Start with low-rated provocation from a client's anger diary.

   b. Instruct the client to play him or herself and the second client to pay provocateur.

   c. Therapist acts as coach for each client. Cues coping by reminding provoked client of two key coping thoughts. Reminds client of opening lines of RCR if forgotten. May suggest switching to a new RCR response. Provoking client is coached to resist until three or four different RCR responses have been made.

   d. Provoked client uses anger as a cue to switch and chooses which RCR response to try next.

   e. Role play should end with successful resolution.

Homework

1. Review all opening lines on a daily basis.

2. In vivo homework:

   a. Using scene from anger diary; pick low-risk individual with whom you have had conflict. Visualize using RCR with that person. Plan out need statement and fallback position.

   b. Actually engage in RCR exchange with that person.

   c. Record results in anger diary.

Sessions 5, 6, and 7

Repeat the role-play switching exercise from session 4. Encourage clients to switch back to old responses already tried. They can acknowledge or negotiate or ask for what they want more than once. As clients become more proficient at RCR, begin using medium, then high impact anger scenes from logs.

Homework for Sessions 5 and 6

Use same homework assignment as in Session 4. Have clients pick a medium-risk person to use RCR with each week. Remind clients to record results in anger log.

Bibliography

AAA Foundation for Traffic Safety. "Report by the AAA Foundation, 1997.

Alexander, F., "Emotional factors in hypertension." *Psychosomatic Medicine.* 1939, 1:175-179.

Ardrey, R. *The Territorial Imperative.* New York: Atheneum, 1966.

Baer, P. E., F. H. Collins, G. C. Bourianoff, and M. F. Ketchel. "Assessing personality factors in essential hypertension with a brief self-report instrument." *Psychosomatic Medicine.* 1969, 7:653-659.

Bander, R., J. Grinder, and V. Satir. *Changing with Families.* Palo Alto, California: Science and Behavior Books, 1976.

Barbour, C., C. Eckhardt, J. Davison, and H. Kassinove. "The experience and expression of anger in maritally violent and discordant, non-violent men." *Behavior Therapy,* 1998, 29:173-191.

Barefoot, J. C., W. G. Dahlstrom, and R. B. Williams. "Hostility, CHD incidence, and total morbidity: A 25-year follow-up study of 255 physicians." *Psychosomatic Medicine.* 1983, 45:59-63.

Bateson, G. "The frustration-aggression hypothesis and culture." *Psychological Review.* 1941, 48:350-355.

Benson, H. *The Relaxation Response.* New York: Morrow, 1975.

Berkman, L., and S. L. Syme. "Social networks, lost resistance, and mortality: A nine year follow-up study of Alameda residents." *American Journal of Epidemiology.* 1979, 109:186-204.

Biaggio, M. K. "Anger arousal and personality characteristics." *Journal of Consulting and Social Psychology.* 1980, 39:352-356.

Blumenthal, J. A., R. Williams, Y. Kong, S. M. Schonberg, and L. W. Thompson. "Type A behavior and angiographically documented coronary disease." *Circulation.* 1978, 58:634-356.

Bry, A. *How To Get Angry Without Feeling Guilty.* New York: New American Library, 1976.

Burns, D. *Feeling Good: The New Mood Therapy.* New York: William Morrow, 1980.

Cannon, W. "Bodily changes in pain, hunger, fear and rage." New York: Appleton-Century-Crofts, 1929.

Cautela, J. "Covert Modeling." Paper presented at the fifth annual meeting of the Association for Advancement of Behavior Therapy, 1971.

Crockenberg, S. "Toddler's reaction to maternal anger." *Merril-Palmer Quarterly.* 1985, 31:361-373.

———. "Predicators and correlates of anger toward and punitive control of toddlers by adolescent mothers." *Child Development.* 1987, 58:964-965.

Davis. M., E. R. Eshelman, and M. McKay. *The Relaxation & Stress Reduction Workbook.* 5th ed. Oakland, Calif.: New Harbinger Publications, 2000.

Deffenbacher, J. L. "Trait anger: Theory, findings, and implications. In *Advances in Personality Assessment.*" C. D. Spielberger and J. N. Butcher, (Eds.). 1992, 177-201. Hillsdale, New Jersey: Lawrence Erlbaum Associates, Inc.

Deffenbacher, J. L., M. E. Huff, R. S. Lynch, E. R. Oetting, and F. Natalie. "Characteristics and treatment of high-anger drivers." *Journal of Counseling Psychology.* 2000, 47:5-17.

Deffenbacher, J. L., and M. McKay. *Overcoming Situational and General Anger.* Oakland, Calif.: New Harbinger Publications, 2000..

Deffenbacher, J. L., E.R. Oetting, R.S. Lynch, and C. D. Morris. "The expression of anger and its consequences." *Behavior Research and Therapy.* 1996, 34:575-590.

Dentan, R. K. *The Semai—A Nonviolent People of Malaya.* New York: Holt, Rinehart & Winston, 1968.

Deschner, J. P. *The Hitting Habit: Anger Control for Battering Couples.* New York: Macmillan, 1984.

Diamond, E. L. "The role of anger and hostility in essential hypertension and coronary heart disease." *Psychological Bulletin.* 1982, 92:410-433.

Dimsdale, J. E., C. Pierce, D. Schonfeld, and A. Brown. "Suppressed anger and blood pressure: The effects of race, sex, social class, obesity, and age." *Psychosomatic Medicine.* 1986, 48:430-436.

Dinkmeyer, D., and G. McKay. *The Parent's Handbook: Systematic Training for Effective Parenting.* Circle Pines, Minn.: American Guidance Service, 1982.

———. *The Parent's Guide: A Systematic Training for Effective Parenting of Teens.* Circle Pines, Minn.: American Guidance Service, 1982.

Dollard, J. R., L. W. Doob, N. E. Miller, and O. H. Mowrer. *Frustration and Aggression.* New Haven: Yale University Press, 1939.

Ebbesen, E., B. Ducan, and V. Konecni. "The effects of content of verbal aggression on future verbal aggression: A field experiment." *Journal of Experimental Psychology.* 1975, 11:192-204.

Eisenberg, S. E., and P. Micklow. "The assaulted wife: 'Catch 22' revisited." *Women's Rights Law Reporter.* 1979, 3:138-161.

Elliot, F. "The neurology of explosive rage: The dyscontrol syndrome." *The Practitioner.* 1976, 217:51-60.

Ellis, A, and R. Tafrate. *How to Control Your Anger Before it Controls You.* Secaucus, New Jersey: Carol Publishing Group. 1997

Esler, M., S. Julius, A. Zweifler, O. Randall, E. Harburg, H. Gardiner, and V. De Quattro. "Mild high-renin essential hypertension: Neurogenic human hypertension?" *New England Journal of Medicine.* 1977, 296:405-411.

Feshbach, S. "The catharsis hypothesis and some consequences of interaction with aggression and neutral play objects." *Journal of Personality.* 1956, 24:449-462.

Friedman, M., S. St. George, S. O. Byers, and R. H. Rosenman. "Excretion of catecholamines in men exhibiting a particular behavior pattern (A) associated with high incidence of clinical coronary artery disease." *Journal of Clinical Investigation.* 1960, 39:758-764.

Friedman, M., and R. H. Rosenman. *Type A Behavior and Your Heart.* New York: Alfred A. Knopf, 1974.

Friedman, M., and D. Ulmer. *Treating Type A Behavior—And Your Heart.* New York: Alfred A. Knopf, 1984.

Frude, N., and A. Goss. 1979. "Parental anger: A general population survey." *Child Abuse and Neglect.* 1979, 3:331-333.

Gentry, W. D. "Habitual anger-coping styles: Effect on mean blood pressure and risk for essential hypertension." *Psychosomatic Medicine.* 1982, 44:195-202.

Gordon, T. *Parent Effectiveness Training.* New York: New American Library, 1975.

Greenglass, E. R. "Anger suppression, cynical distrust, and hostility: Implications for coronary heart disease." in *Stress and Emotion:*

Anxiety, Anger And Curiosity. C. D. Spielberger, and I.G. Sarason, (Eds.) 1996, 205-225.

Gressel, G. E., F. O. Shobe, G. Saslow, M. DuBois, and H. A. Schroeder. "Personality factors in essential hypertension." *Journal of the American Medical Association.* 1949, 140:265-272.

Grunbaum, J. A., S. W. Vernon, and C. M. Clasen. "The association between anger and hostility and risk factors for coronary heart disease in children and adolescents: a review." *Annals of Behavioral Medicine.* 1997, 19:179-189.

Hadley, J., and C. Staudacher. *Hypnosis for Change.* Oakland, Calif.: New Harbinger Publications, 1985.

Hamilton, J. A. "Psychophysiology of blood pressure." *Psychosomatic Medicine.* 1942, 4:125-133.

Hansson, R. D., W. H. Jones, and B. Carpenter. "Relational competence and social support." *Review of Personality and Social Psychology.* 1984, 5:265-284.

Harburg, E., S. Julius, N. F. McGinn, J. McLeod, and S. W. Hoobler. "Personality traits and behavior patterns associated with systolic blood pressure levels in college males." *Journal of Chronic Diseases.* 1964, 17:405-414.

Harburg, E., J. C. Erfurt, L. S. Hauenstein, C. Chape, W. J. Schull, and M. A. Schork. "Socio-ecological stress, suppressed hostility, skin color, and black-white male blood pressure: Detroit." *Psychosomatic Medicine.* 1973, 35:276-296.

Harburg, E., E. H. Blakelock, and P. J. Roeper. "Resentful and reflective coping with arbitrary authority and blood pressure: Detroit." *Psychosomatic Medicine.* 1979, 41:189-202.

Harris, R. E., M. Sokolow, L. G. Carpenter, M. Freedman, and S. Hunt. "Response to psychogenic stress in persons who are potentially hypertensive." *Circulation.* 1953, 7:572-578.

Haynes, S. G., M. Feinleib, and W. B. Kannel. "The relationship of psychosocial factors to coronary heart disease in the Framingham Study, Part III: Eight year incidence of CHD." *American Journal of Epidemiology.* 1980, 3:37-58.

Hazaleus, S., and J. Deffenbacher. "Relaxation and cognitive treatments of anger." *Journal of Consulting and Clinical Psychology.* 1986, 54:222-226.

Hemenway, D., S. Solnick, and J. Carter. "Child rearing violence." *Child Abuse and Neglect.* 1994, 18:1011-1020.

Herman, D. "A statutory proposal to limit the infliction of violence upon children." *Family Law Quarterly.* 1985, 19:1-52.

Hoffman, R. "Moral development." In *Carmichael's Manual of Child Psychology*, edited by P. Mussen. New York: Wiley Publications, 1970.

Hokanson, J. E. "Psychophysiological evaluation of the catharsis hypothesis." In *The Dynamics of Aggression*, edited by Megaree and Hokanson. New York: Harper & Row, 1970.

Houston, B. K., and K. E. Kelley. "Hostility in employed women: Relation to work and marital experiences, social support, stress and anger expression." *Personality and Social Psychology Bulletin*. 1989, 15:175-182.

Jones, W. H., J. E. Freeman, and R. A. Gasewick. "The persistence of loneliness: Self and other determinants." *Journal of Personality*. 1981, 49:27-48.

Kahn, H. A., J. H. Medalie, H. N. Newfield, E. Riss, and U. Goldbourt. "The incidence of hypertension and associated factors: The Israel ischemic heart disease study." *American Heart Journal*. 1972, 84:171-182.

Kahn, M. "The physiology of catharsis." *Journal of Personality and Social Psychology*. 1966, 3 (3):278-286.

Kaplan, S., L. A. Gottschalk, E. Magliocco, D. Rohovit, and W. Ross. "Hostility in verbal productions and hypnotic dreams in hypertensive patients." *Psychosomatic Medicine*. 1961, 23:311-322.

Kawachi, I., D. Sparrow, A. Spiro, P. Vokonas, and S. T. Weiss. "A prospective study of anger and coronary heart disease. The normative aging study." *Circulation*. 1996, 94:2090-2095.

Kellner, R. M., T. Buckman, M. Fava, G. A. Fava, and I. Masuogiacomo. "Prolactin, aggression, and hostility: A discussion of recent studies." *Psychiatric Developments*. 1984, 2:131-138.

Konner, M. *The Tangled Wing*. New York: Holt, 1962.

Korbanka, J., and M. McKay. "The emotional and behavioral effects of parental discipline styles on their adult children." Unpublished paper. 1995.

Koskenvuo, M., J. Kaprio, R.J. Rose, A. Kasaniemi, K. Heikkila, and H. Langinvainio. "Hostility as a risk factor for mortality and ischemic heart disease in men." *Psychosomatic Medicine*. 1988, 50:330-340.

Lazarus, R. S., and S. Folkman. *Stress, Appraisal, and Coping*. New York: Springer Publishing Co., 1984.

Leakey, R. *The Making of Mankind*. New York: E. P. Dutton, 1981.

Lewis, H. K., and M. E. Lewis. *Psychosomatics: How Your Emotions Can Damage Your Health*. New York: Viking Press, 1972.

Lorenz, K. *On Aggression.* New York: Bantam Books, 1971.

Mallick, S. K., and B. R. McCandles. "A study of catharsis aggression." *Journal of Personality and Social Psychology.* 1966, 2:591-596.

Mann, A. H. "Psychiatric morbidity and hostility in hypertension." *Psychological Medicine.* 1977, 7:653-659.

Maranon, G. "Contribution of l'etude de l'action emotive de l'adrenaline." *Revue Francaise d'Endocrinologie.* 1924, 2:301-325.

McKay, M., M. Davis, and P. Fanning. *Thoughts and Feelings: Taking Control of Your Moods and Your Life* 2nd edition. Oakland, Calif.: New Harbinger Publications, 1998.

————. Messages: The Communication Book 2nd edition . Oakland, Calif.: New Harbinger Publications, 1995.

McKay, M., and P. Fanning. *Self-Esteem* 3rd edition. Oakland, Calif.: New Harbinger Publications, 2000.

McKay, M., P. Fanning, K. Paleg, and D. Landis. *When Anger Hurts Your Kids.* Oakland, Calif.: New Harbinger Publications, 1996.

McKay, M., and P. Fanning. *Successful Problem Solving.* Oakland, CA: New Harbinger Publications, 2002.

McKay, M., and P. D. Rogers. *The Anger Control Workbook* Oakland, Calif.: New Harbinger Publications, 2000.

Meichenbaum, D. *Cognitive Behavior Modifications.* New York: Plenum Press, 1977.

Miller, C., and C. Grim. "Personality and emotional stress measurement on hypertensive patients with essential and secondary hypertension." *International Journal of Nursing Studies.* 1979, 16:85-93.

Miller, N. E. "The frustration-aggression hypothesis." *Psychological Review.* 1941, 48:337-342.

Neidig, P. H., and D. H. Friedman. *Spouse Abuse: A Treatment Program for Couples.* Champaign, Ill.: Research Press, 1984.

New York Times. "Cynicism and mistrust linked to early death." Thursday, January 17, 1989.

NiCarthy, G. *Getting Free: A Handbook for Women in Abusive Relationships.* Seattle: The Seal Press, 1982.

Novaco, R. *Anger Control: The Development and Evaluation of an Experimental Treatment.* Lexington, Mass.: C.D. Health, 1975.

Ornstein, R., and D. Sobel. *The Healing Brain.* New York: Simon and Schuster, 1987.

Patterson, G. R. *Coercive Family Process.* Eugene, Ore.: Castalia, 1982.

Pino, C. *Divorce, Remarriage, and Blended Families*. Palo Alto, Calif.: R. & E. Press, 1982.

Rosenman, R. H. "Health consequences of anger and implications for treatment." In *Anger and Hostility in Cardiovascular and Behavioral Disorders*, edited by M. A. Chesney and R. H. Rosenman. Washington, DC: Hemisphere Publishing Co., 1985.

Rubin, I. R. *The Angry Book*. New York: Collier Books, 1969.

Rule, B. G., and A. R. Nesdale. "Emotional arousal and aggressive behavior." *Psychological Bulletin*. 1976, 83:851-863.

Scaramella, T. H., and W. A. Brown. "Serum testosterone and aggressiveness in hockey players." *Psychosomatic Medicine*. 1978, 40:262-267.

Schachter, J. "Pain, fear, and anger in hypertensives and normotensives." *Psychosomatic Medicine*. 1957, 19:17-29.

Schachter, S. *Emotion, Obesity, and Crime*. New York: Academic Press, 1971.

Schachter, S., and J. Singer. "Cognitive social and physiological determinants of emotional state." *Psychological Review*. 1962, 69:370-399.

Schwartz, G. E., D. A. Weinberger, and J. A. Singer. "Cardiovascular differentiation of happiness, sadness, anger, and fear following imagery and exercise." *Psychosomatic Medicine*. 1981, 43:343-364.

Selye, H. "A syndrome produced by diverse noxious agents." *Nature*. 1936, 138:32.

Shekelle, R. B., M. Gale, A. M. Ostfeld, and O. Paul. "Hostility, risk of CHD, and mortality." *Psychosomatic Medicine*. 1983, 45:109-114.

"Seville Statement." *Psychology Today*, June 1988, 34-39.

Siegman, A.W., T. M. Dembroski, and N. Ringel. "Components of hostility and severity of coronary artery disease." *Psychosomatic Medicine* 1987, 49:127-135

Sonkin, D. J., D. Martin, and L. E. Walker. *The Male Batterer: A Treatment Approach*. New York: Springer Publishing Co., 1985.

Spielberger, C. D. *State-Trait Anger Expression Inventory*. Odessa, Fld.: Psychological Assessment Resources Inc, 1988.

Spielberger, C. D., G. A. Jacobs, S. Russell, R. S. Crane. "Assessment of anger: The State-Trait Anger Scale." In *Advances in Personality*, Vol. 2, edited by J. N. Butcher and C. D. Spielberger. Hillsdale, NJ: Erlbaum, 1983.

Straus, M. "Leveling, civility, and violence in the family." *Journal of Marriage and the Family*. 1974, 36:13-29.

————. *Beating the Devil Out of Them: Corporal Punishment in American Families.* New York: Lexington Books, 1994.

Strauss, M. A., R. H. Gelles, and S. K. Steinmetz. *Behind Closed Doors: Violence in the American Family.* New York: Anchor-Doubleday, 1981.

Tafrate, R.C., H. Kassinove, and L. Dundin. "Anger episodes in high and low trait anger community adults." *Journal of Clinical Psychology.* 2002, 58:1573-1590.

Tavris, C. *Anger—the Misunderstood Emotion.* New York: Simon & Schuster, 1989.

"On the wisdom of counting form one to ten." *Review of Personality and Social Psychology.* 1984, 5:270-291.

Tesser, A., R. Forehand, G. Brody, and N. Long. "Conflict: the role of calm and angry parent-child discussion in adolescent adjustment." *Journal of Social and Clinical Psychology.* 1989, 8:317-330.

"The Seville Statement." *Psychology Today.* 1988, (June):34-39.

Walker, L. E. "The battered woman syndrome study." In *The Dark Side of Families: Current Family Violence Research,* edited by D. Finkelhor, R. J. Gelles, G. Hotaling, and M. Straus. Beverly Hills, Calif.: Sage Publications, 1983.

————. *The Battered Woman Syndrome.* New York: Springer Publishing Co., 1984.

Weisinger, H. *Dr. Weisinger's Anger Work-Out Book.* New York: William Morrow and Co., 1985.

Weiss, R. *Marital Separation.* New York: Basic Books, 1985.

Whitting, J. W. M. *Becoming a Kwoma.* New Haven: Yale University Press, 1941.

Williams, R. B., T. L. Haney, K. I. Lee, Y. Kong, J. A. Blumenthal, and R. E. Walen. "Type A behavior, hostility, and coronary atherosclerosis." *Psychosomatic Medicine.* 1980, 42:539-549.

Williams, J. E, C. C. Paton, I. C. Siegler, M. L. Eigenbrodt, F. J. Nieto, and H. A. Tryoler. "Anger proneness predicts coronary heart disease risk." *Circulation.* 2000, 101:2034-2039.

Wolff, H. S., and S. Wolf. "A study of experimental evidence relating life stress to the pathogenesis of essential hypertension in man." In *Hypertension: A Symposium,* edited by E. T. Bell. Minneapolis: University of Minnesota Press, 1951.

————. "Stress and the gut." *Gastroenterology.* 1967, 52:2.

Wood, C. "The hostile heart." *Psychology Today.* 1986, 20:9.

Matthew McKay, Ph.D., is the clinical director of Haight-Ashbury Psychological Services in San Francisco. McKay is the coauthor of twenty popular books, including *The Relaxation & Stress Reduction Workbook, Self-Esteem, The Anger Control Workbook, Thoughts & Feelings, Messages*, and several professional titles.

Peter Rogers is the administrative director of Haight-Ashbury Psychological Services in San Francisco and the past director of the Alcohol and Drug Treatment Program at Kaiser Permanente, Redwood City, California. He is the coauthor of *The Divorce Book, The Anger Control Workbook, Drugs and Your Kid*, and *The Community Building Companion*.

Judith McKay, RN, has made significant contributions to this book through her research on patterns of healthy child rearing and the physiological effects of anger. Her guide for raising children with high self-esteem appeared in the book *Self-Esteem*. She is a nurse in the outpatient medical oncology program at Alta Bates Cancer Center in Berkeley, California.

Some Other
New Harbinger Titles

The End of-life Handbook, Item 5112 $15.95

The Mindfulness and Acceptance Workbook for Anxiety, Item 4993 $21.95

A Cancer Patient's Guide to Overcoming Depression and Anxiety, Item 5044 $19.95

Handbook of Clinical Psychopharmacology for Therapists, 5th edition, Item 5358 $55.95

Disarming the Narcissist, Item 5198 $14.95

The ABCs of Human Behavior, Item 5389 $49.95

Rage, Item 4627 $14.95

10 Simple Solutions to Chronic Pain, Item 4825 $12.95

The Estrogen-Depression Connection, Item 4832 $16.95

Helping Your Socially Vulnerable Child, Item 4580 $15.95

Life Planning for Adults with Developmental Disabilities, Item 4511 $19.95

Overcoming Fear of Heights, Item 4566 $14.95

Acceptance & Commitment Therapy for the Treatment of Post-Traumatic Stress Disorder & Trauma-Related Problems, Item 4726 $58.95

But I Didn't Mean That!, Item 4887 $14.95

Calming Your Anxious Mind, 2nd edition, Item 4870 $14.95

10 Simple Solutions for Building Self-Esteem, Item 4955 $12.95

The Dialectical Behavior Therapy Skills Workbook, Item 5136 $21.95

The Family Intervention Guide to Mental Illness, Item 5068 $17.95

Finding Life Beyond Trauma, Item 4979 $19.95

Five Good Minutes at Work, Item 4900 $14.95

It's So Hard to Love You, Item 4962 $14.95

Energy Tapping for Trauma, Item 5013 $17.95

Thoughts & Feelings, 3rd edition, Item 5105 $19.95

Transforming Depression, Item 4917 $12.95

Helping A Child with Nonverbal Learning Disorder, 2nd edition, Item 5266 $15.95

Leave Your Mind Behind, Item 5341 $14.95

Learning ACT, Item 4986 $44.95

ACT for Depression, Item 5099 $42.95

Integrative Treatment for Adult ADHD, Item 5211 $49.95

Freeing the Angry Mind, Item 4380 $14.95

Call toll free, **1-800-748-6273,** or log on to our online bookstore at www.newharbinger.com to order. Have your Visa or Mastercard number ready. Or send a check for the titles you want to New Harbinger Publications, Inc., 5674 Shattuck Ave., Oakland, CA 94609. Include $4.50 for the first book and 75¢ for each additional book, to cover shipping and handling. (California residents please include appropriate sales tax.) Allow two to five weeks for delivery.

Prices subject to change without notice.